GW01150493

Heritage of Help

Heritage of Help
The Story of the Royal Patriotic Fund

DENIS BLOMFIELD-SMITH

ROBERT HALE · LONDON

© Royal Patriotic Fund Corporation 1992
First published in Great Britain 1992

ISBN 0 7090 4960 9

Robert Hale Limited
Clerkenwell House
Clerkenwell Green
London EC1R 0HT

The right of Denis Blomfield-Smith to be identified as
author of this work has been asserted by him
in accordance with the Copyright, Designs and
Patents Act 1988.

Photoset in North Wales by
Derek Doyle & Associates, Mold, Clwyd.
Printed in Great Britain by
St Edmundsbury Press Ltd, Bury St Edmunds, Suffolk.
Bound by WBC Bookbinders Ltd, Bridgend, Glamorgan.

Contents

	List of Illustrations	vii
	Foreword by HRH Prince Michael of Kent	ix
	Introduction	1
1	Sick Men	5
2	The Royal Commission – Early Years	12
3	The Orphans	20
4	A Covenant for Children	27
5	A New Lease of Life	39
6	A 'Foster' Fund	49
7	Give and Take	57
8	Discord Within and Without	67
9	Incorporation	83
10	A Second Innings on a Worn Wicket	92
11	Ebb and Flow	102
12	A World War and a Nation's Debt	113
13	Coming to Terms	126
14	Fresh Fields in War and Peace	139
15	Dependants and Interdependence	153
16	Money Matters	168
17	New Looks but Old Values	175
18	Constancy and Consistency	190
	Appendices A to T	198
	Index	236

Illustrations

Between pages 134 and 135

1 HRH Prince Albert chairing an early meeting of the Royal Patriotic Fund
2 Patriotic Fund ewer portraying a grief-stricken family being watched over by a Victorian angel
3 Queen Victoria laying the foundation stone of the Commission's Girls' School 1857
4 The completed Girls' School on Wandsworth Common
5 The Royal Victoria Patriotic School, Essendon

Foreword

by HRH Prince Michael of Kent

Prince Albert, Queen Victoria's Prince Consort, was the first Colonel-in-Chief of the 11th Hussars, one of the cavalry regiments in the Light Brigade at Balaclava. He was also the President of the Patriotic Fund when it was first established as a Royal Commission to help the widows and orphans of those whose lives were lost in the Crimean war. Since I am his great-great-grandson, and my old Regiment was the 11th Hussars (Prince Albert's Own), it was an honour for me to be appointed President of the Royal Patriotic Fund Corporation. These close connections with the Corporation's past naturally give me special reasons for welcoming this book.

An important figure in the early history of the Fund was the Actuary for the National Debt. That title was designed to refer to him in his strictly economic capacity, but it also happened to be entirely fitting, because the charity is a symbol of the Nation's debt to those members of the Armed Forces who have given their lives in its service. The Fund has done what it could towards the payment of that debt since 1854, and I am glad to be so closely associated with it.

The story told in this book does not confine itself solely to the part played by the Royal Patriotic Fund, but also affords a fascinating insight into some critical times in the recent history of our nation. That in itself should ensure that it attracts a wide readership.

I have long felt that the Royal Patriotic Fund Corporation is too little known, both to the Armed Forces and to the public at large. I commend this book and hope that it will go some way towards putting that right, as well as giving enjoyment to its readers, and thus contribute to the help the Corporation can provide for Service widows and children.

Michael

Introduction

For a few people towards the close of the twentieth century the end of the Victorian period is just within living memory. By 1900 the camera and the motor car had been invented and there were some 17,000 miles of railways in operation. In the military field, guns had reached a high degree of sophistication; Henry Shrapnel's bullet-filled shell with its time-fuse was already old-fashioned, and the advanced breech-loading rifle designed by Herr von Mauser had long been available. In the world of communications Marconi had followed up Bell's invention of the telephone by developing the use of radio waves, though these were still early days for both; power-driven presses had long contributed to the free availability of the printed word. All this, one might think, should encourage a sense of closeness between the last half of the nineteenth century and the first half of the twentieth.

In writing this story it has seemed to me that the reverse is true. Possibly the very familiarity of some of the scenery somehow adds emphasis to the strangeness of the actors and their actions. A striking example is that of the value set on time and money. It is difficult to envisage a situation towards the end of the twentieth century in which the modern equivalents of the members of the Royal Commission of the 1850s would have what has been described (perhaps maladroitly), as a 'lengthened' discussion about the peccadilloes of one of the clerical staff who had taken somewhat unfair advantage of the opportunities of contact with a 'respectable woman' beneficiary to carry off her daughter. It would be equally hard to imagine, in the late twentieth century, enquiries by a House of Commons Select

Committee and two Joint Select Committees appointed by both Houses of Parliament lasting for six years and devoted solely to the future administration of the Royal Patriotic Fund.

The importance given to the Fund in the nineteenth century was partly, one feels, a measure of the gap in State assistance. Until 1901 widows had no financial help at all from the Government towards their support, or that of their families. Where widowhood was clearly the result of their husbands' service to the State, the sense of responsibility felt by the senior State officials involved was clearly reflected in the focus on this Fund as the central charitable source. Having come into being virtually spontaneously in the early days of the Crimean War, the Fund's scope has since embraced three individual Naval disasters, numerous small wars in Asia and Africa and every major war from 1854 to 1990.

Because of the Fund's close ties with the Royal Family and Governments, it was inevitable that in following the course of its work through the years we should be provided with intriguing glimpses of the actors in much bigger dramas. There was the long delay in the appointment of a new Commission by Queen Victoria because of her prolonged absence from State affairs mourning the death of Prince Albert. There was the rather poignant situation of Lord Raglan, the Commander-in-Chief in the Crimea, and soon himself to be a victim of that war, being one of the members of the first Commission having the care of Crimean widows and orphans as their task. Other great names appeared in the discussions and decision-making about the problems of widows and orphans: Palmerston, Disraeli, Gladstone, all concerning themselves while still in the midst of affairs of State, with detail which in the twentieth century would be delegated quite a long way away from the centre.

This account is also the story of battles and wars: those which have increased the nation's standing and prosperity, and those which have diminished one or the other, but all of which have had tragic consequences for so many thousands of wives and children. From this long history of fighting and hardship though has come much thoughtfulness, hope and happiness. Even the School described by *The Sunday Times*

Introduction 3

in 1984 as towering 'over the surrounding area with an intimidating air of menace, its bristling, gloomy turrets and sinister gargoyles serving as a testament to an era that prided itself on the severity of hard work and high ideals' still boasts a loyal and lively Old Girls' Association. The Victorians looked at things differently.

The need for a full history of the Royal Patriotic Fund was recognized some years ago by General Sir Geoffrey Musson (Vice-President 1974–1983) and well understood and supported by his successors General Sir Michael Gow (himself an author) and the late General Sir Thomas Morony (see the roll of office bearers at Appendix T). This book is the outcome, and I have been greatly encouraged and helped in its production by many past and present members of the Royal Patriotic Fund Corporation; in particular by General Sir Martin Farndale, the Chairman of the Executive Committee and Vice-President, Air Vice-Marshal Sir Bernard Chacksfield, his Deputy (and very knowledgeable indeed about the Royal Victorian Patriotic School) and Major Geoffrey Heywood, Chairman of the Finance Committee and a distinguished actuary, who has been a staunch supporter and helpful source of information about the Institute of Actuaries. I hope that all concerned will feel adequately repaid by the outcome.

I am grateful to the Editor of *The Times, The Financial Times* and *The Sunday Times* for their agreement to the copying of various extracts from their publications of various dates; also to Thorn EMI for providing me with many details of their television hire operations. My task has also been greatly helped by the facilities provided for me by the Cambridge University Library. The Charity Commission has also been most helpful and has provided much essential information.

In a more personal way I have much appreciated the excellent work of Mrs Linda Smith and her daughter at the Anglia Word Processing Centre at Newmarket, and the kindness of Sonia Halliday and Laura Lushington in taking so much trouble with the photography at no cost to the Corporation.

Most of all, as always, I am enormously indebted to my wife for her moral support when things have been difficult, her practical support in endless typing and some very meticulous photography, and, above all, her patience and tolerance throughout.

1 Sick Men

... Whereas, amidst the glorious successes which, through the power of Almighty God, have attended Our arms during the present war, many soldiers, sailors, and marines, serving in Our armies and fleets, have gallantly fallen in battle, or by other casualties during the war; and many who shall hereafter be engaged in conflict, or in the further prosecution of hostilities, may also nobly sacrifice their lives in Our service, while protecting the invaded liberties of Our Ally, and repressing the lawless ambition of Our enemies ...

Thus was the Crimean War characterized in part of the preamble which established the Royal Commission setting up the 'Patriotic Fund' on 7 October 1854. The war had been in progress for only some seven months and the carnage of the Light Brigade's charge at Balaclava had not yet taken place. In fact, the first serious action in which 'Our arms' had been engaged had not occurred until less than a month before, at the battle for the crossing of the Alma River, so that it was the 'other casualties during the war' which had made such an impact on 'Our' subjects; an unusually deep impression in the relatively harsh times of Victorian Britain. These 'other casualties' were caused by disease and malnutrition, and the numbers were indeed disturbing. By 1 December, only some ten weeks after the first engagement, the Expeditionary Force had suffered 4,000 casualties, or about 15% of its strength, and only 1,350 of these had occurred in battle. The bald figures would be worrying enough but to understand fully why the British people were so moved that they demanded, and spontaneously took, action, requires some setting of the scene.
  The War with Russia in 1854 has been variously labelled,

'unnecessary', undertaken because the British were 'bored with peace', and attributed to the indiscretions of rulers, diplomats and politicians, combined with the thirst for glory among military men. Certainly, when viewed from the standpoint of the end of the twentieth century it is hard to understand how the situation was allowed to develop into a war between the great powers. If any single cause were to be sought for this it would probably be the all round lack of rapid, clear communications.

Religion has been a nominal *casus belli* on very many occasions, and every so often it has been the real cause. In relation to the Crimean War it is doubtful if it was more than a pretext. Czar Nicholas I of Russia held a decadent Turkey in contempt; the 'sick man' of Europe was his description of that nation, and he saw the opportunity for a better future for Constantinople in Russian hands, with a Mediterranean dominated by a great Russian fleet. Britain and France, comparatively recent enemies, were at one in disliking this prospect. France, in the person of Napoleon III, took the lead in putting pressure on the Sultan of Turkey to resist any Russian demands. This was done more on the basis of 'I can hurt you more than the Russians' than as encouragement from a staunch ally. The chosen trigger, however, was the decision by Turkey in 1852 to transfer the control of the Christian shrines in Turkish Palestine, from the Greek Orthodox Church to the Roman Catholic Church. On the basis that the Orthodox Church was under Russian protection the Czar demanded that this decision be reversed, that all Orthodox Christians in the Turkish Empire be placed under Russian protection, and that, in order to keep Roman Catholic France from again intimidating Turkey, a Russo-Turkish alliance be formed.

When these demands were rejected by Turkey, the Russians marched into the two Turkish provinces in the Balkans on Russia's south-western border – Moldavia and Wallachia.[1] Britain and France immediately sent warships to the Dardanelles as a deterrent to Russian ideas of westward expansion, and to stiffen Turkish resistance. Thus bolstered, Turkey declared war on Russia in October 1853. When the Russian fleet sank a squadron of Turkish warships in the Black Sea in the following month, the British and French fleets sailed into the Black Sea and Britain delivered an ultimatum to the Russian Naval Headquarters at Sebastopol which would have had the effect of immobilizing the Russian Navy. The last act was an Anglo-French demand that all Russian forces should be withdrawn from Moldavia and Wallachia. This was rejected and in March 1854 Britain and France declared war on Russia. In effect, it was a fight for the Russian ports; and so war came to the Crimean peninsula as well as, for Naval forces, to the Baltic.

To understand what would otherwise be incredible incompetence in every aspect of the conduct of the Crimean War it helps to appreciate that, as a result of the British successes in the Peninsular War against the French in Spain and Portugal in 1813/14 and the final victory at Waterloo in 1815, the Duke of Wellington and the British Army of that period were considered by Victorian Britain to be invincible, and quite capable of routing Russians without needing any special preparations. Although in 1852 the Duke was back in charge of the Army as its Commander-in-Chief, he was in the tenth year of his second tour of duty and there were other crucial differences from the heady days of some forty years earlier. The Duke himself was eighty-three years old and shortly to die. He had also been engrossed in politics for the past twenty years or so. The British Army had not seen action against a major enemy for some forty years, and the very few, very elderly, officers who had seen action under the Duke were more than a little rusty. Senior officers who had not seen action had also not received much in military education or participated in realistic military training. The system of buying commissions was still current so that the only qualification for becoming the officer commanding a company, squadron or even a regiment might be merely the possession of enough money to afford the cost.

It was against this background that an Expeditionary Force of some 28,000 men embarked at Portsmouth in the spring of 1854 to fight a war three thousand miles away in Russia.

The task of clothing, feeding, providing medical care and properly equipping such a force at such a range in unfriendly country had not been understood; if indeed it had even been properly considered. The result was the alarming total of casualties from disease, malnutrition and, when winter came, exposure. Information about this appalling waste and neglect might not have made the impact back in Britain which it did until perhaps there was some good news to set against it, if it had not been that there was one modern feature to this otherwise very old-fashioned Expeditionary Force. It had with it a war correspondent from *The Times*, W.H. Russell.

William Russell was very unpopular with the Expeditionary Force since he refused to accept any censorship of his reports about military dispositions, with the result that it was maintained (including by the Russians themselves) that the only intelligence sources needed by the Russian High Command were copies of *The Times*. Dispositions did not change very rapidly in those days of sieges and there was much substance in this complaint. Without the flow of information about the conditions in the Crimea, however, which emanated from William Russell, the British public would not have been confronted so soon in the campaign with the knowledge that the soldiers it had so enthusiastically despatched in the spring to give Russians a lesson had, by August, suffered heavy casualties from cholera and dysentery. By this time eighty men from one battalion had died from cholera and many soldiers in all the battalions were too weak even to carry their packs, let alone to do themselves justice in battle.

In a despatch dated 19 August it was reported, in *The Times* of 1 September, that the flagship of the British fleet had just buried seventy victims at sea and still had a hundred sick aboard. On another occasion it was decided that the ships which had been anchored offshore should put to sea for a short cruise in order to try to rid the sick of the disease and clear the vessels of infection.

All this was before there had been any serious engagement with the enemy. In consequence the British people were angry and conscience-stricken. The national reaction was a cry for retribution upon the senior officers and Whitehall administrators, and for financial help to provide the soldiers with better clothing and supplies, and to make better provision for their wives and families, widows and orphans.

Such information about the very high rate of casualties from disease and the totally inadequate provision of medical support and proper administration came from other sources as well as from William Russell's despatches. There were frequent letters published in *The Times* from officers and men of the expeditionary force, and letters to families and friends which were quoted in Parliament, which all told the same sorry story.

Although news of the fall of Sebastopol to the Allies was proclaimed on 2 October by the Lord Mayor of London on the steps of the Royal Exchange, and was greeted with national acclaim, this was followed ten days later by a report in *The Times* that casualties in the Expeditionary Force had reached 'at least 4,000', that there was no proper provision for the care of the wounded, and that there were no nurses, even back at the base at Scutari. In fact, Sebastopol remained in Russian hands until almost twelve months later and was to be the cause of many thousands more deaths.

To ameliorate the conditions of the soldiers and sailors to some extent, *The Times* accompanied this report with an appeal of funds for 'creature comforts' for them; remarking that £4,000 to £5,000 could do much to improve their lot.

The casualty list resulting from the battle for the River Alma crossing was published on 19 October and this was followed on 21 October by the announcement in *The Times* that: 'Under a special arrangement of the Peninsular and Orient Company, a number of surgeons, and the staff of nurses organized by Miss Nightingale, will embark at Marseilles on 27th inst ...'

One of the very many deficiencies that Florence Nightingale uncovered at Scutari was subsequently reported in *The Times* to be a fundamental one, an acute shortage of basins. On 26 December 1854 the following letter appeared in *The Times* from the Potteries:

Sir,
In your correspondent's letter from Scutari, under date November 30, we learn that, among other necessary articles which would much contribute to lessen the trials of our wounded and otherwise afflicted soldiers in hospital, basins 'for personal cleanliness or to use in dressing wounds' would be desirable additions to Miss Nightingale's stores. As manufacturers of the articles in question, we beg to inform

you that we shall be glad to forward 500 or 1,000 – say 1,000 – basins immediately on being advised to whose care they can be forwarded for shipment to Scutari.
We are, Sir, very respectfully yours
Samuel Alcock & Co
Hill Pottery, Burslem, Staffs.

Partly as a result of spontaneous giving prompted by the national conscience and partly as a result of *The Times*' appeal, money began to arrive through many different channels and for a variety of purposes. Although in various parts of the country there were individual attempts to introduce some systems to control and make sensible use of these funds, the situation was accurately portrayed in *The Times* on 14 October in these words: 'The public benevolence has hitherto flowed, it may be said, in a rather indiscriminate manner. Good people, as they sent their money to a bank, or put it into the church plate, hardly knew whether they gave it to wives and children, or to widows and orphans, and whether of soldiers or sailors.'

This was the reason that *The Times* was able to announce in the same edition, that: 'Her Majesty has taken the opportunity to appoint a "Royal Commission of the Patriotic Fund", for the collection and distribution of the money pouring in for the widows and orphans of our soldiers, sailors and marines who die in the war.'

Once this had been announced the flow of funds gathered momentum. On 2 November the Lord Mayor of London arranged a meeting at the Mansion House of 'merchants, bankers, traders and other citizens of the City of London, for the purpose of raising a subscription in aid of the Patriotic Fund'. All over the country similar meetings were organized to the same end, and, although there were some who believed that it was 'the bounden duty of the Government of this great country to provide for the funding of those who might fall in their country's service', these were few.

Some details of the Warrant establishing the Royal Commission are reproduced at Appendix A and the membership was impressive. It was presided over by Prince

Albert, the Queen's Consort, and it included many of those actually involved in the conduct of the war such as the then Prime Minister, Lord Aberdeen; his successor in 1855, Lord Palmerston; successive Secretaries of State – at (later for) War, the Duke of Newcastle, Sidney Herbert, and Lord Panmure; the Commander-in-Chief of the Army in the Crimea himself, Lord Raglan, and his fortifications adviser, Lieutenant-General Sir John Burgoyne.

The Commission's task was:

> to make full and diligent inquiry into the best mode of aiding the loyalty and benevolence of Our loving subjects, and of ascertaining the best means by which the gifts, subscriptions, and contributions of Our loving subjects can be best applied, according to the generous intentions of the donor thereof ... And further, to apply, or to order and direct the application of, all such monies in such manner as to you, Our Commissioners, or any three or more of you, shall seem fit ...

The Patriotic Fund thus established by the Royal Commission was the first Service charity to be created as a result of national demand. At the beginning of the century Lloyd's underwriters had established in 1803 'Lloyd's Patriotic Fund' to help soldiers and sailors and their families who had suffered in the Napoleonic Wars, and this fund continued to be in operation (as it is to this day). It set aside £25,000 in 1854 for the families of those killed in action in the Crimea and for soldiers and sailors disabled in the war, and in this way helped greatly in sharing the burden of the Royal Commission. In addition, the experience of those administering 'Lloyd's Patriotic Fund' proved valuable to the Commissioners and the staff of the 'Royal Patriotic Fund' on many occasions.

Footnote

[1] Now part of Romania.

2 The Royal Commission – Early Years

The Commissioners had their first meeting on 18 December 1854 and had further meetings in February, April and May 1855. They had given priority to taking the measures needed to ensure that funds would be collected in an organized manner and over as large a catchment area as possible. Three thousand copies of the Commission had been distributed throughout the Kingdom and the Commissioners arranged, through the 'Commissioners in Aid' so prudently appointed by Her Majesty, the setting up of the local Committees envisaged in the Commission, both in the Kingdom and overseas.

The Commissioners in Aid were:

> the Lords Lieutenant, Sheriffs, and Custodes Rotulorum for the time being of the several counties within Our Kingdom; the Aldermen and Recorder for the time being of Our City of London; the Lord Provost of Edinburgh for the time being; the Lord Mayor of Dublin for the time being; the Lord Mayor of York for the time being; and all other the Mayors, Provosts, Bailiffs, and Baillies for the time being of Our cities, boroughs, and corporate towns; and also all Our Governors-General, Governors, Lieutenant-Governors, and officers administering the Governments for the time being of Our territories and Colonial possessions ...

As can be seen, this was a formidable network with which to tap the generous flow of public contributions to the Fund.
  The Commissioners established this network by a notice issued from its offices at No 16A Great George Street to all the Commissioners in Aid. It is reprinted at Appendix B.

The Royal Commission – Early Years 13

Like the Commission itself this notice was noteworthy for its attention to detail. The fact that it was merely a logical continuation of the Royal Commission was a tribute to the careful planning which had gone into the latter, which, for all its lofty and romantic language, was a very practical document which has stood the test of time.

As instructed in the Royal Commission, the Commissioners also established at an early stage an executive committee which was also the Finance Committee for the Fund. This had its first meeting on 17 January 1855. The first members of the Executive and Finance Committee, nominated by the members of the Commission, were:

The Right Hon. Lord St. Leonards (elected Chairman by the Committee)
Colonel The Hon. James Lindsay, MP
Lieutenant Colonel Shafto Adair, MP
Thomas Baring, Esq., MP
George C. Glyn, Esq., MP
Sir Alexander Spearman, Bt
Vice-Admiral Henry Hope, CB
Major R.J. Little, RM
W.G. Anderson, Esq., (Treasury Representative)
R.C. Kirby, Esq., (War Office Representative)
Captain E.G. Fishbourne, RN (Honorary Secretary)
Captain J.H. Lefroy, RA (Honorary Secretary)

The Commissioners had lost no time in establishing a staff – indeed the date of the staff's establishment was the date on which Royal Commission had been signed. The initial staff, under the two honorary secretaries (one, Captain Fishbourne, was subsequently taken on as a paid secretary), consisted of a Naval Paymaster and an Army Quartermaster (Royal Artillery) as assistant accountants to an accountant provided by the Registrar General, and four clerks. The clerical staff was increased to seven in July 1855.

To the very practical help provided for Florence Nightingale at Scutari by Messrs Samuel Alcock & Co in the form of basins, this firm added in 1855 a production line of splendid ewers,[1] 20cm high, and carrying on one side a black printed scene of the Crimean battlefield with wounded soldiers, and on the other a grieving family. Above the family a very Victorian angel floated watchfully, holding aloft a banner bearing the words 'Royal Patriotic Fund'. The jugs were sold in aid of the Fund. They are now collectors' items and one was sold at auction in 1991 for £340.

Additional publicity was given to the Fund by advertising, but the Honorary Secretaries were careful not to incur undue expenditure, and advertising in the national press was generally limited to those newspapers whose managers would provide space free (such as the *Daily News* and the *Morning Post*) or at a considerable discount.

By the time of the first meeting of the Commission the sum of almost £291,392 had already been contributed by the public to the Fund, and the Commissioners immediately set out to consider what rates of relief should be provided for widows and their families. In assessing from a modern standpoint the total of funds raised and the scales of help given, it needs to be realized that £1 in the mid nineteenth century would be equivalent to about £40 in the 1980s, so that the modern equivalent of 1 shilling then would be about £2.

By the end of their first meeting the Commissioners had approved a 'Provisional Scale of Weekly Relief' for widows. This was calculated according to rank, with a 'Staff Non-Commissioned Officer's' widow at the top level and a 'Drummer's/Private's' widow at the bottom. Increments were given according to the number of children, so that the top rate was 9s a week for a Staff NCO's widow with eight children, while at the bottom end of the scale was a Private's widow with one child at 4s.6d, or, if childless, 3s 6d.

At this first meeting the Commissioners also had before them some questions about eligibility which had been encountered by their Honorary Secretaries. These included:

1. Were the widows of commissioned officers eligible?
2. Could eligiblity be extended to include other dependents if there was no widow or child?
3. Could the wives of prisoners of war be regarded as widows for the time their husbands were prisoners?
4. Would members of Militia Regiments that were stationed

The Royal Commission – Early Years

during the war in the Mediterranean or any other foreign station be considered to be on active service (and their widows, therefore, eligible)?

5. Would crews of HM Ships on foreign stations, other than those adjacent to Russian coasts, be considered on active service unless actually killed in action?

6. Would the widows of civilians 'attending officers as private servants', and who may die of disease, or through enemy action, be eligible?

In answering such questions there seems little doubt that the Commissioners must again have been grateful for the care that had gone into the writing of the Commission, since the phrase '... towards the succouring, educating, and relieving those, who, by the loss of their husbands and parents in battle, or by death on active service in the present war ...' provided them with clear guidance for their answers. These were affirmative to question 1; affirmative to questions 5 and 6, provided that death occurred in action; and negative to the remainder.

Having agreed to the principle that officers' widows could come within the scope of the Fund, the Commissioners considered and adopted some restrictions which would be applicable to them. The first was, that, bearing in mind that officers' widows received Government pensions, 'assistance ought only to be given to them in special cases of great necessity, and that the relief of Non-Commissioned Officers and Privates ought to be regarded as the primary object of the Fund'. The second was that, for the same reason and because funds would be limited, widows of officers above the rank of Captain in the Army, or the equivalent in the Navy, would not qualify for help from the Fund.

The rates proposed for officers' widows within these limits varied between £14 p.a. for a Captain's widow with no children to £62 p.a. for a Lieutenant's widow with three children. The scales were calculated taking full account of the Government pension which would be granted to the widow. In addition, the amounts granted were to vary according to the circumstances of the officer's death; the largest amounts being granted where the officers were killed in action or having some other violent death and lesser amounts being provided where death was from other causes.

In agreeing to all these provisional scales the Commissioners realized that they might be accused of being less than generous. They had, however, to bear in mind that these were early days in the war. The contributions to the Fund had proved to be generous in a very few months, but this could have been a first flush which might dwindle. They were clearly shocked by the number of early – in fact, pre-battle, – casualties so they had sensibly balanced a conservative estimate of the probable flow of funds against a careful calculation of likely claims.

This balance was struck for the Commisioners by the Executive and Finance Committee at its first two meetings, on 17 and 24 January 1855, and the calculations are of great interest for the light they cast on the social structure of the time as well as the picture of the casualties at this stage of the war.

From all the sources available, the Committee assessed the deaths up to 24 January 1855 to be as follows:

At Varna (the port where the allied troops first landed on the Crimean peninsula and before any engagement with the Russians, i.e. from disease) 752

From the battles at Alma, Inkerman and Balaclava (taken from the casualty lists published in the *London Gazette*) 2,301

At Scutari (the base hospitals) up to 7 January 1855 2,044

At Scutari and Balaclava from 8 January to 31 January 1855 (an informed estimate based on an average of sixty a day from sickness) 1,440

Missing 179

Deaths on passage from Scutari 1,300

Deaths in the Navy 800

TOTAL 8,816

The Royal Commission – Early Years 17

Deaths in the trenches since 1 December 1854, at Malta, on passage home to England and after arrival in England estimated at about a further 200 bringing total deaths up to the end of January 1855 to some 9,000. In the event, deaths had reached 10,400 by March 1855.

The Committee's assessment of the probable future claims on the Fund against this background was based on the assumptions that an average of one fifth of the Army and Navy casualties would have been married men and that the average age of their widows would be 30 years.

On this basis the Committee calculated that the number of widows who might need help would be 1,790 and the number of children, 3,000. Life annuities for this number of widows, involving premiums for nineteen years at £9 10s a year for each, would cost £323,095. The maintenance and education of children for ten years at £6 a year would cost £180,000. To these totals were added an estimation of the help that might be needed for some officers' widows (£12,000) and a percentage for administrative expenses over fifteen years. The total of all these liabilities was estimated at £550,095 and the Committee expressed the fear that the cost would be much greater 'if the war continues'.

Over half a million pounds was a very large sum in 1855 so that it was fortunate that the £290,000 raised by mid-December 1854 was not simply an initial enthusiastic response which was subsequently to fade away. By the end of December the total had reached £437,660 and up to the end of March 1855 the Fund stood at about £937,000.

By the time the Executive and Finance Committee had made its second report to the Commissioners in early April 1855 it was clear that there had been an overestimation of the numbers of applicants and an underestimation of the contributions to the Fund. This combination of events enabled the Commissioners to agree a scale of allowances which had been partially revised upwards by the Executive and Finance Committee. At this time contributions to the Fund were being received at an average rate of £10,000 a week and applications for help were being received at the rate of seventy a week for widows and seventy-five a week for orphans.

The investment policy which was operated by the

Executive and Finance Committee in these early stages of the Fund was to acquire a mixture of Gilts and Loans providing interest between 3½% and 6%, so that at the end of March 1855 some £510,000 was invested in Exchequer Bills and Bonds and about £387,000 in Loans and Debentures, the whole bringing in an income of about £37,000.

Bearing in mind the large amounts of money which were arriving from all parts of the world, the initial handling and accounting for the funds were clearly important. Again the careful instructions contained in the Commission had provided for this in detail.

The Paymaster-General, at that time Lord Stanley of Alderley, was appointed Treasurer of the Commission with responsibility for the safe custody of all the money received and paid. The channel for the funds was also specified in the Commission; a separate account to be established at the Bank of England with the title 'Patriotic Fund', from which sums would be paid by drafts and into which all contributions would be received; in both cases on the authority of members of the Executive and Finance Committee or the Secretaries to the Commission.

The exemplary care shown in the arrangements for handling the contributions received by the Fund may appear to have been carried to extremes. For example, the sub-committee appointed to report on the security of the Funds in 1855 recorded that while 'The larger portion of the contributions received have been paid directly to that Account' (the Paymaster-General's account at the Bank of England) 'without passing through the hands of any officer of the Commission', some contributions were 'remitted in letters addressed to the Honorary Secretaries' and these letters were 'opened in the presence of two persons and the remittances are entered by the Assistant Secretary in a day book for that purpose'.

Before concluding that these precautions were rather excessive, it needs to be remembered that the handling of large amounts of public contributions to charitable projects was a new experience in the 1850s, and that these were sometimes very large amounts, particularly those consolidated contributions received from the Empire and from

The Royal Commission – Early Years

local Committees in centres of population in the Kingdom. For example, the £2,000 received from the Lieutenant-Governor of Van Diemen's Land as a result of a collection in Hobart Town is the equivalent in the 1980s of some £80,000.

So far in this narrative the subject of the children of men killed in the Crimean War has merely been mentioned. If this were to give the impression that the Commission gave the proper care of the orphans of the Crimea a low priority, it would be a totally false one. At their earliest meeting, both the Executive and Finance Committee and the Commissioners considered how best to help the children, and this is the subject of the next chapter.

Footnote

1. See illustration facing page 134.

3 The Orphans

The word 'orphan' is not often used towards the end of the twentieth century, because, in common with certain other words which were quite common in the nineteenth century, like 'asylum' (meaning sanctuary) and 'paupers' (meaning those receiving 'poor-law' relief) it has acquired a pejorative implication. The word however, is an accurate and brief description of a person bereaved of one or both parents – usually a child, but for legal (and, consequently, charitable) purposes there are no natural age limits on orphans.

The duties laid on the members of the Royal Commission towards the orphans of those killed in the Crimea were clearly outlined: '... to contribute a portion of those means with which Our nation has been blessed towards the succouring, educating, and relieving those, who, by the loss of their (husbands and) parents in battle, or by death on active service in the present war, are unable to maintain or to support themselves ...'

This simple outline embraced some far from simple tasks, however, as the members of the Executive and Finance Committee soon discovered. There were some families in which the widow, by working, could continue to support and keep some of the children, but not all. In some instances, and for a variety of reasons, homes had to be found for all the children of a family. Education had to be provided for a very wide range of children of all ages; often combined with a substitute home. In many instances children were of an age where they needed to be placed almost immediately in an apprenticeship or in an appropriate training establishment rather than in a school.

The majority of the problems of providing for orphans were relatively long-term matters. It followed that one of the

The Orphans

earliest questions to be solved by the Commissioners was for how long they should accept responsibility for the care of individual children. The decision was made that this responsibility should cease when boys reached the age of 15 years, and girls were 21, or when the latter married, whichever occurred first.

To deal with the many different situations which confronted them, the Commissioners had to make use of a variety of solutions. The chief of these in the early stages were:

> Gratuitous offers of providing for orphans would be accepted 'at the discretion of the (Executive and Finance) Committee'.

> Local Committees would be asked to place children in schools in their several localities, and pay for them if necessary, pending more final, long-term arrangements. If the children were not living with their mothers, board and lodging for them was to be found 'with respectable people'. In all instances where responsibility for education was assumed a Trustee was to be appointed to supervise.

> 'Where orphans are of a fit age to be placed at school or in service, or to be bound apprentice, the (Executive and Finance) Committee to be at liberty to place them out accordingly, and to place any orphans for education in any asylum, industrial school, or other establishment for receiving orphans or destitute children; *but the Committee is not to be at liberty to purchase any perpetual right of presentation, or to endow or enlarge any such establishment. If after all the other claims on the Fund are satisfied a surplus should remain on hand, then the subject of endowments shall be submitted to the consideration of the Royal Commissioners.*'

The italicized passage[1] demonstrates the caution with which the Commissioners had to approach long-term commitments in the first year of the Fund's existence, and it made it necessary for there to be many arrangements made for children which were temporary and in other ways unsatisfactory. It was not surprising that many widows were unhappy with these and that many compromises had to be made.

The situation in which the Commission found itself by the middle of 1855 was that, in addition to some 1,500 widows being provided with allowances, there were 1,835 children for whom allowances and education or other training had to be furnished. The resource available was an invested capital of just over £1 million, producing on annual income of about £38,000 against an estimated commitment of an almost identical sum. At a point in the war which saw the Russians still in control of Sebastopol, with heavy casualties and another winter's campaigning perhaps still to come, it was understandable that the Commissioners were not yet prepared to devote large amounts of capital to extended commitments. Even without the probability of very many more widows and orphans being created, it has to be remembered that communications and social conditions in the mid nineteenth century made the discovery of those in need of help much more difficult than it is in the 1980s. In April 1855 the Executive and Finance Committee was reporting that the rate of applications for help (of seventy-five a week in the case of orphans) did not 'arise so much from recent cases of mortality, as from the time that elapses before the widows are made acquainted with the deaths of their husbands'.

As time went on and contributions to the Fund continued to flow in, the Commissioners did make increases in the scales of allowances for children as well as widows, but not until the war ended in April 1856 did they feel able to allocate large amounts of capital to endowments and in that way to make appropriate permanent provision for Service orphans.

On the recommendation of the Executive and Finance Committee, at its meeting on 19 April 1856, the Commissioners, on 27 May 1856, made the following decisions:

Wellington College
There should be a perpetual endowment in Wellington College to the extent of £25,000 for the sons of military officers: subsequently agreed to provide guaranteed places for 18 pupils.

Royal Naval School, New Cross
There should be a similar endowment in the Royal Naval

The Orphans

School, New Cross, to the extent of £8,000 for 7 sons of naval officers.

Royal Naval Female School, Richmond [now the Royal Naval School, Haslemere] There should be a like endowment in the Royal Naval Female School at Richmond to the extent of £5,000 for 5 daughters of officers.

Royal Naval and Military Free Schools, Devonport [no longer functioning as such] and Seaman and Marines Orphan School, Portsmouth [now the Royal Naval & Royal Marines Children's Home] There should be similar endowments in the Naval and Military Schools of Devonport and Portsmouth to the extent of £2,500 in each for the children of soldiers, sailors and marines: 13 at Devonport and 11 at Portsmouth.

In addition, on 2 July 1856 it was decided to establish a new school for 300 girls between five and fifteen years of age for the daughters of soldiers, sailors and marines. For this purpose the Commissioners had already decided to allocate £15,000 a year for the education and maintenance of the girls and had set aside £160,000 capital to provide this, to purchase or construct a suitable building, and to furnish it.

The requirement for a new school for boys was not considered to be so great. Initial investigations were made into the feasibility of providing a perpetual endowment of such a school, but for only a hundred boys. For this purpose the Commissioners were prepared to set aside the sum of £25,000. As an interim measure some 300 places were filled at a school at Barnet run by the Reverend W. Pennefather.

Clearly, purpose-built schools could not be ready for some time so interim arrangements had to be made, and the Commissioners decided that the capital set aside for the two schools, and not yet committed, should provide the income from interest and dividends, to help the General Fund to meet the cost of these arrangements.

In addition to these endowments for set numbers of pupils already mentioned, arrangements were made with existing appropriate establishments on the basis of payment by the Commission of specified sums annually for each child. Such arrangements were made at 'The Royal Caledonian Asylum' (£17 p.a. for each child), The Orphan Asylum, Wanstead

(£23 p.a. for each child), The Soldiers' Infant Home, Hampstead, and The Royal British Female Orphan Asylum (cost unspecified) and with many local committees which had established homes for up to around twenty children in each, usually supervised by clergymen.

The search for schools or orphanages to look after orphans pending the establishment of the proposed purpose-built establishment for boys, or as a permanent alternative to this, included proposals to set up 'Patriotic Wards' in existing Government operated boys' schools. Those considered were the Royal Military Asylum, Chelsea and The Royal Hibernian School, Dublin, both operated by the War Department, and The Greenwich Schools, operated by The Admiralty. In no case, however, did such arrangements suit either the schools or the Commissioners, so the proposal was dropped and alternatives sought. It being clear that accommodation and educational facilities were needed for a significant number of boys for when vacancies in existing schools or orphanages did not exist, search was made for a suitable building to use as a temporary school. By 1861 the need for such a school had become urgent, partly because of the increasing costs in existing schools, and the Executive and Finance Committee finally found a house at Wandsworth which was taken on a ten-year lease with a view to accommodating up to 200 boys there.

By March 1862 there were 760 children in various boarding institutions in addition to those at the temporary boys' school at Wandsworth (146) and the still unfinished Commission's new girls' school at Wandsworth (268) and those with bursaries (21): the whole totalling 1,195. It needs to be borne in mind that this was only just over a quarter of the total number of children who were being helped by the Commission at that time. The balance being provided, like their mothers, with allowances to help the latter to maintain their families at home.

The story of the Commission's girls' school (which opened in July 1856 and only ended in 1973) has a chapter to itself.

Anyone who has had experience of finding schools for children, even for their own close relations, cannot be surprised to read that placing children who have lost their fathers, in the limited number of institutions available, involved very many hazards. A considerable amount of the time and effort of the Commissioners and their staff was devoted to these problems, so it is right that some should be described.

The case of Mrs 'X' and her son and daughter occupied the time of the Executive and Finance Committee during these meetings in 1857. Also it involved printing a page and a half of a report to the Commissioners. It concerned a sergeant's widow whose son and daughter, with her initial agreement and subsequent endorsement, had been paid for by the Commissioners to attend two separate Protestant schools. The girls' school appeared to satisfy all concerned, but Mrs 'X' complained about the boys' school. The complaints were proved to be unfounded but the mother was told that if she was not satisfied she could take the children home. Having said that she was satisfied, she then asked that the children be moved to a Roman Catholic asylum, on the grounds that although her husband was Protestant she was a Roman Catholic. 'She was informed that there was no desire to interfere with any right she might possess as a guardian over these children, but that no assistance would be given in their removal to a Roman Catholic asylum, as their father was a Protestant, and as she had stated that it was his wish that they should be educated as Protestants, and further, as they had been up to that period educated as such.' The boy duly left school and joined his mother. The girl did not wish to leave and said that she wanted to continue to be a Protestant.

Mrs 'X' was not prepared to accept this and a writ of habeas corpus was obtained. The case was argued in the Queen's Bench Division and the daughter was delivered to her mother as the Court instructed. Meanwhile the girls' school had made her a Ward in Chancery and asked that the Court should appoint Protestant guardians. This was agreed by the Court and the girl returned to her Protestant School.

Meanwhile, as a result of the case it had been discovered that Mrs 'X' was already married to another man when she 'married' Sergeant 'X', so that she herself was actually not entitled to help at all.

A much more public and time-consuming controversy also

arose over religious denomination. The Commissioners and their staff were faced on two separate occasions with public allegations that they had discriminated against Roman Catholic widows and orphans. The first was brought by the Duke of Norfolk in June 1857, and the second, later that year, from the Roman Catholic Archbishop of Dublin. Both were on the same general lines: that in spite of generous contributions to the Fund from Roman Catholics all over the world, the benefits from the Fund were devoted *primarily* to Protestant children and that little, if any, help was given to Roman Catholic children to be brought up in the Roman Catholic religion. These charges and their repercussions are covered in some detail in the next chapter.

It is likely that this experience had the lasting effect that the Commissioners were careful in the future to emphasize in their reports the strictly neutral nature of the education provided for orphans in schools and orphanages used, as far as religious questions were concerned, or to specify the Roman Catholic persuasion where it existed. They were at pains to emphasize the non-denominational aspect of their own school for girls, the 'Royal Victoria Patriotic Asylum', which was about to be built in 1857.

Footnote

1. Author's italics

4 A Covenant for Children

The Royal Commission's decision, at its meeting on 30 April 1856, to use a significant proportion of the capital of the Fund for 'perpetual endowments' for the education of orphans of those killed in the Crimea, including the establishment of its own schools for girls and boys, was a momentous one. It implied a commitment extending far beyond the near limits of the, already concluded, Crimean conflict; although at the time it is not clear that this had been fully appreciated by the Commissioners.

The Executive and Finance Committee had already set up a sub-committee to study the arrangements for the girls' school and this, in turn, lost no time in requesting the Reverend F.C. Cook, HM Inspector of Schools, connected with the Church of England, to provide some detailed recommendations about the objectives of such a school, its control and staffing, the type of accommodation required, and some of its running costs. His report was considered by the Committee in July 1856 and he was asked to obtain a plan and estimates based on his proposals.

The Committee also decided that the site for the school should be within twenty miles from London, and that enquiries should be made for a suitable site of between five and fifteen acres. Some sites subsequently considered were at Feltham, Holloway, Hampton, Harlesden, Willesden, Shooters Hill, Slough and Sudbury (Middlesex).

On the face of it, the Committee favoured the Sudbury site and appointed a sub-committee of three, including the Reverend F.C. Cook, and assisted by an architect, to inspect this site and to tender for its purchase to Miss Copeland, the owner, if it appeared satisfactory. The architect nominated was Mr Major Rhode Hawkins, who was the architect to the

Committee of the Council of Education.

At about this time it seemed probable that Kneller Hall might be purchased and appropriately converted into the school for girls. While still considering what expenditure might be needed to make this building suitable, however, an important development occurred. Earl Spencer offered a large and very desirable site on Wandsworth Common at the very reasonable price of £50 an acre and the Executive and Finance Committee strongly recommended that the Commissioners authorize the purchase of up to fifty acres. The Commissioners were more than pleased with the offer of such a central and prominent site, and increased the area to sixty-five acres. They also fully endorsed the Reverend F.C. Cook's full proposals. Because these provide a rare picture of a Victorian establishment of this type, the proposals are given in full at Appendix C. Some, however, warrant mention here.

The object of the 'Institution for three hundred girls, between five and fifteen years of age' was specified as 'to afford such a practical education to the girls as may qualify them for domestic service, or other similar occupations'. To the ears of those brought up in the latter half of the twentieth century, this may sound hard-hearted, and a very limited aim. But in the 1850s this was simply a recognition of reality, and it was based upon evidence provided by experts with ample experience of similar establishments.

The course of instruction was recommended to include a system of industrial training as well as all the subjects taught in 'a good national school', with due attention being paid to 'practical and economical matters'.

The staff proposed for the school was a Superintendent (also to double as Housekeeper), three 'Governesses' and three Assistant Teachers, and a domestic staff of one cook, three housemaids, a laundry-woman, a porter and a medical attendant. The Chaplain was also to be the Secretary, and was to be a crucial member of the staff as he was also to be held responsible for the instruction in the school, the Superintendent being responsible for everything else.

The pupils were to be divided into three 'departments' of a hundred girls each. Those who came into the school between the ages of 5 and 8 would go through two of the

A Covenant for Children

departments, but older girls, who were expected to be more difficult to manage and to need firmer discipline, would enter the third department.

Once the girls became fifteen years old, it was planned that some would be employed as pupil teachers for the younger girls, others as domestic staff in the school, and it was hoped that the balance of the anticipated thirty-five or so girls likely to reach that age each year would be found domestic situations outside.

The anticipated annual running costs of the school were some £600 to £700 for salaries and £3,000 for board and clothing.

All this sounds modest enough and, even in the 1850s, not likely to cause much of a public stir. Not many Royal Commissions, however, sponsor a major building on a prominent site within three miles of Westminster, and even fewer are composed of so many distinguished figures presided over by The Queen's Consort. Thus it was that, at their meeting on 8 June 1857, the Commissioners 'resolved – that His Royal Highness Prince Albert be requested to solicit Her Majesty to be graciously pleased to lay the Foundation Stone of the intended Asylum and sanction its being called "The Royal Victoria Patriotic Asylum for Orphan Daughters of Soldiers, Seamen and Marines".'

Events moved fast and, at a quite grand ceremony on 11 July 1857, Queen Victoria laid the foundation stone with an appropriately engraved silver trowel.

The extra fifteen acres of land purchased from Earl Spencer were more expensive than the original fifty, but still a bargain, so an extra £900 was approved for the purchase. The lowest tender for the construction of the building was £31,607, including the cost of internal fittings, and came from Messrs George Myers and Son. This was accepted and the expectation was that the Asylum would be ready for occupation by Christmas 1858.

The Commissioners needed to make an interim arrangement for a number of girls for whom arrangements could not be made at existing schools through endowments already made, and because, in any event, they wished to begin to train staff for the Wandsworth establishment. They, therefore, rented 'Lime Grove', Putney, as a temporary school and in July 1857 the first Matron/Superintendent was appointed. This first appointment was not an unqualified success in that within a year the Matron's partiality to alcohol had rather outweighed her otherwise efficient performance of her duties. She was allowed to resign, and a successor, Miss Clavell, was appointed, together with a Chaplain, the Reverend William Kirkby.

Meanwhile, the building of the permanent Royal Victoria Patriotic Asylum was proceeding. It had been designed as a 'prestige' building in the 'Gothic' style then fashionable. Its architectural importance was acknowledged by all concerned in the early stages of its construction, care being taken to spend an additional £600 on iron railings round the grounds next to the Tooting Road in place of a solid fence, tree planting, and landscaping the ground because 'The Asylum being a National Monument, the Committee felt it right to open it to view of passengers travelling on the South Western Railway, by sloping the ground, so as to admit a view of the principal front of the building.'

A contrary view a century and a quarter later is provided by an article in *The Sunday Times Magazine* of 29 July 1984 which described the building as 'the kind of building that gave Victorian architecture a bad name. It towers over the surrounding area with an intimidating air of menace, its bristling, gloomy turrets and sinister gargoyles serving as a testament to an era that prided itself on the severity of hard work and high ideals'.

The planned date of Christmas 1858 for the first occupation of the building was, perhaps, unrealistic from the start. In the event (partly because of a strike by the builders' workmen) it could not be occupied until 1 July 1859 and at that time parts of the main building were still not completed. In addition, ancillary buildings such as the Infirmary, the Chaplain's house, farm buildings, the 'engine house' and a round Lodge had still to be constructed.

The partial occupation of the new school at Wandsworth ahead of completion was made necessary because the lease of the Lime Grove premises at Putney came to an end and places had to be found for 240 girls. The cost of maintaining the temporary girls' school at Putney had been £5,500 for the two years of its occupation.

A Covenant for Children

Looking at the broader picture of child care by the Fund, the number of children for whom some form of relief was being provided stood at 4,380 at the end of 1859. This was 780 more than the total estimated only two years earlier, and was in spite of a rather horrifying mortality figure of 341 children, only one of whom had been in the Commission's own establishment. It is apparent that many of these deaths were due, at least in part, to neglect and malnutrition – sometimes starvation. The Executive Committee reported that the 'moral and physical improvement in the children after being placed in asylums is readily perceptible. There is no reasonable doubt but that the lives of many have been saved by the food and care which they have received'.

The number of children who had been placed in various schools and other boarding institutions by the Commission at this time was 778, excluding those in the Royal Victoria Patriotic Asylum. The annual overall cost of the help given to children in relief, lodging and education was running at about £80 per caput or some £33,000 and the total cost of building the school at Wandsworth had eventually totalled £47,000.

With the girls' school operating, if not yet fully completed, there was still no permanent solution in sight for the Fund's school for boys. There had been an offer from Lord Northwick of Thirlestone House at Cheltenham, but the tenure would have been for only seven years, and the buildings would have needed £6,000 spending on them to convert them for use as a school. The Commissioners had accumulated £32,000 to provide temporary accommodation for the boys, and a house was found at Wandsworth, reasonably near the Royal Victoria Patriotic Asylum, on a lease of ten years, and by 1862 there were 146 boys at what was described as the 'Boys' Temporary Home'.

At this time there were 268 girls at the Royal Victoria Patriotic Asylum and some 900 children placed at twenty-five boarding establishments, the latter including twenty-one officers' children between the Royal Naval Female School, Richmond, The Royal Naval School, New Cross, and Wellington College. In addition, of the 4,513 children who had been receiving help since the Commission was established, 609 had become apprenticed, obtained posts or had become adults, and, sadly, 419 children had died.

Very soon after the decision to build the Royal Victoria Patriotic Asylum was made in 1856 the time of the Executive and Finance Committee was almost monopolized by problems of the education of orphans in general, and those of the Royal Victoria Patriotic Asylum in particular. So dominant was this, that in 1863 when Lord Colchester, the Chairman of the Committee, found himself at odds with the Committee over the question of discipline at the Victoria Asylum, he found it necessary to resign from the Committee because 'The business of the Executive Committee has now resolved itself chiefly in the management of the Schools of the Fund, especially of the Victoria Asylum.'

To see why this was so (and it undoubtedly was) it is necessary to look at three events involving the school which brought much unfavourable publicity.

The first of these, chronologically, was the charge of discrimination against those of the Roman Catholic faith. As already mentioned in a previous chapter, this charge was laid during 1857 in two different forms by the Duke of Norfolk and Archbishop Cullen of Dublin respectively.

The Duke of Norfolk, in a letter to the Right Honourable Sidney Herbert, one of the Commissioners and the Secretary of State for War (or 'Secretary-at-War'), registered three complaints:

> that, while Roman Catholic children in Scotland and Ireland could be placed in Roman Catholic establishments there by the Commissioners, those in England were denied similar facilities.

> that endowments had been given to Church of England establishments which could only be attended by Roman Catholics with the consequence of 'almost inevitable destruction of their faith: that similar endowments had not been given to Roman Catholic institutions'.

> that the Duke could quote 'some instances of the great hardships poor Catholic widows undergo, from the manner in which they are treated by those to whom the management

A Covenant for Children

of the Patriotic Fund is intrusted, and the way in which the rules are administered'.

The Archbishop, whose letter was printed in *The Times* on 5 October 1857, made four charges in much the same vein. These were:

> that Catholic clergymen in Dublin had applied to the managers of the Patriotic Fund 'in favour of the widows and orphans of soldiers killed in the Crimea; yet, as far as I could learn, not one shilling was then obtained by such application'.
>
> that 'when relief was granted in Dublin, a parson was always employed to administer it, and, I have heard, that he generally selected a Protestant Church or vestry as the place for doling it out'.
>
> that 'the good Sisters of Mary and of St. Clare, and other religious communities, offered their services to the managers of the Patriotic Fund for the education, at a very trifling expense, of the female orphans of the Catholic soldiers'. They had, the Archbishop wrote, received responses but 'I believe there was not one single orphan committed to their care in Dublin, and I suppose the same may be said of the rest of Ireland'.
>
> that while grants had been made 'to Protestant institutions and for Protestant education, not a shilling voted, it would appear, to give a Catholic education to Catholic orphans'.

These charges were naturally taken very seriously by the Commissioners, and the Executive and Finance Committee devoted much effort and time to ensuring that the Commission could refute them successfully. In rebutting the general charges of partiality in the Duke of Norfolk's first two complaints the Commission was able to point out that there were three ways in which help with accommodation and education was given to the orphans of soldiers and sailors. The greater proportion attended 'local, national and other schools' with the help of the Fund, without any religious consideration being specified by the Commissioners and based upon the choice and decision of the mother. The second category of children were those who needed boarding accommodation as well as education and these were placed in establishments of the appropriate religion; again, depending upon the choice of the parent or guardian. Contrary to the Duke's allegation that suitable Roman Catholic allocations were made only in Ireland and Scotland, all the Roman Catholic establishments receiving Crimean orphans in the summer of 1857 were in England.

The third way in which the orphans were housed and educated was in the Commission's own establishments, and these were to be open to children of all denominations 'on the principle arranged by Act of Parliament for Union District Schools'. Even so, if the parent or guardian of a Roman Catholic Child did not wish the child to attend the Commission's School, financial assistance would be given to enable the child to attend elsewhere.

The Duke of Norfolk's complaint of 'instances of great hardship', when challenged, resolved itself into one occurrence of one widow 'kept a long time in suspense' and this, it appeared, was due to delay in the school's agreement to accept the child.

The charges made by Archbishop Cullen, because they were publicized in the columns of *The Times*, called for a similarly public response, and were firmly refuted by the then Chairman of the Executive and Finance Committee, Lord St. Leonards, in a letter to *The Times* on 5 October 1857. Regrettably this, which is reprinted at Appendix D, did not satisfy the Archbishop who continued to make unsupported general allegations of discrimination against Irish Catholics. Where the Commission was able to extract specific complaints, these were investigated and eventually, after voluminous correspondence, the Archbishop appears to have withdrawn into reluctant silence, but not until Christmas Eve 1857 when presumably his other duties claimed more of his time, or perhaps he was satisfied at having brought about no less than sixty appendices to the Royal Commission's Second Report to Her Majesty The Queen.

The second occurrence which called for the full attention

of the Commission over a long period was a tragic death at the Wandsworth School and the circumstances which surrounded this. Before describing these events and their repercussions, it is right to recall the conditions prevalent in the age in which they occurred. They were hard times: times in which infant mortality was at a high rate; deaths from epidemics of diseases virtually unknown in the late twentieth century were common; ten per cent of the children coming on the books of the Commission were dying before reaching maturity; disposal of sewage was often primitive (at the Boys' School, at one point, there was a glowing report upon the cesspool, to the effect that there were very few solids visible because they were regularly removed to the manure heap for use on the gardens); and at one large 'District' School in London the staff consisted of 'a master, a mistress, needle-mistresses and laundresses' for 450 girls who slept 'two in a bed, 50 or 60 in a room'.

The death of Charlotte Barnett at the Royal Victoria Patriotic Asylum occurred on Tuesday, 7 January 1862. Charlotte was an orphan pupil, who, being about seventeen-and-a-half years of age, was employed as part of the domestic staff at the school. As such, she was still subject to the discipline of the school and was being punished for being rude to one of the laundresses on the previous day. Her punishment, given at the direction of the Chaplain, but carried out by the Lady Superintendent, was to be locked into the Lady Superintendent's bathroom. Her midday meal was taken to her at about 3 pm, and some matches were left with her so that she could light the gas light. The head housemaid visited her at about 4.30 pm and found her 'in good health'. When, however, she went to see her again at about 8.30 pm to take her some tea she found Charlotte badly burnt and lifeless. The linen window blind appeared to have caught fire, together with a chair and all the girl's clothing.

That this incident could have happened without anyone's knowledge seems remarkable in an establishment housing over 300 girls, and can best be explained in the words of one of her friends, Sarah Reardon, who gave evidence at the inquest:

At about six o'clock I was in a room immediately under that

bathroom, and I then heard a screaming and a knocking overhead. A girl named Walters came in and said, 'I wonder what that girl is doing walking up and down now.' I went outside and went with Jane Duncan half way upstairs. At the moment one of the teachers passed across the hall and called to Duncan, who went away, and I returned to the portresses room, yet I did not make known to anyone what I had heard.

Thus the unfortunate Charlotte burnt to death while her colleagues went about their business. The assumption was made that in lighting the gas, with matches and perhaps newspaper spills, she somehow set fire to the blind and then her clothes, or vice versa, and a verdict of 'accidental death' was returned.

Although those were harsh times, the Commissioners were clearly concerned at several aspects of the tragedy. The first of these being the glaring weaknesses in supervision. The Executive and Finance Committee decided that 'two of the school mistresses – the one in charge of the Asylum during the temporary absence of Lady Superintendent, the other, to whom the first alarm was communicated – had both been culpably remiss in disregarding the information they received'. Both teachers were dismissed.

As a more constructive and permanent step to improve the supervision of the school, the Committee appointed a 'Ladies' Committee'[1], of thirteen members, to visit the school each month and to report its recommendations to the Executive Committee. This move led to a much more searching enquiry into the administration of the school, and to the discovery of more serious flaws than irresponsible supervision.

The aspect of the whole affair which most disturbed the Ladies' Committee after two visits, taking evidence and generally seeing the running of the school, was the way in which pupils were punished. The Committee expressed considerable disquiet at the use of solitary confinement and corporal punishment for girls, particularly where the latter had been administered to girls in their teens. The feelings of most of the Committee members were that the system of supervision which entailed the decision about punishments being in the hands of the Chaplain was wrong (although the punishments were implemented by the Superintendent). Equally wrong, they considered was the laxity in supervision which failed to ensure proper control while the Lady Superintendent was not present (as in the Charlotte Barnett affair), and which allowed thefts to occur without detection, and girls to return to the school having been employed in work outside and having been dismissed as unsatisfactory.

The Ladies' Committee called for the dismissal of both the Chaplain and the Lady Superintendent, as well as the establishment of a system of referral to the Ladies' Committee (and, if necessary, the Executive Committee) of serious misdemeanours by the girls or of complaints or appeals by them or their mothers. The Ladies also pressed for the responsible head of the establishment to be a woman and for the prohibition of corporal punishment.

There followed several meetings of the Executive Committee and the Ladies' Committee on these matters throughout 1862, with the former taking a more lenient attitude towards the Chaplain and the Lady Superintendent on the lines that, while they had erred this had been partly due to lack of guidance and supervision by the Executive Committee and that, with the establishment of the Ladies' Committee and clear guidelines, they would perform their duties well. Several members of the Ladies' Committee were sufficiently dissatisfied with what they regarded as lack of support from the men that they resigned.

However, 1863 found the Chaplain and the Lady Superintendent still in office but, as has been mentioned earlier, Lord Colchester, Chairman of the Executive Committee, unable to agree with the other members of the Committee that limited corporal punishment could be inflicted at the girls' school, and resigning. His place as Chairman was taken by the Right Honourable H.T.L. Corry, MP.

On the more positive side at the Royal Victoria Patriotic Asylum the Infirmary was finished and taken into use (thus releasing two extra dormitories in the school for additional children), a second Lodge was completed and occupied, and the building of a chapel was authorized.

Education was being provided by the Commission at the end of the 1863 fiscal year for 573 boys and 640 girls. Of this total, 148 boys were in the Commission's Boys' Temporary House at Wandsworth and 282 girls at the Royal Victoria Patriotic Asylum there; the balance attending those establishments listed at Appendix E. In addition, 20 children of officers' widows were benefiting from the Commission's bursaries at Wellington College, The Royal Naval School, New Cross and The Royal Naval Female School.

The number of children receiving help in the way of allowances at that time were 4,581, and in the period 1862–3 thirty-one children had been apprenticed to traders, forty-five had 'entered service', two had joined the Army and thirteen had joined the Navy. It is another reminder of the mortality rate in the mid nineteenth century that, in the twelve months since 1862 deaths of those on the Commission's books amounted to sixty-five, of whom twenty-three were children and the rest widows who only seven years after the end of the Crimean War, cannot have been of great age.

Footnotes

1. The members of the Ladies' Committee were: Mrs Adair*, Mrs Brown, The Lady Colchester*, Mrs Cook*, Miss Burdett Coutts, Mrs Fishbourne*, Mrs Kirkby*, Mrs Lefroy*, Lady Sarah Lindsay*, Mrs Frank Morrison, Mrs William Prescott, The Hon. Miss Sugden, The Hon. Mrs Wellesley.
   * Wives of Executive Committee Members.

5 A New Lease of Life

The 1860s continued to be a trying time for the Royal Commission. In addition to being the year of the domestic tragedy at the Commission's school at Wandsworth, it was a year of national loss from the death of Prince Albert, the Prince Consort; the leader of so many aspects of life in Victorian Britain, and the President of the Commission. With his death causing so many gaps in the nation's affairs, and an absolute hiatus in so many of the Queen's activities, it was inevitable that consideration of a permanent replacement in the Commission should be put in abeyance. By common consent, the Duke of Newcastle filled the breach as Chairman of the Commission until a more permanent solution could be found.

It has been seen that school problems had become predominant in the business of the Commission and its Executive Committee, and the repercussions of affairs at the Wandsworth Girls' School continued to beset these two bodies. The Commission's third report to Queen Victoria, dated 28 July 1862, had, perforce, included, not only the death of Charlotte Barnett with all the details which emerged at the inquest, but also the incidents of corporal punishment, and the associated large scale resignations from the Ladies' Committee; because the Executive Committee allowed the Chaplain and Superintendent to remain in charge at the school and did not forbid corporal punishment. The resignation of Lord Colchester as Chairman of the Executive Committee because he objected to this last decision was not the end of the matter, because in May 1863 Mr John Abel Smith tabled a question in the House of Commons, for answer by the Under-Secretary of State for War, as to whether he was aware of the affair, and to ask what steps had been taken to prevent a recurrence.

It was not long before the atmosphere of uncertainty and distrust surrounding the school's administration led to the voluntary resignation of both the Chaplain and the Superintendent, and, after the revelation that there had been cases of hysteria among the girls for which they had been sent to 'mesmerists' in London, the school Medical Officer was invited also to resign.

It did not help the Royal Commission at this time that it really was no longer properly constituted. There was no officially appointed President, with the result that the calling of meetings and the rendering of reports to Her Majesty were both intermittent. The situation was exacerbated by the death of the acting President, The Duke of Newcastle, in 1864. The Duke of Somerset signed the report of July 1864, but was clearly aware that the standing of the Commission was somewhat dubious by that time. There had been a considerable reduction in the number of Commissioners (from thirty-six to twenty-six), there was no President, and, most importantly, various major projects had been undertaken that had not been envisaged in the original Commission and which would have long term effects on the Commission's work and funds.

The Duke of Somerset had made the suggestion to The Queen that the Duke of Cambridge would be a most appropriate President for a new Commission. The subject does not seem to have been pursued very energetically however, partly for the reasons already given, but also because the Duke of Somerset decided that he would not take any further responsibility for the Commission's affairs in the light of yet another administrative difficulty; this time in the Commission's own office.

The Naval Captain who had been the Royal Commission's Secretary since its establishment, had corresponded with a schoolmaster who had been dismissed for using corporal punishment injudiciously at the Barnet school, where some three hundred orphans supported by the Commission were being educated. This correspondence, in which the Secretary had been less than tactful concerning actions of the Executive Committee and the Commission, was passed to the Duke of Somerset by the same John Abel Smith who had tabled the Parliamentary question about the troubles at Wandsworth. The outcome of this was a reprimand for the Secretary, and the latter's resignation. This resignation, however, was not accepted by the Commission and this incurred the displeasure of the Duke of Somerset, who thought that it should have been. The general situation at the time is well illustrated by the following exchange in the House of Lords on 1 June 1866.

A question was raised by Lord Nelson who asked the Duke of Somerset (then First Lord of the Admiralty) whether, since there had been no meeting of the Royal Commission for almost a year, any steps were being taken to form a new Commission, and, when it was proposed that the Commission would hold a meeting for the purpose of receiving reports from the Executive and Finance Committee and of approving a report to Her Majesty The Queen.

The Duke explained his disagreement with the retention of the Secretary and said that, in consequence, he had not wished to be associated any further with the work of the Commission and had retired from it at the Commission's meeting on 10 March 1865. Before doing so he had informed the Commission of Her Majesty The Queen's assent to the proposal that HRH The Duke of Cambridge should be appointed President of the Commission.

The Duke of Somerset went on to say that:

> Before he dissociated himself from the Royal Commission, he had considered that a new Commission should be appointed because on the large fund(s) which had been subscribed for the Crimean War all the legitimate claims were exhausted, and in his opinion, they ought to become available for other purposes connected with the Army and the Navy.

The (somewhat testy) exchange continued with Lord Nelson claiming that, since the President had resigned, there was no method of calling future meetings of the existing Commission, and the Duke of Somerset retorting that he never had been the President but had taken the chair at the Commission's request after the death of the Duke of Newcastle.

There seems little doubt that, with the death of Prince Albert and the other misfortunes of the early 1860s, the higher direction of the Royal Commission was not working harmoniously, since members, and recent members of the Commission (such as Abel Smith, Lord Nelson and the Duke of Somerset) were communicating with each other in this way through the very public medium of the Houses of Parliament.

The Royal Commission met, somewhat pointedly, in the week after the exchange in the House of Lords, when Lord Nelson proposed that Earl Grey should take the chair.

There followed something in the nature of an inquest in which the Chairman of the Executive Committee, Lord Nelson and Sir John Pakington gave some convincing reasons why they had considered that the Duke of Somerset was 'acting either as President of the Royal Commission, or else as the Member of the Government who had undertaken to carry out the necessary arrangements preparatory to the issuing of a new Commission'.

The conscience of the Commission having been cleared, the members addressed a letter to the Marquis of Hartington, the Secretary of State for War, as follows:

My Lord,
    At the last Meeting of the Commissioners of the Patriotic Fund on 10th March 1865 the Duke of Somerset informed the Commissioners that he had determined to resign the Chairmanship of the Commission; he also stated to the Commissioners that he had addressed Her Majesty on the subject of a new Royal Commission, of which His Royal Highness the Duke of Cambridge should be President, to which Her Majesty had assented. Under these circumstances the Commissioners at a Meeting held this day, have desired me, as Chairman on this occasion, to request that your Lordship will have the goodness to inform them when Her Majesty's Government are likely to have completed the arrangements for the issue of a new Commission.
                      I have the honour, etc.
                                Grey

Earl Grey was asked to remain as Chairman for the purposes of dealing with the Government about the new Commission but otherwise the Earl of Hardwicke was

A New Lease of Life

elected to chair future meetings of the existing Commission.

The Commission duly approved a belated report to The Queen – this explained that the uncertainty about the appointment of a new Commission had led to the 1865 Report not being rendered, and it emphasized that a number of important issues must await this appointment.

There were, however, some positive developments during these otherwise difficult years. The first was the eventual resolution of the awkward question of the Rodriguez legacy. When it had first become known to Her Majesty's Consul in Manila in 1857 that Don Francisco Rodriguez, who had died on 30 April, had bequeathed the whole of his property to be applied to the relief of 'the Families of English subjects wounded or dying in the Wars', the Consul duly reported this to the British Government and asked for instructions.

The Prince Consort was asked at the time by the Government whether the Patriotic Fund would be able to administer the property, and on the Commission's behalf replied that 'the Royal Commissioners, anxious to acknowledge the compliment paid to the nation by the deceased, would gladly undertake the distribution of the property, and for this purpose a separate account should be kept, to be called the 'Rodriguez Fund Account'.

In fact, because of objections by relatives, the Prince Consort was to die before some of the money from the will was finally released in 1863. The will itself, because of its unique contents and place as a foreigner's tribute, is reprinted at Appendix F. The total sum eventually available to the Fund in 1866 was £7,380 16s 4d.

In this way, the Royal Commission received the first of many funds that arose from causes other than the War with Russia and which were entrusted to it by Her Majesty's Government. Perhaps it served to make still more manifest the increasingly awkward situation in which the Commission found itself. It was some years after the end of the Crimean War and almost all immediate applications for help for widows had been met, very many of the Crimean orphans had embarked on their adult lives, and an increasingly large proportion of the still substantial funds were being devoted to long-term causes such as the Royal Victoria Patriotic Asylum and numerous educational endowments at other schools. An example of the latter which occurred as late as 1864 (eight years after the end of the Crimean War) was the grant of £10,000 to the School for the Daughters of the Officers of the Army for ten bursaries in perpetuity. There were other, equally deserving, institutions seeking long-term financial assistance so that, by 1866, the need for a new Commission was becoming urgent.

The first attempt to remove the doubts and uncertainties that now surrounded the work of the Commission was the publication of the Patriotic Fund Act 1866 (29 and 30 Victoria cap. 120) which was the first official Government intervention in providing some degree of Parliamentary control over the application of funds.

It was soon apparent, however, that this Act, while adequate in introducing governmental authority, was too brief to provide the necessary detailed direction and authorization (in some instances retrospectively) for the administration of funds well into the future, when the immediate cause for the establishment of the Patriotic Fund had ceased to require large scale use of the funds available. Promptly, therefore, this Act was repealed and superseded by the Patriotic Fund Act, 1867 which, in turn, became the basis for the 'Supplementary Commission' of 28 March 1868 which was, at last, the 'new' Commission so long awaited. Some provisions of the 1867 Act and the Supplementary Commission are shown in detail at Appendices G and H but those which were most important to the future of the Fund were as follows:

First of all, the Act confirmed the appropriation and application of the Patriotic Fund that had taken place under the original Royal Commission, and this included the endowments of both the Royal Victoria Asylum and the Boys' School.

Secondly, the Act authorized future 'Supplementary' Commissions by Her Majesty to continue to apply the Patriotic Fund for the relief of widows and orphans of those Servicemen who lost their lives in the war with Russia.

In addition, however, the Act included authorization for the Fund to be used to help the children of Servicemen who lost their lives 'in any other war' or 'in the Services of the Crown'.

A New Lease of Life

The Act confirmed the Royal Commission's provisions concerning the parts to be played in the administration of the Fund by the Paymaster-General, the Governor and Company of the Bank of England, and HM Treasury.

In a new development which, with the Act itself, well and truly officially involved the Government for the first time in the operation of the Fund, the First Lord of the Admiralty, the Secretary of State for War and the Paymaster-General were appointed trustees of the Patriotic Fund.

Finally, 'any Supplementary Commission' was authorized to direct that the Rodriguez Fund should be applied for the same, or similar, purposes as the Patriotic Fund.

The Supplementary Commission issued on 26 March 1868 followed the provisions of the 1867 Act very closely, but it also restored the strength of the Commissioners, both in calibre and in numbers (forty-three). Presided over by His Royal Highness the Duke of Cambridge, the new Commission included, in addition, the Dukes of Somerset and Wellington, the Earls of Shrewsbury, Shaftesbury, Lauderdale, Dalhouse, Hardwicke and Chichester; Earl Grey, Earl Nelson and Earl de Grey; Lords Petre, Rokeby, St Leonards, Fermoy, Chelmsford, Lyveden; and a distinguished list of Commoners including William Gladstone, Benjamin Disraeli, two Field Marshals and several Admirals and Generals.

The warrant for the new Commission contained the same extension of the benefits of the Fund as had the 1867 Act to children orphaned in 'any other war' or as a result of loss of life 'in the service of the Crown'. This regularized the position of the Patriotic Fund Schools and other long-term educational endowments which clearly would involve helping children orphaned long after the war with Russia had come to an end.

A very influential figure in determining the probable future commitments of the Patriotic Fund, and whose calculations had guided the Royal Commission since the Executive and Finance Committee of the Fund first began to look to the future in 1858 and to attempt to measure its probable liabilities against its resources, was the 'Actuary of the National Debt', Alexander Glen Finlaison.

This was the beginning of a relationship with the

profession of actuaries which continues to this day, albeit in a different form. In the 1860s the role of the 'Actuary of the National Debt' in the Commission was to prepare and submit the statement of accounts of the Fund and to provide the Executive and Finance Committee (and, through that body, the Commission) with estimates of existing and probable assets and liabilities. In making these assessments, Mr Finlaison went into considerable detail to produce his actuarial 'computations'. As an example, in his 1863 report he analysed the statistics of the remarriage rate of widows over six years and reached the conclusion that 'It will probably not be incautious if the rate of reduction' [in the number of widows needing help] by remarriage and other causes is therefore placed at 2 per cent per annum.' At that time, of course, the average age of those widowed by the war with Russia was only about 35 years. By the time Mr Finlaison's successor – his son – had provided his last 'computations' for the Commissioners – in 1900, shortly before his death – it was over 70.

The appointment of the Supplementary Commission in 1868 provides an appropriate moment to compare Mr Finlaison's calculations at that date with those he provided in 1858.

	No.	1858 Cost £	No.	1868 Cost £
Allowances to widows of Warrant Officers, NCOs and rank and file	3,200	45,760	2,953	28,266
Allowances to widows of Officers	123	5,904	164	5,929
Total of Widows	3,323	51,664	3,117	34,195
Education of primary school children from home	2,600	10,400	942	5,463
Boarding school education	700	10,500	519	9,082
Boarding school education (Officers' children)	227	2,837	264	5,268
Royal Victoria Patriotic Asylum – Girls	300	5,000	285	5,000
Totals	7,150	80,401	5,127	59,008

The main difference was in the unsurprising fact that twelve

A New Lease of Life

years after the end of the war with Russia the number of orphans of primary school age was greatly reduced. Combined with the inevitable effect of mortality, this demonstrates the very adequate reason why it was necessary to extend the scope of the Commission to 'any other war', at least as far as the children were concerned: a development which was destined to result in lasting benefit for generations of Service orphans to come.

The broader financial picture as calculated by the 'Actuary of the National Debt' at the end of 1868 showed the Commission's investments with a total market value of £794,470 producing an income of £54,821. The foreseeable liabilities of the Commission at this time were £623,793 so that, after setting aside a reasonable sum as a reserve, something over £100,000 was adjudged to be available for capital expenditure if necessary.

In the ten years since Mr Finlaison's first computations, the capital of the Fund had diminished by £957,071. Of this total, the purchase of land, building, endowment and running costs of the Royal Victoria Patriotic Asylum accounted for some £218,000, endowments set aside for the Boys' School and paid to other schools for rights of nomination totalled £71,000, and annuities had been purchased costing £668,071.

The decision to purchase annuities, planned to mature at various dates from 1865 to 1885, was first made in 1855 when 'from the great and increasing number of applicants' it seemed probable that, in spite of the very large sum contributed to the Fund, the income from investments alone would not suffice to meet the commitments of allowances and education costs.

For all the careful provision made for the handling of funds, as described in Chapter 2, in the spring of 1868 the Commission discovered that one of the clerks in the office of the Fund had embezzled money due to widows who had remarried and were living abroad. The circumstances, as reported to The Queen by the Commissioners in 1869 were:

> It was Mr Harvey's duty on receiving the money to give vouchers for the amounts, and to obtain and send the Post Office orders. Instead of obtaining the orders and forwarding

them he appropriated the money to his own use, and abstracted from the office any letters of inquiry which arrived from the widows. This created difficulty and delay in ascertaining the amount embezzled when the dishonesty was discovered; inasmuch as it was only at a later period, when subsequent letters were received asking for the allowances, that it was possible to find out whether or not he had transmitted the money. Mr Harvey was forthwith dismissed; he had been 12½ years in the office. The ascertained extent of the defalcation is £247. His father stated his utter inability to make good the money. In compliance with our instructions, proceedings were taken for the prosecution of Mr Harvey, the Clerk in question; and a warrant for his apprehension was issued by the magistrate at the Bow Street Police Court. Subsequently, Mr Harvey's father addressed a Memorial to His Royal Highness the President, praying, for reasons alleged, that his son might not be prosecuted. The Committee reported that this Memorial contained many mis-statements, and we much desired the prosecution to be continued.

The value of £247 in the 1860s is illustrated to some degree by the report by the Commissioners to The Queen in their Tenth Report in June 1871 that 'The defaulting Clerk, Mr Harvey, alluded to in our Eighth Report to Your Majesty, returned from America, and gave himself up to the Police. He subsequently pleaded guilty, and was sentenced to nine months' imprisonment with hard labour.'

An interesting situation (but not suggested to be in any way related), which it is difficult to envisage occurring towards the end of the twentieth century, was that from December 1866 to December 1869 there had been no audit of the Fund's accounts. Repeated applications to the Treasury for audits had come to nothing so the Commission appointed a retired Inspector of the Audit Office (William Andoe) to carry out the outstanding audits. The Commission was then able to report to The Queen in its Ninth Report in 1870 that 'The Lords Commissioners of the Treasury have sanctioned the Audit by Mr Andoe to the end of last year; and have directed the Controller and Auditor-General to undertake the Audit from and after that period.'

On the whole, it was with a fairly clear conscience as well as a new team that the Royal Commission entered the 1870s.

6   A *'Foster' Fund*

The increased scope provided by the 1867 Patriotic Fund Act was soon being exploited by the Commission and by the Services themselves. Following the lead given in the Supplementary Commission, enquiries were made of the Admiralty and the War Office to establish the probable numbers of Service orphans of wars subsequent to the war with Russia. Casualties of the Indian Mutiny were to be excluded from the total because a Special Fund had been established to help widows and orphans stemming from the mutiny.

The War Office agreed to call for a return to provide the Commission with the Army figures, and, after obtaining more detail from individual regiments, the Actuary was able to arrive at a reasonably accurate total of widows and orphans. The Admiralty considered that the quality of the information which they could provide 'with much labour and research' and at considerable expense would probably not meet the Commissioners' requirements. However, the Actuary considered that he could make a reasonable estimate based on the Navy's Annual Statistical Reports. He was able to report to the Commissioners in February 1870.

The 'Actuary of the National Debt' (and it was still Alexander G. Finlaison) considered casualties from actions in Bengal, China and New Zealand and, after careful analysis reached the conclusion that the probable numbers of orphans to be helped would be thirty-seven where fathers were commissioned officers and fifty-one where fathers were not. Based upon these figures he foresaw their annual support costing £1,157 which represented a capital commitment of £7,741.

Based on these calculations, the Commissioners approved

the inclusion of 'Orphans of Other Wars' as beneficiaries of the Patriotic Fund; to be dealt with in the same way as those of the Russian War, but with some restrictions. These were, that the late father and mother had to have been 'in the married state' while the father was serving in the war (it is just possible that there could be a few who might not satisfy this condition); also, that, when considering claims, the Executive Committee should categorize the orphans as follows:

1. Those whose fathers had lost their lives in battle.
2. Those whose fathers had lost their lives within six months from wounds, or from disease contracted during the war.
3. Those whose fathers had lost their lives within twelve months of the end of the war, from disease contracted during the war.

Having considered the funds probably needed to meet this commitment, the Commissioners also decided that they could authorize an expansion to the number of 'Special Cases' which could be brought within the scope of the Fund.

The category of 'Special Cases' had been established by the Commission in 1866. The need for this arose because the Executive Committee, with the Commissioners' approval, had found it necessary to reject numerous applications from widows where there was inadequate evidence that the husbands' deaths had been attributable to the Russian War or where the marriage had taken place after the war was over, and sometimes after the men had left the Service. As regards the latter category, the rule was established that no allowance, or other help with orphans, could be granted if the marriage had taken place after 31 December 1857.

The rigid application of this rule would sometimes have given rise to hardship for the orphans whose fathers had given good service to their country. The Commissioners had therefore authorized the Executive Committee 'to assist in Special Cases, at their discretion, in educating, and in providing Outfits and Apprentice Fees for orphans who, by existing rules, are excluded from the benefits of the Fund'.

The Executive Committee established four classes of 'Special Cases'. These were:

A 'Foster' Fund

Class 1 Where the father's death was attributable to service in the Crimea but where the marriage had taken place after 31 December 1857. (No marriage after 31 December 1860 was regarded as qualifying, however).

Class 2 Where marriage had taken place before the end of the war but where the father's death could not be proved to be attributable to the war.

Class 3 Where the date of marriage failed to qualify but where there was good medical probability of the father's death being attributable to his service in the war or where 'meritorious services' were established.

Class 4 Where the father had served in the war and where great destitution, numerous family or chronic disease were involved.

In 1867 the Executive Committee included in its list of 'Special Cases' 356 children of non-commissioned ranks and seventy-two children of officers. By 31 December 1868 these numbers had increased to 538 and 119, and three years later the total on the books had increased by 100%. Although these large numbers were all 'on the books' of the Fund, only just under 50% of these were actually receiving education allowances or attending schools at the expense of the Fund at any one time.

The involvement of the Admiralty and the War Office in the Patriotic Fund, which had been brought about by the 1867 Act of Parliament, had, the effect of bringing the Fund firmly into focus as the 'official' Service Fund. It had the structure, resources and experience to receive and dispense funds, so that the extension of its scope already apparent in 1870 proved to be only the beginning.

On the night of 6 September 1870 HMS *Captain* was lost in the Bay of Biscay. There were very few survivors and a *Captain* Fund was set up almost immediately by a committee of naval officers formed at Portsmouth. In April 1871 the Commissioners were approached by this committee with the request that they might take over a proportion of the *Captain* Fund and undertake its distribution.

The naval officers managing the *Captain* Fund were all

serving and considered that they could neither provide the organization or the continuity to administer the funds properly. They felt that the disaster had been a national one and that, as far as help for widows and orphans was concerned, the relief provided would precisely correspond with the scales and arrangements of the Patriotic Fund. Certain allocations had already been made by the *Captain* Fund Committee to relatives of the victims and, where these were parents, the Patriotic Fund would be asked to administer these.

The Commissioners agreed that the Executive Committee should take over these responsibilities and that two naval officers (Rear-Admiral Ryder and Captain Field) should be added to the membership of the Committee to deal with *Captain* Fund questions. It was also agreed that a separate account should be kept and that this expense of administering the Fund should be charged to this. The total amount received by the Commission for the *Captain* Fund on 1 January 1872 was just over £45,000, of which some £5,000 was in the form of gratuities granted by the Admiralty, to be paid out by the Commission on the Admiralty's behalf.

The subscribers to the *Captain* Fund also asked the Commissioners if they would consent to operate a 'Royal Naval Relief Fund' to take up any balance not needed by the *Captain* Fund and to receive subscriptions and donations for the more general relief of distress among 'the widows, children and parents of Officers, Seamen, and Marines of the Royal Navy'. After taking legal advice, the Commissioners initially balked at this proposal, but after an official approach by the Lord Commissioners of the Admiralty to Mr Cardwell, the Secretary of State for War, and detailed study and reassurances by the Executive and Finance Committee, the Commissioners agreed on 8 July 1874 to operate the 'Royal Naval Relief Fund'. It was made clear, however, that the Commission would not be involved in raising any funds.

The seal of approval for the Royal Naval Relief Fund was duly given by Queen Victoria in a Commission issued to the Commissioners for the Patriotic Fund on 7 June 1875 – the Fund being 'either for the immediate relief of any special objects of destitution, arising among the widows, orphans and other relatives of deceased officers, sailors, and marines who have served in Our Fleets, or for the relief of such other objects of destitution as many come within the meaning and purpose of such benevolence'.

At this stage, and until 1878, there was no money in the Royal Naval Relief Fund. The *Captain* Fund Committee, which had the idea of this general Naval Fund as the recipient of the balance left over from the *Captain* Fund and for subsequent subscriptions and donations, had not yet been able to arrive at any final balance and was still using the *Captain* funds to the full. It was not until there had been another Naval tragedy that some money became available.

On 24 March 1878, in a squall off the Isle of Wight, HMS *Eurydice* foundered with the loss of all but two of the crew. As in the circumstances of the loss of HMS *Captain*, a fund was set up in Portsmouth, with a naval committee to raise money and administer it for the benefit of the families of those lost.

However, this Committee considered that the structure and machinery of the Patriotic Fund was in the best position to administer the *Eurydice* Fund on the same lines as the *Captain* Fund. The Royal Commission was duly approached and accepted this additional Trust, subsequently authorizing the Executive and Finance Committee to take on this task following the same principles as for the *Captain* Fund and using the Patriotic Fund scales of assistance.

The money to meet the *Eurydice* commitment was transferred to the Commission in two parts. It was calculated that to pay appropriate allowances to families of those lost would require a capital of £19,000, and this amount was credited to the *Eurydice* Fund. There remained to the Naval Committee a balance of £3,150 which was transferred to the Royal Naval Relief Fund, thus providing it with some substance for the first time.

The next Service orphans to fall within the shelter provided by the Patriotic Fund Commission were those whose fathers failed to survive the wars with the Ashantee tribe in the southern part of West Africa. There were sixty-one of these children – sixteen of them the children of officers. These orphans were brought within the scope of the

Patriotic Fund as 'Orphans of Other Wars', and widows were not included as beneficiaries until the Patriotic Fund assumed full responsibility for the 'Ashantee War Fund' in 1888. Until that year this Fund had an unusual background. It was inaugurated as 'The Gold Coast Relief Fund' in 1874, and the funds were held by the Army Agents, Cox & Co. The Committee responsible for raising the funds paid allowances to seventeen Naval and eleven Army widows, using cheques which were honoured by Cox & Co. Orphans were not included as beneficiaries (which was why they were helped by the Patriotic Fund as 'Orphans of Other Wars'). The value of the 'Ashantee War Fund' when eventually established by the Patriotic Fund was just over £2,000.

1879 began with yet another Naval tragedy. On 2 January that year, as a result of an explosion in HMS *Thunderer* (it was the second in that ship), some funds were raised for the care of the relatives of those killed. These amounted to just over £2,000 and the *Thunderer* Explosion Fund Committee asked the Executive Committee of the Patriotic Fund if it would undertake the administration of this. The Commissioners agreed, provided that the funds could be administered as part of, and on the lines of, the Royal Naval Relief Fund.

The need for help on a much larger scale was incurred later in 1879 as a result of casualties in the Zulu War. Three Funds were opened for public subscription; the 'Zulu War Fund', initiated by an appeal in the press by Colonel James Gildea and managed at the Mansion House; the 'Isandlwana and Rorke's Drift Fund' and the 'Zulu War General Fund' both of which were raised by Committees composed of military, naval and militia officers. The amounts raised by these three funds finally reached over £27,000 and the number of widows and orphans who needed help was 262 of whom 104 were widows. These separate Funds were maintained for only a few months before their administration was taken over by the Patriotic Fund. They were amalgamated under a Royal Warrant dated 22 August 1879 as the 'Zulu War Fund'. The amalgamated fund reached a total of just over £25,000, and it was thought that the allowances granted by the Commissioner would soon exhaust this total – this proved not to be so and the fund still had a substantial surplus well into the 1890s.

In 1880 the Royal Navy suffered another loss. HMS

A 'Foster' Fund

Atalanta was lost with all hands on a voyage from Bermuda to England. The date she foundered is still not known but in the early summer, after the loss was confirmed, a committee was formed in Portsmouth to raise and administer funds to help the widows, orphans and other dependants of the officers and crew. The Lord Mayor of London subsequently broadened the structure for the administration of the *Atalanta* Fund to make it nationally based, and in March 1881 the Royal Patriotic Commissioners agreed to accept responsibility for the Fund, and for its administration on the same lines as the 'Royal Naval Relief Fund'. The amount concerned was £9,275 and those initially on the books for help were twenty-nine adults (including three widows and two mothers of officers) and forty-seven children (including eleven children of officers).

By 1881 the 'Foster Mother' Fund, the Patriotic Fund, had been given seven additional Funds to administer: the extra money available totalling some £103,000 and the extra liabilities amounting to 259 widows, 340 orphans and 172 other dependants, the majority of whom represented long-term commitments in the form of allowances. Also at this time the 'Mother' Fund was caring for 2,370 widows and 104 orphans of the Crimean War together with 361 orphans who qualified as 'Special Cases' and fifty-eight who were 'Orphans of Other Wars'. This was a very heavy burden; particularly bearing in mind that the girls' school ('The Royal Victoria Patriotic Asylum') was costing £10,200 a year to run, and the boys' school, £4,600, while another £2,000 a year was being paid to other educational establishments.

The 'Actuary for the National Debt', in his role as monitor of the Commission's finances, had been concerned for some time at the rate with which these commitments were going to diminish the Patriotic Fund's capability to meet them. By the time he had struck the balances in the accounts early in 1880 it was clear that the Fund had a surplus of assets over liabilities of only just over £12,500. However, as the Actuary reported to the Executive Committee and the Commissioners had to report to the Queen, this took no account of a commitment made in 1874. This was a decision that £30,000 should be set aside at once to make provision for the education of the orphans of Roman

Catholic soldiers and sailors, and that the interest accruing to this sum, should be added to it until the Commission employed the money for its intended purposes: a rider which meant that by 1880 the sum set aside would have been £35,855. This had still not been spent on the education of Roman Catholic orphans and, by the Actuary's computations, it exceeded the cash available by just over £23,000. Furthermore, Mr Finlaison considered that if the Commissioners were to continue the policy of giving extra allowances to widows when they reached the age of 60 an additional £32,000 would be needed in 1880/81. In short, the Patriotic Fund was over-extended and some radical action was essential. As the Fund's Secretary was to put it in evidence to a House of Commons Select Committee in 1895, 1881 was to become a year in which 'the most important epoch in the history of the Patriotic Fund Commission' was to begin.

7 Give and Take

At this range, and at first sight, it is difficult to see why Colonel Young, the Secretary to the Commission in the 1890s, should have regarded the 1881 Act as epoch-making.

The event which gave rise to it was the Actuary's report in 1880, already described, which came to the conclusion that 'it now becomes a subject of imperative necessity to consider what part of the benevolent programmes of the Commissioners should be relinquished'. Yet – with hindsight – it could be argued that the apparent financial crisis which faced the Commissioners was, to some extent at least, an artificial one.

Taking all the specific funds into account, and including those maintained for the boarding schools for girls and boys, the market value of investments was just over £700,000. This was aside from the value of the Patriotic Fund's school properties. To arrive at the apparent deficit of some £50,000, the Actuary had calculated liabilities consisting of estimates of potential applications from widows and orphans, of probable increases in the value of allowances granted, of possible additions to school premises, and of reserves needed to meet various contingencies.

The Actuary's son, Alexander John Finlaison (who was to succeed his father as Actuary to the Commission in 1882) was to question the term 'liabilities' in evidence before a House of Commons Select Committee in 1895. As he saw it, he did not 'apprehend that the Royal Commissioners ever had any liabilities in the sense in which that phrase is generally used ...'. He did not know 'that the Commissioners had ever made any definite promise with reference to the rates of pensions they contemplated to pay in the future, or how far they had embarked in the maintenance of the schools they then had under their control'. Mr Finlaison, the younger, felt that rather than accepting these potential costs as firm liabilities, his father was advising the Commissioners in 1880 'that they were contemplating engaging in a larger expenditure than the amount of funds which they were managing would be able to satisfy'.

The other factor which made the Patriotic Fund's situation appear in deeper trouble than a more concrete balance sheet would have revealed was the view taken by the Commissioners that, apart from capital expenditure on schools, they were free to spend only the income derived from investments. Lord Nelson underlined this in his evidence to another Select Committee in 1900; defining the figure of 'liabilities' as that calculated to be the amount of principal needed to provide the income necessary to meet all possible commitments. This was based on the premise that the funds under the Commissioners' control were 'all permanent funds, and we can only deal with the interest of these funds'.

Standing firmly on these assumptions, the Commissioners reported to The Queen on 6 May 1881 that 'we must abandon the idea of completing the full endowment of the Boys' School for 200 boys' (this had been estimated to cost £60,000), that 'the school must be closed, and we have directed the Executive Committee to take measures to provide, as speedily as possible, for the boys at present in the school, and to reduce the expenditure with a view to closing the school before the end of the year'. Some of the funds thus released could then be made available to implement the long overdue commitment specifically to provide education for Roman Catholic children.

The Commissioners concluded that 'it will be necessary that an amending Act of Parliament be obtained': this not only to cover the closing and selling of the Boys' School and the use of the funds for the education and maintenance of Roman Catholic children but to create 'a permanent governing body for the management of the Girls' School, under the Charitable Trusts Act, as that school may now be considered a fully endowed charitable institution for the benefit of the daughters of soldiers, sailors and marines'.

These, perhaps rather technical, reasons for requiring a

new Act of Parliament would seem to be unlikely precursors of any dramatic development in the Patriotic Fund's history. It was the effect of the apparent financial difficulties on the War Office and the Admiralty which propelled the Commission into a new era. The Secretary of State for War, Mr Childers, had been alerted to the apparent deficiency in the Commission's funds as a result of the 1880 Annual Report to the Queen and, in an interview with the Chairman of the Executive and Finance Committee and the Secretary to the Commissioners on 12 August 1880, had asked for the Actuary's report up to June 1880 which was to prove so crucial. The joint view of Mr Childers and Lord Northbrook, the First Lord of the Admiralty was that 'in their opinion, so serious a deficiency in the assets of a body pledged to pay annuities to the widows and children of officers and men of the Army and Navy, who have died in the service of their country, demands the immediate and most serious attention of the Royal Commissioners'.

In this way the Ministers of the Crown for the Naval and Military Departments were firmly intervening, and signifying the long-term responsibility which they envisaged for the Commission in providing annuities for Service widows and orphans. This was reflected in the 1881 Act in its provision 4 that:

> It shall be lawful for Her Majesty from time to time, by supplemental Commission under Her Royal Sign Manual, to direct the Commissioners of the Patriotic Fund to apply the Patriotic Fund and the income and accumulations thereof or any parts thereof ... for such purposes for the benefit of the widows and children of officers and men of Her Majesty's military and naval forces, and in such manner as may be directed by the said Commission, and so far as any direction in the Commission does not extend, as the Commissioners from time to time think expedient.

The significant change from the 1867 Act was that the restriction of help for those 'in other wars' or 'in the service of the Crown' to Service children no longer obtained: indeed, the Patriotic Fund was now firmly established as a permanent fund (to quote the War Office letter of 12

August) 'pledged to pay annuities to the widows and children of officers and men of the Army and Navy, who have died in the service of their country'.

The weight which the War Office and the Admiralty attached to the health of the Patriotic Fund may have been on principle – though, bearing in mind that the Government still provided no pension for the widows of servicemen, this would seem less than justified – but it may also have been that these Departments were very conscious that developments in South Africa were liable to put some strain on the only source of regular help for Service widows and orphans.

The Boer War (more strictly, the Second Boer War) was still eighteen years away, but the Paul Kruger-led rebellion to reverse the British annexation of the Transvaal was brewing, and 1881 was to see Britain's major defeat by the Boers at Majuba in what amounted to the First Boer War. In the event no special fund was opened to assist with any applications resulting from casualties in this conflict, but the situation in South Africa must have sharpened the concern that a healthy source of funds should be available. (The 'Transvaal War Fund' subsequently established was, in effect, a Boer War Fund related to 1899 onwards.)

The 1881 Act having cleared the way, in its second provision, for the sale of the Boys' School and for 'the said purchase money and also the part of the endowment appropriated for the Boys' School' to be 'carried to and form part of the Patriotic Fund and be applicable for the purposes to which the rest of that fund if for the time being applicable', the school was disposed of for £32,000, and a further £28,400 from the Boys' School endowment fund also became available. These sums enabled £35,000 to be used for the education of Roman Catholic children and the balance to help the liquidity of the Patriotic General Fund which was then able to show a surplus balance of over £73,000.

The boys from the Boys' School were dispersed, partly to St Saviour's Grammar School at Ardingly, and partly to friends' homes. Also resulting from the 1881 Act, a Board of Governors was established for the Girls' Royal Victoria Patriotic Asylum consisting of four members of the Executive and Finance Committee; General Lord

Chelmsford, G.C.B., General Sir Edward Hodge, K.C.B., Frederick W. Gibbs C.B., Q.C., and Joseph Woolley, LL.D.

One of the results of the Patriotic Fund coming more under the spotlight of Government Departments was that a review of the administration of the Fund and its expenditure was undertaken. The two elements of these under scrutiny were the management team and the arrangements for the handling of applications and payment of allowances (generally described as 'annuities').

The staff established in 1855 had consisted of Captain Fishbourne, R.N. and Captain Lefroy, R.A., who were Honorary Secretaries (Captain Fishbourne later being taken on in a paid capacity), an Accountant with two assistants and seven clerks. At the end of 1867 Captain Fishbourne retired and was replaced by William Henry Mugford, a Naval Paymaster who had been one of the assistants to the accountant. Mr Mugford was assisted by a chief clerk/accountant, four clerks and two temporary clerks.

Captain Lefroy, who, as an honorary secretary had been a member of the Executive and Finance Committee, soon achieved prominence in the latter capacity but also in the wider sphere of his profession. By 1856 he was a Lieutenant Colonel, a Colonel by 1859, a Brigadier-General by 1864, a Major-General and full member of the Royal Commission by 1869, and a KCMG by 1877, a Lieutenant-General by 1878, and General Sir J. Henry Lefroy by 1885; bearing in mind that his progress must have been earned outside his Patriotic Fund activities his commitment to the Fund was even more remarkable. In terms of length of service he actually outdistanced that loyal Actuary, Alexander Glen Finlaison, whose computing skills were used by the Fund from 1858 to 1881, but whose contribution was then continued by his son, Alexander John Finlaison until the latter's death in 1900.

This characteristic of long service was maintained in the lower echelons of the Fund's staff. In 1880 a review of the office arrangements showed that two senior clerks had been with the Fund for twenty and twenty-five years respectively, the Chief Clerk and Accountant for almost twenty-six years, and the two junior clerks, the shorthand writer and the

Office Keeper had all served for nine or ten years. Mugford himself, who had become Secretary only in 1867, had been with the Fund since its inception in 1854. This look at the administrative staff after twenty-five years showed no extravagance. After accepting responsibility for an additional five funds together with two schools, the initial staff had, by 1880, been reduced by five.

The limited communications which had perhaps contributed to the problems of warfare in the 1850s, were also a factor in making contact with those who needed the Patriotic Fund's help. The network of 'Commissioners in Aid' (described in Chapter 2) had, as its initial task, the channelling of public subscriptions to the Fund, but through the local committees (usually Ladies' Committees) which they established they also constituted the first source of recommendations for help from the Fund and of local practical help in finding homes for orphans. As time passed and public knowledge of the Fund increased, applications for help were made by individuals or others (usually clergymen) on their behalf; concurrently, however, some of the local committees tended to take a decreasing interest.

The importance of having proper authentication of applications for help is an obvious one but, not always easy to achieve. There was usually no problem in obtaining marriage and death certificates but awareness of disqualifying illegalities was not so easy to attain. The problems created by a bigamous marriage were mentioned in Chapter 3, but difficulties in verifying details in the Service records of men were not often encountered, because the Corporation was concerned, in the main, with widows. However in accepting responsibility for administering the balance of the Balaclava (Light Brigade) Fund after the Crimean War the Corporation had also had to consider applications from soldiers and sailors.

One such application was received from an ex-soldier, Mr S. His story was that having had three years' service in the infantry and then a similar period in the cavalry, on each occasion 'purchasing his discharge', he had re-enlisted in a cavalry regiment again in 1853. He had taken part in the charge of the Light Brigade, had been wounded eleven times and had been assessed by his Troop Commander as having

'The conduct of a first class soldier, and in the Crimea altogether exemplary'. He had taken a voluntary discharge in 1863 after just over nine years' service in the same regiment. He had been helped with £30 from the Balaclava (Light Brigade) Fund before its administration was taken over by the Royal Patriotic Fund, and after the Fund was transferred he applied for further help.

The Royal Patriotic Fund delved rather further into the case and found a slightly different picture of Mr S. He had been tried in 1860 for desertion, spent two years in prison and finally discharged (hardly voluntarily) in January 1863 with the assessment as 'an incorrigible and worthless character'. Such discoveries did not necessarily preclude assistance (though they helped to do so in this instance).

Local help is always necessary in establishing the eligibility of applicants for charitable assistance, and it is also an excellent method of distributing funds if trustworthy representatives exist in sufficient number who are prepared to undertake the task. From early days most of the allowances provided by the Patriotic Fund had been disbursed by the 'Staff Officers of Pensioners'. These officers were employed by the Government to pay Naval and Military Pensions to Sailors, Soldiers and Marines and, until 1882, the Government had approved their also undertaking the payment of Patriotic Fund allowance – initially on a percentage commission basis – from 1881 as part of their normal duties. For the payment of pensioners the Government had arranged that its 'Staff Officers' (at local Pay Offices) should become postmasters and the pensions would be paid using 'Post Office Orders'. With the agreement of the Post Office, allowances from the Patriotic Fund from July 1882 onwards were also to be paid by 'Post Office Orders' through local Post Offices. The Patriotic Fund was to provide a schedule of names at the Charing Cross Post Office, the special 'Post Office Orders' would be provided for the Fund Secretary, and sent by him to the beneficiary who, armed with her 'Life Certificate' (provided by the Fund), could collect her allowance from her local Post Office. This is recorded in some detail, partly because it is a very early example of the use of postal orders, and because of the coincidence that over a hundred years later the Fund, after numerous moves in London, settled within a hundred yards of Charing Cross Post Office.

The Life Certificates mentioned were (and still are) the link between the Fund and beneficiaries. The Fund despatched them to beneficiaries quarterly. They were returned, giving the latest details of the widows' financial situation, keeping the Fund informed of any change of address or other circumstances, and certifying that the widow concerned was still alive.

In the 1880s an odd, but fortunate, balance seemed to be struck – of campaigns undertaken and consequent hardships being accompanied by new resources created to help contend with them. The Second Afghan War, which ended in 1880 was followed by the Egyptian/Sudanese campaign between 1882 and 1885 but, on the credit side, a Greek merchant in Alexandria, Sir Constantine Zervudachi, donated £1,300 to His Royal Highness, the Duke of Cambridge as President of the Patriotic Fund Commissioners, intended, in the first instance, for the relief of widows and orphans of the Egyptian campaign and, both for this campaign and the Afghan War the wives and families of soldiers and sailors benefited from the initiative of Colonel Gildea.

Colonel Gildea's contribution began with a letter to *The Times* about the need for funds to help the widows and orphans of those killed in the Afghan War. This was the way in which Gildea had started off the 'Zulu War Fund' and by summer 1881 £3,200 remained in the 'Afghan War Fund' when it was offered to the Patriotic Fund Commissioners for their disbursement. The offer was not accepted because the amount was regarded as too limited to warrant administering as a separate fund, since it was likely to be absorbed very rapidly. Meanwhile, however, it undoubtedly helped to lessen the claims on the Patriotic Fund.

The appeal for funds by Colonel Gildea related to the Egyptian campaign was opened with another letter to *The Times* in 1885. Initially he showed concern for those wives and families of husbands sent to serve overseas, and in particular those who were not 'on the strength' of these Regiments, that is to say, whose husbands had not received approval to marry and whose wives or other dependants would not receive the Government's 'separation' allowance. Funds for this purpose naturally could not benefit the Patriotic Fund but the relevance to the latter was indirect and subsequent: firstly in that this Gildea appeal, and the organizing of local committees to administer it, led to the birth of the Soldiers' and Sailors' Families Association (SSFA), and because collaboration between the Patriotic Fund and the Association began at this time.

In 1882 the Commissioners for the Patriotic Fund had informed the Service Departments that they would be ready to consider the care of any daughters orphaned in the Egyptian campaigns, and co-operation between the Patriotic Fund and SSFA began by the latter letting the Commissioners know when any of the wives and children in their care became widows and orphans.

The Patriotic Fund took a significant additional step in 1884 in providing help for widows and orphans created by the campaigns in Egypt and the Sudan through the decision by the War Office in May 1884 that the Fund hitherto administered by the War Office, the 'Soldiers' Effects Fund' should be transferred to the Commission.

This Fund, which stood at just over £44,000, had been accumulated from the unclaimed estates of soldiers dying intestate and was transferred under a Warrant signed by the Queen in June. So that from the 1 July 1884 the Commissioners were able to take over the commitment to pay allowances to twenty-three widows previously being helped by the Egyptian War Fund (part of what later became the 'Imperial War Fund') and then to provide help for additional widows and orphans under the Commissioners' normal conditions. By January 1885 eighty-nine widows and 156 orphans were on the books of the 'Soldiers' Effects Fund' under the Commissioners' administration.

The initial beneficiaries were all as a result of casualties in the Egyptian campaigns and the Secretary of State for War made it clear, when transferring the Fund, that he wished 'its benefits should be confined to the relatives of those who lost their lives in war since July 1882'. The Royal Warrant directed that the Fund:

> Shall be applied in payment of such compassionate, annual

or other allowances, to the widows and children or other dependant relatives of soldiers dying on service or within six months after discharge, and generally in such manner for the benefit of such widows and children or other dependant relatives of soldiers dying as aforesaid, as the said Executive Committee [of the Royal Commission] ... shall, from time to time think fit, preferential consideration being given to the widows and children of soldiers on the married establishment ...

This warrant then specified a similar series of classifications as already encountered in the original Patriotic Fund linking deaths closely to active operations or military duty. It did not, however, tie the Fund at all to the Egyptian or Sudanese campaigns, but with the separate directive from the Secretary of State for War, that it should apply from July 1882, it would clearly be applicable to future conflicts. Meanwhile 'Our said Commissioners shall be at liberty to invest the said "Soldiers' Effects Fund" upon such investments as they or any three or more of them shall from time to time think fit ...'

These investments might not have all those many years to accrue.

8 Discord Within and Without

By 1900 the names of Botha, Kruger, de la Rey, de Wet and Smuts came to signify considerable discomfiture for the nation; and, within it, Milner and Rhodes versus Kitchener, and the military feuds between Roberts on one side and Buller and Wolseley on the other hardly represented harmony. In parallel the Members of Parliament for Devonport, H.E. Kearley, and for Chesterfield, T. Bayley, were to become names as unwelcome to most of the Royal Commissioners. The seeds of these dissensions were sown by 1895; those which were to germinate in South Africa being fertilized by the operations of Cecil Rhodes' British South Africa Company in the late 1880s, and showing rapid growth after the Jameson raid into the Transvaal in 1895. The first public signs of the growth of dissatisfaction with the Patriotic Fund's affairs occurred in 1893.

On 27 March in that year Mr Bayley, MP for Derbyshire (Chesterfield) asked the Secretary of State for the Treasury:

> Whether his attention had been called to the Report of the Auditor for the National Debt Office, in auditing the Accounts of the Royal Patriotic Fund for the years 1891 and 1892, in which he stated that the requisite administrative authority for the payment made for office salaries etc. not having been obtained, he was again unable to certify the accuracy of the disbursements made under that head, but learned from the minutes of the Executive and Finance Committee that the matter is under investigation and suggests that this should be brought into accordance with requirements of the Supplementary Commission of 26th March 1868 with as little delay as possible, as this is now the third year in which he has had to take exception to these payments; and what steps, if any, have the Royal

Commissioners of the Patriotic Fund taken to carry out the Auditor's Report of 1892?

The Treasury Secretary, Sir J.T. Hibbert, pointed out that the question should have been put to the Secretary of State for War, but said that he himself 'was in a position to state that a scheme has been sanctioned for the office establishment referred to and the necessary Royal Warrants have been signed and reached the Office of the Commission for the Patriotic Fund on 18th instant'.

This exchange looks inoffensive enough: indeed, hardly worthy of any Secretary of State's time, and unlikely to lead to any further developments. It was, however, a straw in the wind. It soon became clear that there were many (and Mr Bayley was just one) who considered that there was cause for concern about the way in which the Royal Commission was administering the various funds entrusted to it.

There were several strands to this pattern of unease. It was felt that the Commissioners were too grand and remote; that there was a lack of contact and of sympathy with those in need. The opinion of some was that funds raised for a particular purpose should all be exhausted in that cause and not used subsequently more widely: another view was a somewhat vague feeling that, once money was in the hands of the Commissioners, they hoarded it; again there were others who saw extravagance in their administration. In general, there was little doubt that, however ill-founded, a feeling was gaining ground that the Royal Commission was not perhaps the best body to handle the relief of all the widows and orphans of nineteenth-century wars. Developments in South Africa were to give greater urgency to this feeling as the end of the century approached.

The exploitation by Cecil Rhodes' British South Africa Company of Mashonaland and Matabeleland (later to be called Rhodesia) followed by its attempt to retake the Transvaal in 1895 by means of a combination of the 'Jameson Raid' and an uprising in Johannesburg were stages along the long fuse which had been smouldering since 1881 and which was to keep South Africa stirring for many years. The troublesome combination, over which the British Government seemed at times to have little control, was that

Discord Within and Without

of the gold and diamond mining houses in partnership with the 'Uitlanders' – the mostly British immigrants who were there for the diamonds and the gold. The State which was the target of the rebels was that of the Boers, whether in the Transvaal, Orange Free State or Natal: a State which was determined to keep South Africa 'Afrikaans'.

By 1895 the pressure from various quarters for there to be an enquiry into the workings of the Royal Commission for the Patriotic Fund had achieved its object, and the sources and more specific causes of complaint began to be clearer.

The terms of reference of a House of Commons Select Committee order an 21 February 1895 were: 'To inquire into, and report on, the administration and financial position of the several Funds controlled by the Commissioners of the Royal Patriotic Fund, and of such other Funds as may be administered by other bodies or persons for the relief of Widows, Orphans and dependent Relatives of Soldiers, Sailors and Marines.'

Included in the fourteen members of the Select Committee were the two MPs whose names were already known to the Commissioners and were to become even more familiar over the next few years, Kearley and Bayley. It was the Secretary to the Royal Commission for the past eight years, Colonel John Smith Young, who found himself answering some hundreds of questions on behalf of the Commissioners over the next year at the expense of his normal duties for the Patriotic Fund.

It is doubtful whether the Select Committee inquiry provided any real guidance for the future operations of the Funds controlled by the Royal Commission, but it certainly provided a window on the activities of Service Charities at the end of the nineteenth century, and it illuminated the attitudes of the growing number of Service Charities to each others' place in the field of Service 'welfare' (an expression which would have meant little at the time).

After some long sessions of questioning Colonel Young about the way in which the Commission administered the various Funds entrusted to it, it was apparent that the MPs Kearley and Bayley were to follow the lines of enquiry already mentioned, of lack of local contact, failure to spend funds to the full on the causes for which they were contributed, and lack of efficient control in general.

The questioning of representatives from other Service Charities revealed other concerns. In the early years of the Patriotic Fund the only other institution operating a fund for the welfare of the Services was Lloyds, with the Underwriters' 'Patriotic Fund' which had been founded in 1803. By 1895, however, the two 'Patriotic Funds' had begun to be joined by other Service Charities, and the Select Committee took evidence from the representatives of these, pursuing, in particular, the line that there might be some overlapping between Charities in the help they were giving.

The first of the representatives from other charities to give evidence to the Select Committee was Colonel Gildea, whose first venture into raising money for Service families had been his letter to *The Times* which had led to the setting-up of the Zulu War Fund, and who had followed this with a similar appeal in 1885 during the Egyptian Campaign. From the latter came offers of help from ladies to form local Committees all over the country, and this developed into the Soldiers' and Sailors' Families Association, with the primary role of helping the wives and families of men 'of all branches of the Land and Sea Forces': a role extended to include widows and orphans, because, Colonel Gildea said in evidence: '*Our finding that the Patriotic Fund Commission was very much limited, and that they were not likely under any circumstances, as far as we could learn, to help those not on the strength*' (that is, those who had married too young or who, for some other reason, had not had their regiment's permission to marry).

At various points in his evidence Colonel Gildea remarked upon the Patriotic Fund Commission that: '*As far as the widows are in question, there are very many cases to which the Patriotic Fund Commission, under present circumstances, do not give any help whatever.*'

And concerning the fund raised as a result of the loss of HMS *Serpent* in November 1890 which was given to SSFA to administer, rather than to the Patriotic Fund: '*Well, I must confess that there was a very strong feeling at the time, especially on the question of expense, in the administration of the Patriotic Commission ... the cost of administration by the Patriotic Fund Commissioners "was excessive" ... there was a*

Discord Within and Without

very strong feeling that there was a want of sympathy in the Patriotic Fund administration.'

At further points in the evidence that Colonel Gildea gave to the Select Committee he added to his criticism of the way in which the Commission was administering its funds. Possibly arising from these comments and from the figures before the Committee, the Committee Chairman pointed out that Colonel Gildea's Soldiers' and Sailors' Families Association appeared to be guilty of the charge being brought against the Commission of accumulating capital by failing to spend its income. On the Chairman enquiring as to what plans Colonel Gildea had for the surplus, the following exchange took place:

Colonel Gildea	'Well, I consider we should have to go a good many years before we have sufficient laid by to meet the contingencies that would come upon us in the case of any war.'
Chairman	'Then you are building a "by-and-by Fund", if I may use the phrase?'
Colonel Gildea	'To a certain extent. And may I add another matter, which is also somewhat of a personal one, that it may be difficult when I am not here to get anybody to give their whole services for nothing.'

Colonel Gildea's services were rewarded by 1901 with a CB and CVO.

The sources of the next evidence against the Royal Commission – and this is the way that it appeared – were the homes of the Royal Navy – Portsmouth and Devonport.

From Miss Weston, who ran the 'Royal Sailors' Rests' at Devonport and Portsmouth, from a Portsmouth priest and other Portsmouth witnesses, the Committee heard of the lack of sympathy for Naval widows from the Commission, that there was 'always something that bars applicants' for help and, indeed, that 'the men of the Navy have no confidence at all in the Royal Patriotic Commission' (this latter from Miss Weston).

The Select Committee had not finished its task at the end

of the Parliamentary Session and was reconstituted in February 1896. Before it made its report later in 1896 the Committee had taken evidence from representatives of a further seven small funds. From all this evidence the criticism distilled was that:

> the Royal Commission was not constituted in a way which enabled it to have sufficiently close contact with those who needed its help;
>
> the funds raised for particular purposes had not been adequately drained in support of those purposes;
>
> the Commission tended to refuse help on occasions for a few, on the basis that it would establish a precedent for the many;
>
> the Commission had not made adequate efforts to have its scope broadened where this would have enabled funds with restricted application to be more fully expended.

At the same time, the enquiry demonstrated that there was no other existing Services Charity that could undertake the type of long-term relief which the Commission could provide. On the other hand it showed that there was some degree of overlapping where new organizations were covering the same cases.

In sum, the Select Committee concluded that:

> while the Commission 'under the wise direction of the Prince Consort' may have been correctly constituted to meet the conditions at the time of the Crimea War, it no longer had public confidence';
>
> some Commissioners should be Members of Parliament and some should come from the business community, from whom so much of the funds had come;
>
> two representatives on the Commission should represent the warrant and non-commissioned ranks of the Services;
>
> more publicity should be given to the Commission so that those in the Services should know of the funds available;
>
> to bring the operations of the Commission more under the supervision of Parliament, provision should be made in the Service Estimates for a token sum for the Commission, not necessarily more than £100 to achieve

Discord Within and Without

the same object as was the situation with ordnance factories.

For those who had pressed for the enquiry and for some of the accusers from other charities, but most particularly for Messrs Kearley and Bayley, this outcome of almost a year-and-a-half of deliberation was hardly satisfying. After about six months of lack of reaction even to these mild conclusions, Mr Kearley asked the First Lord of the Treasury 'whether the attention of the Government has been directed to the Report and Recommendations of the Select Committee appointed to inquire into the administration of the various funds controlled by the Commissioners of the Royal Patriotic Fund'. At this point Mr Kearley departed from the conclusions of the Committee and lifted from the proceedings some selected deductions of his own, such as:

> ...that there is immediately available from the total assets recently valued at £1,086,000 for the further relief of widows, children and dependent relatives of soldiers, sailors and marines who have lost their lives in the service of the Crown, a surplus approximating to half a million sterling; and whether any steps have been taken for the prompt issue of a Supplementary Commission under Clause 4 of the Patriotic Act of 1881, to deal with such surplus funds which have accrued, and may hereafter accrue, as recommended by the Committee? ...

Mr A.J. Balfour, then the First Lord of the Treasury, replied that the Committee's recommendations were being studied by the Secretary of State for War and the First Lord of the Admiralty and that he could not discover in the Report the passage quoted by Mr Kearley.

It took two more Parliamentary Questions and until 6 May 1897 before the then First Lord of the Treasury answered that 'the Supplementary Commission which the Committee had recommended had been issued on 3 April 1897 and was already being acted upon by the Commissioners'.

By the Spring of 1899 it was clear to some that if the

British High Commissioner for South Africa, Sir Alfred Milner, had his way, British troops would soon be committed to military operations of some sort in at least one province in that country. The last opportunity for avoiding such a conflict was the conference at Bloemfontein, the capital of the Orange Free State, which took place from 31 May to 5 June 1899. There was very little likelihood of a meeting of minds between the main protagonists, President Paul Kruger of Transvaal and Sir Alfred Milner. The latter somewhat contemptuously broke off the conference and called for a large military force to be despatched to Natal (considered to be vulnerable to attack by the Boers from Transvaal and the Orange Free State).

Various attempts were made during the summer by those who saw the folly and wastefulness of a war in support of the mine-owners and Uitlanders, but with Joseph Chamberlain, the Secretary of State for the Colonies, still putting this trust in Milner, there was little chance of any final agreement being reached. On 9 October a Boer ultimatum was handed to the British Agent in Pretoria which was bound to be rejected as a large part of the force of 8,000 British troops was already landing at Durban.

The situation as regards the military preparations for war in South Africa was gravely prejudiced by a weak Secretary of State for War and the jealousy and competition which had survived the Crimea War between the 'Indian' and the 'African' Generals; that is between those whose active service had been in India, such as Roberts, Sir George White and Penn Symons, and those whose military successes had been in Africa, such as Wolseley and Buller. The lack of both trust and a spirit of co-operation between the British military commanders in the 1890s was a handicap not experienced by the Boers.

Neither these problems, nor the fact that the British force was neither equipped nor trained for the type of mobile warfare with which they were about to be faced, were probably widely realized at the beginning of 1900. It was, however, quite clear by then that Britain had a serious war on its hands: British garrisons at Kimberley, Mafeking and Ladysmith were besieged; major defeats were suffered at the hands of the Boers at Magersfontein, Colenso and Spion

Discord Within and Without

Kop; in all, by February 1900 British casualties were over 5,500 – killed, wounded and missing (the latter mostly prisoners of war). This showed the foresight of the combined efforts of Parliament, the Patriotic Fund Commissioners and the Lord Mayor in mounting in October 1899 an appeal to the nation for a Mansion House Fund for 'the widows, orphans and other dependents of officers and men of Her Majesty's Forces who may unfortunately lose their lives in the war operations in South Africa'. (The relevant correspondence is at Appendix J).

The British public, horrified by this cavalier treatment of their Army by the Boer commandos and shocked by such early losses, gave generously to the Mansion House 'Transvaal War Fund', so that by December £386,685 had been received of which £257,364 had been earmarked for the relief of widows. By February 1900 some £250,000 had been passed from the Mansion House Fund to the Patriotic Fund to disburse to widows and orphans of the South African battles. This was put into a new fund, and by July about £400,000 was held by the Commission in the 'Transvaal War Fund'.

It was this continued employment of the Royal Commissioners to look after widows and orphans in spite of the prolonged criticism of the Fund that brought forth another concerted attack from Messrs Kearley and Bayley; this time in the debate in the House of Commons on 8 February 1900 on the Queen's Speech. Mr Kearley, in a well-researched analysis of the state of the different Funds under the control of the Commissioners, concluded that the Patriotic Fund was managed by 'the permanent secretary and a small coterie' and that they 'entrench themselves behind such great names ... but who take no active part in the administration of the Fund'. He deduced that 'These great names make up what is called in financial circles a good "front page". The Fund is not properly administered. A million of money is concerned; it wants proper control, and I hope the Government will now take steps in the matter.'

Mr Kearley's long speech was followed by enthusiastic support from Mr Bayley who, alleging that the provision of annuities for the widows of soldiers and sailors by charity 'has failed and failed ignominiously' and that they should be provided with Government help on the same lines at the (recently introduced) Employers' Liability Bill 'whereby the dependents of any person killed or any person injured had a claim against the employer concerned'. In other words, charitable relief should be replaced by a Government pension.

As in the past, there were those who stoutly defended the Commission and its staff. Admiral Field (MP for Eastbourne) while admitting that there were some grounds for calling for wider and more flexible use of the funds, asserted that 'The Patriotic Fund Commissioners have worked laboriously and well, particularly the Secretary, who is one of the ablest men I have ever come across in administering charitable funds.'

He went on to maintain that the public mind 'had been unduly poisoned against the administration of the Fund'.

The Financial Secretary to the War Office, in his reply to the debate, showed that there was some Government sympathy for Mr Kearley's proposal that immediate and effective action to 'ensure that accumulations and available surpluses of various funds administered by the Royal Patriotic Commissioners should be applied for the benefit of the widows and children of officers and men of Your Majesty's military and naval forces who lose their lives in the war in South Africa.'

Finally, the First Lord of the Treasury, Mr Balfour, promised that 'the Government, or those who represent us, will do their best to consider with those who are responsible for the new funds and the old funds some method of general organization by which those funds may be turned to the best advantage.'

It seems doubtful whether the critics of the Commissioners would have been greatly encouraged that the outcome of this debate should be the setting up of another Committee; this time, however, it was a 'Committee of Inquiry' entitled 'The Committee on War Relief Funds', headed by Lord Justice Henn Collins, with the broad terms of reference 'to consider, with the assistance of the managers of the various charitable funds available for the relief of persons who have served or are serving in the field, or of the families of such persons, how these funds may be distributed

Discord Within and Without

with the least waste and to the best advantage of those for whom they were intended.'

This committee started to take evidence on 12 March 1900 and finally reported on 29 May that year. Not surprisingly, much of the evidence had already been presented to the House of Commons Select Committees, although the Henn Collins Committee was more concerned with the question of possible overlapping among Service Funds than the former had been.

It must have seemed rather ironical to Lord Chelmsford, who had been a prominent Commissioner in 1880 when the Secretary of State for War and the First Lord of the Admiralty had been concerned about 'so serious a deficiency in the assets' of the Commission, that he should be told by Lord Justice Henn Collins: 'You see, your fund has been fortunate. It has been so extremely fortunate that it has got you into trouble. You have had such large surpluses, unlike most charitable organizations, which have none. It is suggested that your actuaries have allowed a somewhat extravagant margin for contingencies ...'

He would perhaps have been excused if he had remarked on the difficulty of pleasing everybody: a conclusion which would be given greater emphasis by the deduction of the Henn Collins Committee in their Report that 'it is impossible before the conclusion of the War to be certain whether the fund in the hands of the Patriotic Commissioners will suffice to provide pensions even on the present scale'. Lord Chelmsford might have been forgiven if he had subsequently advented to the earlier allegation of the 'somewhat extravagant margins' of actuaries.

The recommendations of the 'War Relief Funds Committee' can hardly have satisfied any of those concerned. They were:

> 'that relief should in all cases be administered locally through committees on the spot;
> that such committees should include nominees of the central as well as the local funds;
> that representatives of the principal local and central funds be called together in London for the purpose of forming a consultative council, who should provide for

the formation of local committees and carry into effect the conclusions at which we have arrived, and which are embodied in this Report.

In the Report, however, the following passage would have given more comfort to those who based their criticism on the Commissioners' lack of contact with those needing their help:

> We desire to record our opinion that unless they [the Patriotic Fund Commissioners] 'radically change their present method of administration so as to make it at once more businesslike and more elastic and also take steps to ensure complete and cordial co-operation with the persons distributing local funds, the public confidence, which has been rudely shaken, will never be restored, and thus the only central fund in the country for the permanent relief of widows and orphans of soldiers and sailors will cease to exist. This would be a great public misfortune. It is of the utmost importance that the flow of subscriptions should not be interrupted at the present crisis, and if the Patriotic Fund Commissioners adopt the suggestions here made we venture to hope that funds will be entrusted to them adequate to the needs of the present war.

The very general recommendations of the Henn Collins Committee clearly needed further thought and discussion amongst those concerned before they could be developed into any new organization for helping service families in a more efficient way than hitherto. The Royal Commissioners, in their Annual Report of July 1900, recorded that 'much misapprehension exists as to our methods of administration, but for the moment we refrain from endeavouring to correct such misapprehensions'. They also stressed their desire to co-operate with others working to help widows and orphans and to this end appointed a sub-committee of eight, with Lord Davey in the Chair, to consider how the Henn Collins' recommendations could best be carried out by the Commission.

There were certain recurrent themes in these studies of the affairs of the Patriotic Fund and the apparent reaction of the Government to them: firstly, that the responsible official

Discord Within and Without 79

view was that, for all its faults, the Patriotic Fund was the only organization suitable for use as a national instrument for the financial support of widows and orphans of men of the armed forces; secondly, that to operate efficiently the Fund needed close co-operation with one or more organizations with local representatives; and, thirdly, there were strong arguments for a greater element of Government control.

The studies and subsequent debate had also focused the Government's attention on the possibility that reliance on charitable donations to support widows and orphans could prove irresponsible in the face of the long casualty lists arising from the war in South Africa.

The outcome of these factors was that before the conference of Fund representatives, called by the Lord Mayor of London as a result of the Henn Collins' recommendations, could meet on 31 July 1900, the Secretary of the Treasury had written to the Secretary to the Commissioners in the following terms:

> I am authorized by the First Lord of the Treasury and the Chancellor of the Exchequer to state for the information of the Patriotic Fund Commission, and of the small committee of which Lord Davey is Chairman, that Her Majesty's Government propose to ask Parliament to approve of the grant of small pensions by the State to the widows and orphans of men killed in action, or dying of wounds received in action, or of disease resulting from exposure on active service; so soon as the necessary rules have been settled after examination by a small committee of experts, who will be appointed to deal with the matter. All subscriptions by the public will then become available for such additions to the uniform State Pension as may be found desirable, after enquiry by a local Committee into each particular case, as recommended by the War Relief Funds' Committee [i.e. the Henn Collins Committee].

At this time the funds of the 'Transvaal War Fund' were being used to help some 1,550 widows and orphans of those killed in South Africa and ninety-one other dependants such as parents and sisters, and fresh applications were being received at the rate of about twenty a day. Others, particularly widows and orphans of mobilized militia and reservists were being helped from the 'Soldiers' Effects Fund'. The rapid escalation of the Boer War liability is illustrated by the numbers being helped less than six months later, which were 2,392 widows and orphans and 1,500 other dependants.

On 8 February 1901, HRH The Duke of Cambridge, the President of the Commission[1] wrote to the First Lord of the Treasury:

> Dear Mr Balfour,
> The duration of the War and the increasing list of casualties in South Africa make it evident that a vigorous effort must be made to provide for those who have suffered in the service of the Nation.
>
> I understand that His Majesty's Government will submit to Parliament, on its reassembling, a scheme of State pensions for the widows and children of soldiers and sailors who have lost their lives on active service, and that it will be a feature of the proposal that the pensions so granted will be supplemented by the united efforts of private benevolence.
>
> This is a new departure and Parliament will doubtless require to be assured that the administration of the public and private funds which have been raised, or will be raised, for the relief of disabled soldiers and sailors, or for pensions to widows and children, is organized on principles which will prevent overlapping and secure efficiency.
>
> I need not say to you how heartily the Patriotic Fund Commissioners will concur in proposals directed to this end, but I am afraid that the movement for bringing existing funds into correspondence and co-ordination has not progressed sufficiently to enable you to give a decisive answer to the questions which will be put.
>
> The Patriotic Fund Commissioners venture to hope that His Majesty's Government[2] may themselves take up the question, and in that event I desire to say how anxious we are to co-operate with and assist you, and I can assure you that no question of our Charter will stand in the way of measures which the Government may think desirable.
>
> Yours sincerely,
> George

Mr Balfour, acknowledging that 'the country owes a great debt of gratitude to those who have administered the

Discord Within and Without 81

Patriotic Fund', agreed that there would be a demand for some 'change in the machinery by which private charity is distributed'. The result was yet another committee: this time a Joint Select Committee of both Houses of Parliament with terms of reference:

> ...to consider the various Charitable Agencies now in operation, and the funds available for relieving widows and orphans of soldiers and sailors with a view to insuring that the funds subscribed by local and private benevolence are applied to the best advantage in supplementing a scheme of Government Pensions for widows and orphans of soldiers and sailors who have lost their lives in war.

The committee, under the chairmanship of Lord James of Hereford, reported on 26 July 1901 that even with the proposed Government pensions 'the necessity of rendering assistance by voluntary effort will still continue'. The committee foresaw that the Government pensions would need to be supplemented by charitable help; that immediate help would be needed before any pension would be available; that widows who had married 'off the strength' would need to depend exclusively on charitable help; that the widows and orphans of colonial soldiers would also have to depend on voluntary help; and that 'other dependents' would need similar assistance. To provide this dual State and Charitable help, the committee recommended the setting up of two separate Official Boards, one Naval and one Military, which should take over all the funds in the hands of the Commissioners and administer these as well as the State pensions: the Boards also to be responsible to Parliament.

The Duke of Cambridge gave Mr Balfour the Commissioners' views on these recommendations, agreeing with the need for local committees but seeing the requirement for 'an authoritative central body so constituted as to command the confidence of the public' and of these local committees: this powerful central body to take the place of the Patriotic Fund Commission. The Commissioners considered that pensions should continue to be paid by the Admiralty and the War Office.

These views accorded with the ideas of the Council set up

at the Mansion House under the presidency of the Earl of Derby as a result of the Henn Collins' recommendations and, clearly, Mr Balfour also saw problems in official Government bodies disbursing a mixture of State pensions and charitable annuities, not to mention a possible reluctance on the part of the public to give their voluntary contributions to State Pensions Boards. Consequently, when the tenacious Mr Kearley questioned him on 24 April 1902 in the House of Commons about the Government's response to the Joint Select Committee's Report, Mr Balfour replied that:

> The plan which I think would be the best to adopt with regard to the matter in which the honourable gentleman has shown himself persistently so much interested, would be to frame a general Central Council representing the chief local authorities in the Kingdom, and which should include a certain number of persons appointed by the Crown to represent the two great services and the authorities distributing Government pensions. The Council so constituted could only act through an administrative and financial committee. By this machinery we hope, not only to provide a body competent to allocate the funds of the Royal Patriotic Commission, but also one which shall be in close touch with the Government pension authorities on one side and with the local charitable organizations throughout the country on the other. As the honourable gentleman is aware, legislation will be required in order to transfer the property of the Royal Patriotic Commission to the new Council.

Driven by long casualty lists from South Africa, an elephantine gestation period was almost over.

Footnotes

1 At this time the top three signatures of the Royal Commission were 'George, George and Edward of Saxe-Weimar' being Field Marshal HRH The Duke of Cambridge, Rear Admiral HRH The Duke of Cornwall and York, and Field Marshal His Highness Prince Edward of Saxe-Weimar.
2 Queen Victoria had died in 1901.

9 Incorporation

Colonel James Gildea, founder and treasurer of the Soldiers' and Sailors' Families Association; Lieutenant-Colonel Thomas Tully, Secretary of the Royal Military Tournament (held annually since 1878 when Major-General Burnaby arranged the first at the Agricultural Hall in aid of Service funds nominated by the Duke of Cambridge); James Millington, Secretary of Lloyd's Patriotic Fund; Miss Agnes Weston, founder of Sailors' Rests at Devonport and Portsmouth; Major-General J.F. Maurice, General Officer Commanding, Woolwich District: all these witnesses consulted during the prolonged enquiries into the Patriotic Commission's affairs were genuinely concerned with the welfare of servicemen and their families, even though there may, in some instances, have been an element of contention involved, and it would have been very surprising if there had not been some substance in their criticisms of the Royal Commission. The Commissioners themselves had already showed an awareness of some of the weaknesses, in the study conducted by a special committee of five of their number in 1895; namely, that there was insufficient local contact with applicants; that without this there was considerable danger of overlapping in the new era of proliferating charities as well as an undesirable apparent lack of sympathy; and that the restrictions on the purposes of the many individual funds under the Commission's control resulted in many having surplus money while applicants for help from other funds were disappointed through lack of resources.

This pointed up a common dilemma in the field of charitable organizations. Money subscribed by the public for a special purpose needs to be safeguarded in its administration by a body of trustees and, to ensure that it is impartially administered, these are usually drawn from disinterested fields. These trustees need to ensure that the funds under their control are employed solely for the purposes for which they were raised, and not diverted to other purposes. Yet, at the same time, all those who give their services to such charities would always wish to use their resources to help as many genuine applicants as possible, and, from the point of view of the public in general and applicants in particular, a general pool of money controlled by a small full-time staff and disbursed on a person-to-person basis, would be popular, but it would also be the most easily liable to abuse.

While, therefore, there was some justice in the criticisms made of the Royal Commission, there was also some injustice. On the one hand there were accusations that the funds were impersonally administered by a 'front' of distinguished names; yet concurrently there were charges that control was in the hands of the Secretary and 'a small coterie'. The trustees – as all trustees – needed to find a course between the Scylla of being vulnerable to allegations of 'hoarding' and the Charybdis of being 'unable to meet their liabilities'. In their Annual Report of 1902, their penultimate year as a Royal Commission and the second they had addressed to King Edward VII, the Commissioners demonstrated that they had not, after all, made such a bad job of maintaining this course. It provides an excellent summary of the Commission's work for Service widows and orphans over a period of almost fifty years:

> The Patriotic Fund Commission has been in existence since 1854, and, in the interval, 17 Funds for the relief of widows, orphans and dependents of sailors and soldiers losing their lives in the service of the State, have been entrusted to our administration.
> Of these –
> 3 were raised directly by ourselves through the Lord Mayor of London with co-operation of local authorities.
>
> | | |
> |---|---:|
> | In 1854, Patriotic Russian War Fund | £1,471,371 |
> | In 1893, HMS 'Victoria' Relief Fund | £   73,261 |
> | In 1900, Transvaal War Fund | £ 466,353 |
> | | £2,010,985 |

Incorporation

8 were raised by other Bodies and placed under our administration to obtain economy and uniformity of principles in administration –

In 1871, HMS 'Captain' Relief Fund	£ 45,163
In 1878, HMS 'Eurydice' Relief Fund	£ 19,000
In 1878–1879, Royal Naval Relief Fund	£ 5,277
In 1879, Zulu War Fund	£ 27,361
In 1881, HMS 'Atalanta' Relief Fund	£ 9,275
In 1886, County of Forfar Fund[1]	£ 846
In 1888, Ashantee War Fund	£ 2,272
In 1890, Light Brigade (Balaclava) Relief Fund[2]	£ 2,950
	£ 112,144

2 were formed by direct donations to us by individual donors –

In 1883, the Zervudachi Fund	£ 1,300
In 1884, the Thurlow Fund[3]	£ 500
	£ 1,800

4 were placed under our administration by the Government –

In 1864–66, the Rodriguez Fund	£ 6,213
In 1884, the Soldiers' Effects Fund (up to 1901)	£ 133,830
In 1897, Indian Army (European) Effects Fund[4]	£ 4,800
In 1899, Patriotic (Army) Fund[5]	£ 2,390
	£ 147,233

Making a Grand Total of	£2,272,162

The number of beneficiaries placed upon these Funds has been:

Widows of		Children of		Other dependents of	
Officers	Other Ranks	Officers	Other Ranks	Officers	Other Ranks
452	9,897	944	14,215	34	2,149

The Commissioners go on to answer more specifically some of the criticisms made of their administration: to the charge that they 'hoarded' funds, they point out the uncertainties of investment, even in the Gilt-edged market, together with the uncertainties as to the number of applicants and the periods for which their support would be necessary, concluding that they had to be guided by the best actuarial advice from the Council of the Institute of Actuaries. They offered as evidence of the success of their husbandry that, from the original cash contribution to the 'Russian War Fund' of £1,471,371, expenditure over the years on relief had been £2,661,893 and securities with a nominal value of £443,077 were retained; in part as endowment for the maintenance of the girls' school and in part to meet pension liabilities for beneficiaries.

In answer to the accusations of extravagance in costs of administration, the Commissioners provided the following figures:

The total expenditure of the Commission from 1854 to 1901, inclusive was	£2,921,139
Of that total, 47 years' cost of management, 1854 to 1901 was	£ 150,039

or 5.13 per cent of the expenditure

On the question of the lack of local contact raised by some of the critics, the Annual Reports since 1898 showed that the Commissioners had made some efforts in this respect in that they listed local committees comprising cross-sections of inhabitants for the following areas:

Portsmouth and neighbourhood
Leeds and neighbourhood
Devonport, Plymouth, Stoneham and neighbourhood.
The cities and towns of Birmingham, Belfast, Chatham, Cork, Dover, Dublin and Woolwich
The County of Norfolk

The problem of surplus resources being held in specifically restricted Funds had been a real one, caused by the necessity for Trustees to adhere to the restrictions then in force. This was resolved by a Supplementary Commission of 28 December 1899, based upon the Patriotic Fund Act of 1899,

Incorporation

which enabled the Commissioners to use such surpluses 'for the benefit not only of widows and children, but of other dependants of officers and men of Her Majesty's military and naval forces'. A solution satisfying the need to reduce surpluses in certain funds, while not pleasing those who maintained that money subscribed for a particular purpose should not be employed in any other.

These opening years of the twentieth century marked the end of a long association: that between the Commission and the Finlaison family. The loyal and excellent service provided for the Royal Commission by father and son has already been described. The coincidence of the death of the son, Alexander J. Finlaison, and the beginnings of the 'Transvaal War Fund' presented the Commissioners with a problem since the £400,000 which the Mansion House Fund transferred to the Commission, and the probable total casualties from that war, clearly demanded the skills of an accomplished actuary to calculate the scope and necessary limits of the help to be given. It was fortunate for the Commission that Alexander J. Finlaison had been a past President of the Institute of Actuaries, and that the Institute had had both the standing in the country and the confidence in its valuations to have been undaunted and unaffected by the criticism already related. Consequently, as reported in the April 1901 report of the Institute:

> ...it was obvious that the Commissioners would need actuarial assistance such as would be received without question, not only by those who had previously raised objections, but also by the multitudes interested in the funds, whether as subscribers or possible beneficiaries. Happily there are many whose attainments and position would be recognized without dispute; and yet it was felt that, better than any individual opinion, if the President and the Council of the Institute, as representative of the profession in this country, was, for the sake of patriotism, in their joint capacity to advise the Commissioners, no reasonable person could then deny that the Commissioners might with the utmost confidence base their action on an opinion so obtained. ...A new departure was therefore taken, in that the President (Mr Higham) placed himself informally in communication with the authorities, and made the sug-

gestion; and it was accepted without hesitation, as being certain to ensure the absolute confidence of the public.

The letter from Mr C.D. Higham making the formal offer to the Secretary of the Patriotic Fund ended with the words: 'Though I am bound to point out that the Council cannot bind its successors, I have the gratification of assuring you that those now serving on it would welcome the opportunity of contributing something of any skill they may possess in the service of their King and Country.'

Not surprisingly, the Commissioners accepted with alacrity – in less than a week – and in this way an important element in the Patriotic Fund's future structure was established.

Another buttress to the Patriotic Fund's future strength which also appeared at this time was the clear confidence shown by the Government in the Fund. This was demonstrated in the first instance in the rescue of the 'Indian Mutiny Relief Fund'. This was a trust fund set up by former trustees, Alderman Finnis (at that time Lord Mayor of London), Mr Thomas Hankey (a governor of the Bank of England), Mr Philip Cazenove (a stockbroker), and General Tremenheere (late of the Royal Engineers). After some years the trustees wished to hand over this responsibility, so the fund was paid into the Court of Chancery and administered by a Committee. In 1901 an actuarial valuation of the Fund found it to be insolvent to the extent of just over £11,000, and in 1902 the Government asked the Patriotic Fund Commissioners to take over the Fund's administration.

The second manifestation of this confidence occurred in 1901. The weight of the Boer War casualties, apart from the individual tragedies that they entailed, had brought about a critical situation concerning the financial support of the families involved. The Patriotic Fund Commissioners found that between the start of 1901 and the end of that year the number of Boer War widows on their books had risen from 84 to 2,392 widows and orphans and 1,500 other dependent relatives. The Commissioners had already taken advantage of the wider scope that had been provided by the Secretary of State for War in the 'Soldiers' Effects Fund' by using it

Incorporation

(including some of its capital) to take some of this burden. Some £2,000 of the capital of the Patriotic Fund had also had to be added to the income of the Fund to meet commitments. All these factors had led to anxiety as to whether the Transvaal War Fund resources would be adequate to meet probable future calls. Clearly the situation demanded Government action and the decision was made in the spring of 1901 to grant State pensions to the widows and orphans of those losing their lives on active service. For the initial implementation of these pensions, however, the Government again showed their reliance on the Patriotic Fund; the Fund paying out no less than £8,664 from its own resources in advances to families on the Government's behalf: a point made by the auditor of the Fund's accounts in April 1902.

By 1903, therefore, the stage was set for the birth of a new organization and one which, for all that it needed to include the generally accepted recommendations of the many enquiries, would be based upon the tried – and evidently trusted – Patriotic Fund.

It was on the 11 August 1903 that the instrument forging the new structure was enacted by King Edward VII's Government. By the Patriotic Fund Reorganisation Act, 1903 the 'Royal Patriotic Fund Corporation' came into being on 1 January 1904 and took over all the assets, duties and liabilities of the Patriotic Fund Commission, which was simultaneously dissolved.

The method by which the control of the Fund had been made more representative of the nation, which had contributed so much in lives in the various actions and so generously in money to help those bereaved, was by a very broad membership. This comprised:

The Lord Lieutenants of Counties
The Chairmen of County Councils
The Lord Mayors and Mayors of every County Borough in England, Wales and Ireland
The Lord Provosts and Provosts of 'every Royal, parliamentary or police burgh in Scotland with a population of or exceeding 50,000'

The way in which the new Corporation was brought

further under Government influence than its predecessor had been was partly by the additional memberships of twelve to be appointed directly by the Sovereign. Five of these were accounted for by one member representing the Treasury, two representing the Admiralty and two representing the Secretary of State for War. In addition, the Paymaster-General was to be the treasurer of the Corporation and, with the Bank of England, act as the Corporation's banker. The Treasury was made responsible for the audit of the accounts.

The members composed a Council, and the Council itself had the powers to co-opt up to seven more members who represented other charitable funds with similar purposes to that of the Corporation.

The tenure of appointments was to be three years and after the first three years the number of members directly appointed by the Sovereign was to be reduced to six; the balance of six was to be in the gift of the Council.

This total membership exceeded three hundred, so it clearly could not deal with the detailed handling of the Corporation's affairs. The Act of Parliament recognized this in specifying that 'The powers and duties of the Corporation shall be exercised, and performed by the general council of the Corporation, consisting of the whole of the members, and by an executive committee appointed from among the members'. The executive committee was to consist of at least twelve and not more than twenty members, including the representative members appointed by the Sovereign; and the Vice-President of the Corporation was to be its Chairman.

In the field of local contact, the Act empowered the Council to appoint local committees 'for purposes connected with the fund': this wording making it possible for such committees to be involved in fund-raising if necessary, because the Act also authorized that 'The Corporation may from time to time solicit and receive contributions from the public and donations of property for the purposes of the Corporation, and may also receive any such sums as may be granted by Parliament.'

The last Report of the Royal Commissioners to King Edward was dated 31 December 1903 and it summarized the

Incorporation

contribution of the Corporation since its inception in money terms. The detail is shown at Appedix K and it shows the Commission to have administered a total of nineteen funds since 1854, contributions to which had been £2,516,518; to have expended £3,081,152 in its work, and to have available to transfer to the Corporation £1,203,321 in securities (at par value) and £3,399 in cash.

It may have had its faults but perhaps there had not been much wrong with its husbandry.

Footnotes

1. Set up by the county to enable two widows to be paid 5s a week.
2. The balance of a fund set up by public subscription for necessitous survivors of the Charge of the Light Brigade.
3. Established from donations by Major Thurlow and Captain Thurlow for 'deserving girls' admitted to the Royal Victoria Patriotic Asylum.
4. Unclaimed estates of European members of the Indian Army administered as in the 'Soldiers' Effects Fund'.
5. With the passing of the 1899 Patriotic Fund Act surpluses in funds could be applied more broadly and the War Office felt able to entrust the Commissioners with the administration of what had been 'The Quarter Master General's Fund', then retitled.

10 A Second Innings on a Worn Wicket

The first task of the newly created Corporation had been apparent since July 1903: it was to find adequate resources to meet the ever-increasing commitment of providing proper levels of support for the victims of the South Africa War.

By the end of 1903 the public had contributed, through the Lord Mayor of London's Mansion House appeal, just under £493,000 for widows, orphans and other dependants of soldiers and sailors who had lost their lives in the 'Transvaal' War. As the Commissioners' final report to King Edward VII recorded: 'That sum is virtually exhausted in providing for allowances and other payments already granted, and fresh claims are daily received.'

The problem in collecting more funds was that the war had ended some six months earlier so that it had been difficult for some time to maintain public interest and generous support for the original appeal. At the same time the after-effects of the war were still being widely experienced and this meant that wives and children were still being bereaved as well as there being many 'late-comers' appearing on the Fund's books.

The Commissioners felt that it was essential that the rates of support given to Transvaal War widows and orphans should be the same as those provided for the beneficiaries of their other funds, and that, if cheeseparing was to be avoided, the public must be asked for more help.

They arranged a conference of the Lord Lieutenants of Counties and the Lord Mayors and Lord Provosts of the principal cities on 17 July 1903 to consider 'what steps might and should be taken to ameliorate the prospects of the Transvaal War widows'. This conference unanimously adopted the following resolutions:

It is desirable that the allowances granted to the Transvaal War widows should be on the same scale as those granted to widows in previous wars, but that the Report of the Council of the Institute of Actuaries, dated 31st December 1902, shows that to accomplish this object a capital sum of £231,000 would be required in addition to the fund at present at the disposal of the Patriotic Fund Commissioners, and that since the date of the Actuarial Report the roll of widows has been considerably increased and will continued to increase for some time to come.

This resolution did more to state the problem than to provide any solution but the Commissioners reported optimistically in their swan-song:

As the Lord Lieutenants and Chairmen of County Councils and Municipal Authorities will be members of the Royal Patriotic Fund Corporation, we have confidence that steps will be taken to secure the same provision for the Transvaal War widows as we have, by the liberality of the Nation, been able to provide for the widows resulting from former wars and from accidents at sea to some of Your Majesty's ships of war.

At the beginning of 1903 the Transvaal War Fund had been helping over 4,000 widows, and over 2,500 children and other dependent relatives: by the end of that year a further 277 widows, 369 children and 26 dependent relatives had been added to the list of beneficiaries. Bearing in mind that 22,000 men on the British side had been killed in the Boer War and that, in addition, four times as many had been wounded, there were good grounds for believing that significantly greater resources would be needed. Many widows would have been receiving the new government pensions but these amounted only to between five and ten shillings a week, together with one shilling and sixpence to two shillings a week for a child: furthermore, the pensions were only effective from 1901. There were the pre-1901 widows still dependent upon allowances from the Corporation and even for those on pensions there was still a gap to be filled between these sums and the amount needed to maintain a home and family.

The importance of the new Corporation getting rapidly into its stride was emphasized at its inaugural Council meeting on 21 January 1904 by the Royal President, His Royal Highness The Duke of Connaught, who had been appointed by his eldest brother King Edward VII in place of the President of the Royal Commission, His Royal Highness The Duke of Cambridge, who had resigned because of ill-health, and was to die the same year.

In his opening address, The Duke of Connaught included clear directions as to the urgency of providing executive and consultative bodies to deal with considerable arrears of applications, to appeal to the Nation to provide adequate resources for the widows and orphans of the Boer War, and to provide properly qualified management for the Royal Victoria Patriotic Asylum for Girls. The Duke set the prevailing tone for the future, as well as providing encouragement for members, but referring to the Corporation as a 'National Trust' and saying: 'I can assure you of the personal interest and support of His Majesty the King, and I trust in the discharge of our duties and responsibilities we shall have the confidence and support of the Nation and of all His Majesty's subjects.'

The trustees of the Corporation who had been appointed by the King, in addition to the President, were the nominees of HM Treasury, the Admiralty and the War Office, and were:

Lieutenant Colonel Lord Edmund Talbot, MVO, DSO, MP.	
Sir Francis Mowatt, GCB.	HM Treasury
W Hayes Fisher Esq, MP.	Nominees
H E Kearley Esq, MP.	
Sir Richard Awdry, KCB, Accountant General of the Navy	Admiralty
C.H.R. Stansfield Esq, Director of Greenwich Hospital	Nominees
Lieutenant-General Sir Thomas Kelly-Kenny, GCB Adjutant General	War Office
Frank Marzials, CB, Accountant General of the Army	Nominees

A Second Innings on a Worn Wicket

There were thus four vacancies to be filled in order to reach the minimum strength stipulated in the Act for the Executive Committee, and the appointment of these was the responsibility of the General Council. The President took the initiative in proposing four candidates, namely The Earl of Dartmouth, The Earl of Powis, The Lord Mayor of the City of London and D J Shackleton, MP.

The Duke of Connaught explained to members in his opening address the special grounds for suggesting these trustees from the long list of distinguished names available: 'The Lord Mayor will naturally speak with authority for our great. Municipal Institutions, Mr Shackleton for Labour and Lords Dartmouth and Powis are not only Lords Lieutenant of Counties but men also who have devoted themselves to raising and administering local funds for sufferers by the recent war.'

These twelve were unanimously elected to the Executive Committee of the Corporation as the result of a resolution proposed by the Marquis of Ripon, the Lord Lieutenant of the North Riding of Yorkshire, and seconded by Lord Rothschild, the Lord Lieutenant of Buckinghamshire; two of the impressive list of fifteen Lord Lieutenants, who together with the appointed members, six mayors and ten Chairmen of County Councils constituted the attendance at the first Council meeting at the Royal United Service Institution in Whitehall.

The Council lost no time in pursuing another of the President's priorities; that of providing a properly constituted management for the Royal Victoria Patriotic Asylum.

The President kept up the pressure by himself chairing the first meeting of the Executive Committee only ten days later, 1 February, at the old headquarters of the Commission, 53 Charing Cross. This meeting refined the organization of the Corporation by establishing two sub-committees of the Executive Committee, a 'General Purposes' Committee composed of seven members and a Finance Committee of five members; both Committees to meet 'so often as shall be thought necessary for the transaction of that business and that they report to the Executive Committee which shall sit regularly once in every month.' The Earl of Dartmouth was elected Chairman of the

Executive Committee and Sir Francis Mowatt was elected chairman of both the sub-committees.

The Executive Committee delegated the problem of raising more money for the Transvaal War Fund to the General Purposes Committee. If any additional spur had been necessary for early action in raising more money this was provided by the restrictions which the Executive Committee found themselves having to impose in the Transvaal Fund of not providing help to dependent relatives, other than widows and orphans, discontinuing help with medical fees, and limiting help with funerals to £3.

The Council met again in the third week of June and, at the Duke of Devonshire's suggestion, resolved to set up a consultative committee, well-qualified in various ways, to consider, and report to the President, the best means of organizing an appeal for funds.

This committee consisted of:

Sir James Ritchie – Lord Mayor of London
S Hope Morley – Governor of the Bank of England
Earl Spencer
Earl of Derby
Lord Rothschild
Lord Balfour of Burleigh
Lord Iveagh
Lord Strathcona
W Hayes Fisher, MP

On 15 July 1904 the Committee issued an appeal 'to the generosity of the Nation', setting out the size of the problem and continued:

> We believe that the Country would wish that the Transvaal War widows should be permanently provided for on the same scale as those who were made widows in consequence of the Crimean War.
> We therefore make this the basis of our appeal, and though there are many appeals before the Country, we believe the cause of the widows, orphans and other dependants of our sailors and soldiers, killed in action or losing their lives as the result of wounds or diseases

A Second Innings on a Worn Wicket

contracted in war, is a sacred one, and one which the Nation has ever been and will be willing to support by adequate contributions.

The appeal, after providing some detail of the reasons why this new appeal had become necessary, ended:

> The Lord Mayor of London having consented to re-open the Mansion House Fund for Transvaal War Widows and Orphans we invite donations, which we shall gladly welcome either in single sums or in instalments spread over two or more years. But the smallest contributions will be thankfully received.
> Donations may be sent to:
> The Secretary's Office
> Mansion House, London
> or to
> The Bank of England,
> to the credit of the Transvaal War Fund for Widows and Orphans for administration by the Royal Patriotic Fund Corporation.

The appeal was signed by the Royal President and all the members of the Committee, was sent to all members and given to the national and local press throughout the Kingdom.

Within a week the Lord Mayor received the following letter from General the Right Honourable Sir Dighton Probyn:

> BUCKINGHAM PALACE
> July 21, 1904
>
> Dear Lord Mayor,
> I am commanded by the King to forward you the enclosed cheque for 200 Guineas as a donation to the fund which His Majesty is glad to see you have reopened on behalf of the Transvaal widows and orphans.
>
> The King further commands me to say that he sincerely hopes the public will respond generously to this great national charity.
>
> Yours faithfully
>
> D M Probyn, General
> Keeper of His Majesty's Privy Purse

This Royal example was quickly followed by a contribution of 100 Guineas from the Prince of Wales, and other substantial donations were received from various County Funds through Lord Lieutenants, from Mayoral Funds, and through the initiative of some newspapers. Nevertheless, in the five months to the end of 1904 the total received in response to the July appeal had not quite reached £13,000 out of the estimated £231,000 needed. In addition to the difficulty already mentioned, of maintaining a sufficiently high public interest two years after the end of the Boer War, the 1904 appeal was launched in a period of financial depression. It was also in competition with other appeals for large amounts in aid of more immediate and inviting purposes.

As the Council reported to the King, it was only reasonable to accept the situation and to wait for a more favourable time to lay stress on the appeal. It was recognized that the big deficit disclosed by the Institute of Actuaries had been a long-term difficulty; one which would arise in the years ahead on the assumption that the current scales of assistance were at least maintained.

This shortfall in a specific Fund raised once again the division of opinion within the Executive Committee as to the proper use of money contributed by the Public for a limited purpose. The point at issue was that, where there are several funds administered by one organization and there are surpluses in some of the more limited funds while others would run into deficit if common scales of help were applied, should more lavish help be given to exhaust the smaller funds, or, should funds be consolidated so that common standards be maintained?

With great consistency, Mr Kearley, a critic of the Commissioners in the days before incorporation, continued to maintain that 'whenever a fund is subscribed by the benevolence and liberality of the public for a specific set of sufferers it should be administered in accordance with the undoubted intentions of the donors, which we believe at all times to be that the whole of the money so subscribed shall be gradually, but completely, distributed in the shape of pensions and gratuities for the widows, orphans and dependants, for whom the appeal was made'. However, only one other member of the Executive Committee supported Mr Kearley's view, the majority believing that common scales of assistance should be observed in all the funds rather than varying these in order to exhaust specific funds which had accumulated surpluses because of light commitments.

The conversion of Mr Kearley from poacher to gamekeeper by his appointment to the Council of the Corporation and to membership of both the General Purposes and the Finance Committees, and indeed to Chairman of the latter did not seem, in this instance, to have changed his convictions in this respect.

Another name, previously familiar as a prominent witness in the enquiries into the administration of the Royal Commission, and now co-opted as a member of the General Council of the Corporation, was that of Colonel James Gildea, now advanced to Colonel Sir James Gildea.

He, together with Admiral Sir Nathaniel Bowden-Smith, KCB, was co-opted as representing a charitable fund 'founded for the like purposes as the Corporation' under the First Schedule, Paragraph 1 (f) of the 1903 Act: the former representing the Soldiers' and Sailors' Families Association and the latter The Royal Naval Fund.

Strong support for the consolidation of some of the eighteen different funds which the Corporation had inherited from the Royal Commission, came from the Institute of Actuaries in its report to the Council in June 1904 when it 'felt bound to urge', with the proviso that the interests of each specific fund were safeguarded by the Corporation's regulations, that 'such a consolidation of the assets would greatly facilitate the general administration of the Funds, and will in time become almost a necessity'.

This idea certainly found favour with the Corporation, although the 'safeguarding' of the interests of individual funds was bound to be a stumbling block. As things were there was a very strong family resemblance between the old Commission and the new Corporation: the most significant differences being the much closer involvement of Members of Parliament and Government Departments among the trustees, the closer association of Lord Lieutenants, Chairmen of Councils, Lord Mayors, Mayors and Provosts, in major decisions, and the formation of specialist

Committees of manageable size able to meet frequently and take a keen interest in the administration of the Corporation and its school.

There were no dramatic changes in the office staff in 1904 and Colonel Young remained in charge as secretary. The office had to move, however, because 53, Charing Cross was to be demolished. Charing Cross consisted of the spear-shaped area comprising the Trafalgar Square end of Whitehall on the East side and a short distance down the West side of Northumberland Avenue. The move was not too far: merely across Admiralty Arch, along Pall Mall and into Waterloo Place to Number 17, known as Seymour House. The Executive Committee held its first meeting there in August 1904.

At the end of 1904 there were on the books of the Corporation receiving help 4,469 widows, 4,424 children and 234 other dependants. The majority of these were in the Patriotic Fund, the Transvaal War Fund and the Soldiers' Effects Fund – some of the small funds supported less than ten beneficiaries thus underlining the need for consolidation.

The Executive Committee studied this problem and decided to recommend the amalgamation of ten funds into one 'Patriotic Fund', namely:

Patriotic (Russian War 1854–56) Fund
Patriotic (General) Fund
Ashantee War Fund
Zulu War Fund
HMS 'Captain' Fund
HMS 'Eurydice' Fund
HMS 'Atalanta' Fund
HMS 'Victoria' Fund
Rodriguez Fund
Zervudachi Fund

The Council was content with this proposal; but it needed legal concurrence. Treasury Counsel advised that the most that the Corporation could achieve in the way of consolidation, without seeking special powers, would be to combine the two elements of the Patriotic Fund itself and also absorb the Rodriguez and Zervudachi Funds. This

A Second Innings on a Worn Wicket

advice led the Council, somewhat surprisingly, to conclude that no consolidation of funds should take place at all.

Some changes were made, however, at the General Council meeting on 24 May 1906. The Transvaal War Fund was still lacking in sufficient funds to apply the same scales of allowances to widows as older funds operated by the Corporation; so that the decision was made not to restore the allowances of widows who had been widowed a second time after remarriage.

On the other hand, the Council also agreed that 'in dealing with the surpluses on any funds at the disposal of the Corporation, remaining after providing for all claimants thereon upon the scale of allowances approved by the Corporation at the Annual Meeting of 27th June, 1905, the policy of the Corporation shall be to retain and apply such surpluses for relief to widows, children and dependants of Officers and Men of the Army and Navy needing assistance and not provided for by any special fund'.

By 1906, with over 9,000 widows, orphans and dependants created by wars and other operations over the past fifty years still being helped to the extent of over £72,000 a year (a considerable sum at the beginning of the century), some members of the Corporation must have felt considerable concern that future events could make such numbers insignificant. War plans of the 'Great Powers' were already refined to a considerable extent. Alliances were being made and dissolved. Military commitments and interdependent mobilization plans were advancing to situations where it seemed that the only direction and development could be forward into conflict. Even those members with no access to privileged information must have felt something of a chill at the outlook as Germany squared up to France over French claims in Morocco.

11 Ebb and Flow

With the balance of power in Europe swinging first one way and then the other the charity providing the main support for Service widows would have wished to have financial resources on a scale sufficient, not only to meet existing commitments comfortably, but also to face with some confidence the sort of fresh burden which the world situation threatened to introduce. The Corporation in its first ten years was not in this satisfactory state, and the pattern of its decisions and activities in this period reflects members' awareness of this vulnerability.

In its first year, for example, the Corporation could not see its way to achieve its strongly felt wish that there should be standard scales of allowances for widows, irrespective of which fund was involved. In 1904 the widow of a Private or Able Seaman who had been a victim of the Crimean War, a naval disaster or the Zulu War would be receiving a basic allowance of nine shillings a week while the rate for a similar widow of the Boer War, from the Transvaal War Fund would be seven shillings; and this differential of two shillings a week pertained through all the non-commissioned ranks. What is more, these amounts for Boer War widows were reduced by the amount of the Government pensions, where these were given.

At this time the post of Commander-in-Chief of the British Army was abolished and replaced by a 'Chief of the Imperial General Staff' and the Corporation's Executive Committee made an immediate plea to the War Office for the release to the Corporation of funds which had hitherto been under Lord Roberts' control in his appointment as Commander-in-Chief; the 'Army Compassionate Fund' and the proportion of the Royal Military Tournament Profits

Fund which had always been paid into the C-in-C's Fund. The Corporation's case was based on the grounds that it was 'the Statutory Body appointed to administer charitable funds for the benefit of widows and other dependants of soldiers and sailors'; its strong supporting argument was that it had insufficient funds adequately to meet calls on the Transvaal War Fund.

Although the Duke of Connaught put the case, the request was rejected in January 1905. It was clear that members felt strongly that the Corporation, as well as having the best possible use for those funds, was the appropriate body to administer them, so, after further detailed study of the history, objects and methods of administration of the 'Army Compassionate Fund', the Secretary of State for War was asked to receive a deputation from the Corporation further to discuss the case. He replied in May that he did not 'consider that any advantage would be obtained by the reception of a deputation' for this purpose.

For a time, Committee members were heavily engaged both in routine affairs and with one of those internal clashes which are inevitable on occasions in charitable organizations. However, with the failure of the renewed national appeal, described in the last chapter, the Chairman of the Executive Committee, Mr Hayes Fisher, MP, was invited to take advantage of an opportunity to talk to the Secretary of State for War about the Corporation's claims; with the addition of a bid for the administration of the War Office 'South African War Widows and Orphans Fund'. It certainly seemed a fair argument that civil servants appeared to overlap with work performed by charities.

Mr (later Lord) Haldane evidently gave Mr Hayes Fisher a sympathetic hearing in July 1906 and asked for a personal letter setting out the previous correspondence and present position in some detail. The Secretary of State gave the assurance that this would receive his personal attention. His answer in October, however, was still firmly negative.

One of the more whimsical efforts being made by the Corporation to improve the income to the Transvaal War Fund in these early years was to include, in the renewed appeal to the public for funds, His Majesty's High

Commissioner for South Africa. From Viscount Milner, on whom, perhaps more than any other individual, must rest a high proportion of the responsibility for the Transvaal War, came the reply that, in his view, 'it would be well to postpone until better times in South Africa any definite effort to secure contributions'. It was presumably with entirely straight faces that the General Purposes Committee replied 'expressing concurrence with Lord Milner's views, and leaving time and manner of launching Appeal in South Africa to his discretion'.

Concurrently with all these efforts to improve the income to the Corporation, various economy measures were investigated. Applications for help from the Transvaal War Fund were to be classified, A,B, C and D, and only those in Class A were to be accepted at once. The other categories either being accepted, only after the Finance Committee had considered that funds would allow, or being rejected. Stringent criteria of this type were continuing to be applied up to 1907, when the Duke of Connaught had to report to the Council that in 1904 and 1905 the Corporation had been forced, through shortage of funds, to reject 1,400 out of 2,000 applications and that to monitor applications on this scale had called for over fifty meetings of the General Purposes Committee in three years: further that the Corporation was spending £30,000 more than its investment income and needing to sell shares at a time of 'monetary depression' in order to meet the commitment. In June 1907 he had to tell the Council that 'we are within measurable distance of exhausting' surpluses 'and having to cease accepting further cases for relief'. In the annual report to King Edward for 1906, the Corporation had already recorded that fresh cases for help from the Royal Naval Relief Fund could not be accepted at that time.

Against this background it was not surprising that at the June 1907 Annual Council meeting the following resolution, moved by the Earl of Derby and seconded by the Duke of Devonshire, was unanimously adopted:

> That in view of the certainty of a considerable number of soldiers who served in the War in South Africa dying within the next few years from wounds or disease contracted in that

War, and realizing that the resources of the Royal Patriotic Fund Corporation for relieving the widows and orphans of such soldiers are exhausted, the Corporation resolves that the Chancellor of the Exchequer be asked to receive a Deputation, in order that the financial position of the Corporation may be made known to His Majesty's Government, and that this Corporation may have placed at its disposal a sum of money sufficient to enable it to continue to accept for adequate relief further cases of widows and orphans of those whose deaths are proved to be the result of wounds or disease contracted in Service in the South Africa War.

The Chancellor of the Exchequer and the Secretary of State for War duly received the Chairman of the Executive Committee, Mr Hayes Fisher, the Earl of Derby and the President of the Institute of Actuaries. The Ministers agreed that the period of eligibility for Government pensions for widows whose husbands' deaths were caused by the South Africa War should be extended from two years after duty in South Africa to seven. As the Corporation reported 'The boon thus conferred forms a precedent for similar treatment of widows and orphans resulting from future wars' – a revealing demonstration of the threat felt at that time.

The Corporation's other request had been that it should be reimbursed by the Government for its expenditure on allowances for widows and orphans resulting from the South Africa War for the years up to the time that the Government agreed to War Pensions from 1 April 1901; namely for 1899, 1900 and the early months of 1901. This was rejected and in spite of well-argued submissions by the Corporation between November 1907 and May 1908 the most the War Office would do was to reply that it neither had the power or the funds to agree, and to suggest that future submissions should be directed to the Treasury. A further deputation was planned, but the 1908 Budget measures together with the chancellor's concession to South African War widows, described earlier in this chapter, made it unnecessary to pursue this rather unequal contest any further.

The Chancellor's 1908 Budget made provision for the first time for the granting of 'Old Age Pensions'. These pensions were granted to those of both sexes over seventy years of age whose annual income did not exceed £31.10 shillings a year. This measure was bound to affect the Corporation's commitments. By this time, however, the Corporation's financial situation was already showing the benefit of the Chancellor's concession to South African War widows, so that the Executive Committee did not feel itself bound to deduct from its allowances to these widows over 70 the amounts that they could henceforth receive from the Government. Instead, the Corporation decided that: 'Widows on Funds specially subscribed publicly in connection with certain Wars and Naval Disasters having allowances at annual rates lower than £31.11 shillings should, if over 70 years of age and on attaining that age, receive on and after 1st January 1909, a uniform allowance of £31.11 shillings[1] per annum.'

This decision was taken because members of the Corporation felt that: 'It would be unfair to add to the burden of the taxpayer the cost of Old Age Pensions for such widows when we had specially-subscribed Funds in hand sufficient to meet the increased allowances of £31.11s. per annum.'

(This early instance of a charity helping out the Exchequer [often repeated in the years to come] was subsequently queried by an 'Honorary Agent' at the 1910 Council Meeting in the terms 'Is it wise to save the Chancellor of the Exchequer?')

In addition, the Corporation felt able to provide additional allowances for widows from the Patriotic General Fund. All this was a far cry from the situation of stringency some twelve months earlier. Following the Chancellor's extension of help to 'Transvaal War' widows and the introduction of the new Old Age Pension, the Corporation had certain of its Funds actuarially revalued to determine the extent of the lessening of the burden on these. The Actuary, Mr F. Schooling, was able to report that at 31 March 1909 surpluses of assets over liabilities in the three more general funds would be £112,405; most of this being in the Patriotic General Fund which, as a result of the payment of Old Age Pensions, had had its annual commitment reduced by about 66%. This encouraged the Corporation to extend the conditions of eligibility for help from the Patriotic

Ebb and Flow

General Fund to the many widows of those who had served in campaigns and 'gave long and meritorious service' – whether or not the husbands' deaths were attributable to the campaigns.

The year 1908, in addition to signalling a turning-point in the Corporation's financial position, also saw the end of hostilities between the Member of Parliament of Devonport, Mr H.E. Kearley, and the Secretary, Colonel Young. The contest had its origins in the former's persistent criticism of the Royal Commission in 1893 and his subsequent clashes with the Secretary throughout the hearings of the Select Committee in 1895 and 1896. After Mr Kearley became a member of the new Corporation, and the Chairman of its Finance Committee, he continued to provoke most of the Committee members, and the Secretary in particular, by his repeated attempts to change the Corporation's policy from being one of uniform treatment of beneficiaries of all the Funds to the exhaustion of the resources of individual funds upon those for whom the funds were raised. Mr Kearley had only one ally in his campaign to this end, Lieutenant-General Sir Thomas Kelly Kenny (whom he had proposed for membership).

These two remained in the minority, and the extra administrative work which they provided for the Secretary is apparent, stemming largely from their insistence that their motions and proposals – usually by letter – should be recorded, not only in Minutes but also in the Annual Report. The Executive Committee was further aggravated in 1905 by the 'leaking' to the Press of the draft Report of the Committee to the Council which thus publicized the conflict about policy which Mr Kearley and General Kelly Kenny were promoting. This particular incident ended in the resignation of General Kelly Kenny; with something of a flourish, since he sent copies of his letter of resignation to the Prime Minister as well as the Duke of Connaught. The Corporation's records on the subject are discreet but it is clear that the General, as well as Mr Kearley, did not feel that due weight was even given to his views and, in particular, by the Secretary, who, he alleged, misrepresented him. As for the Secretary, his irritation comes through in Minutes and resolutions in terms such as 'Mr

Kearley expressed at some length ... 'The Executive Committee, having exhaustively considered ...'

Mr Kearley, however, appeared unlikely to follow his colleague's example: indeed, he seemed to be spurred on in his somewhat maverick course, pressing his personal views and making use of the press. In a speech in his constituency on 3 January 1906 he took some personal credit for the 'agitation he himself started [applause] as money had not been distributed as freely and liberally to the widows of the men who were actually killed ...' The speech led to numerous applications from the Devonport area, many ineligible.

Throughout the spring and early summer of 1906 Mr Kearley lost no opportunity to attack the Secretary; with little success, however, as Colonel Young was staunchly supported by the rest of the members. It was clear that their patience with Mr Kearley's disruptive tactics was nearly exhausted. When, therefore, Mr Kearley's three-year term as a member appointed by King Edward came to an end that year, he disappeared from the Corporation's records; unsung it seems. In contrast, towards the end of 1907 Colonel Young was given a knighthood. It was, perhaps, rather regrettable that throughout 1907 he had been taking up much of his time and that of the Executive Committee in presenting, at great length and with voluminous evidence, the case that he was inadequately paid for the remarkable job that he did. He sent an impassioned plea to the President, the Duke of Connaught, and, as it is something of a classic of its kind, it is printed in full at Appendix L. Bearing in mind the grant of a knighthood at the end of the year, this letter could perhaps be considered as less of a complaint; more of a citation. The eventual decision of the Executive Committee that his salary could not be increased any more, but that 'whenever the Secretary should decide to retire – a matter which the Committee did not desire to press upon him – it would be the duty of the Committee to submit to the Treasury a recommendation as to his retiring allowance, and that it would be their wish to make a generous recommendation in this respect having regard to the Secretary's special services.' Whether or not the Committee desired to press retirement on Colonel Young, this decision had an unsurprising result. Six weeks later he tendered his resignation: departing with £400 a year and his knighthood in October 1909, after there had been an unsuccessful trial of one successor and a successful apprenticeship of another who became his relief, Major E.A. Stanton, the late Governor of Khartoum.

The first Annual Report signed by Major Stanton, and issued in July 1910 bore a black border. The death had occurred on 6 May of that year of King Edward VII, who had received the first Annual Report of the new Corporation and whose likeness appeared (and still appears) on the Corporation's seal.

A copy of the special address from the Corporation to King George V which appeared at the beginning of the Annual Report for 1910 is at Appendix M.

Although the help given in the education of orphans no longer occupied the Executive Committee to any great extent, thanks to the effectiveness of the efforts of the General Purposes Committee in dealing with cases and the Management Committee of the Royal Victoria Patriotic Asylum, the support for large numbers of children continued unabated and from time to time impinged on the other Committees.

The move into the new reign was marked by the recognition that, as recorded in the 1909 Report, the word Asylum is 'now mainly used to denote an Institution for the insane', so that 'with the approval of HRH the President and on the recommendation of the Committee of Management' the Wandsworth establishment became the Royal Victoria Patriotic School. At this time it had forty-three girls under ten years old, 166 girls under thirteen years and eighty-four above that age, the latter learning 'laundry, kitchen and household duties'. The average annual cost of each child at the school, exclusive of any maintenance cost of the property, was just over £19, and the number of girls at the school rarely seemed to fall much below 290. The responsibility for the girls' education had been assumed by the London County Council since the end of 1906; the Corporation bearing the responsibility and cost of housing and boarding.

The total number of children 'on the books' of the Corporation in 1910 were just over 3,700 of which eighty were being cared for by the Roman Catholic Orphans' Fund and 323 paid for at various boarding schools.

The Royal Victoria Patriotic School had been in existence for just over fifty years and expensive repairs were needed to the roof, the guttering, the pointing in the brickwork, and the flooring. The cost of these repairs over a period of two or three years was anticipated to amount to somewhere between £7,000 and £12,000 and, after considering other alternatives and consulting the Treasury Solicitor on the possibility of transferring some of the surplus from the Transvaal War Fund to an endowment for repairs to the School, the Executive Committee decided that the necessary funds should be provided by loans from the General Fund at 3½% interest payable by the School Fund. During 1910 and 1911, £10,000 was loaned and spent on repairs.

The Fund which was causing some anxiety at this time was the 'Soldiers' Effects Fund'. The capital value of this fund fell by nearly £12,000 between 1909 and 1910 and the annual income was steadily decreasing to below £5,000, while the expenditure was equally steadily increasing until it stood at over £12,000 by 1910. At the 1910 Council meeting the Duke of Connaught foresaw the exhaustion of the Fund in comparatively few years but added that, if this happened, 'some similar fund would almost of necessity have to be created by those who were responsible for our Army': the Fund at that time being one of the few devoted to helping widows (in 'exceptional cases'[2]) children and other dependants 'of soldiers dying on service or within six months after discharge from the Army'. The outlook for the 'Soldiers' Effects Fund' was to remain a gloomy one for some years partly because, as education in the Army improved, few soldiers died intestate. Strong representations were made by an impressive deputation to the Secretary of State for War (Colonel Seely), consisting of ten members of the Executive Committee led by its Chairman on 26 November 1913. Both sides agreed on the need but the Secretary of State was not prepared to approach the Chancellor for it and the Corporation saw little prospect in an appeal to the public.

In general, the Corporation could not be accused at this time of 'hoarding'. In 1910 the total income was just under

Ebb and Flow

£40,000 and the expenditure was almost £66,000. Unfortunately, Mr Kearley was not there to applaud. Less pleasing for Mr Kearley, with his belief in funds being totally exhausted on those for whom the funds were initially raised, would have been the Corporation's decision to use the surplus in the 'Victoria' Fund to establish a 'Special Navy Fund' for an equivalent purpose to that of the 'Soldiers' Effects Fund'; and to use the surpluses in the 'Patriotic (Russian War) Fund', 'Zulu War Fund', 'Captain Fund' and 'Eurydice Fund' to form a 'Special Army and Navy Fund' for very deserving and special cases not eligible for help from any existing Funds. By the end of 1913 these two new Funds were providing allowances for 172 widows, 205 children and 20 other dependants.

The 1911 Council meeting was the last to be chaired by the Duke of Connaught until 1913 as he had been appointed Governor General of Canada. However, he remained President of the Corporation throughout.

There was undoubtedly a spirit of flexibility and urge to help amongst the management of the Corporation in 1911 and 1912. To make more funds available the Corporation proposed to sell twenty acres of the farm land at Wandsworth, which was surplus to the school's needs, to the London County Council. This caused some concern in Wandsworth and Battersea that the land might be used for building and the two Councils first opposed the sale and then determined to acquire it from the London County Council to ensure its continuing use as open space. The sale to the LCC eventually went through; the price being £11,000 together with £1,000 to provide a dividing wall and railing.

On the expenditure side, this flexibility was manifested by an application to the Charity Commissioners to make use of an accumulation of capital in the Transvaal War Fund of nearly £100,000 by extending the scope of that fund to include as many as possible of those necessitous widows and orphans whose husbands had served in the South Africa War, although their deaths might not be considered attributable to it. This application was approved and duly instituted.

The total numbers 'on the books' of all the Corporation's funds at this time were just over 3,000 widows, 3,500 children and 276 other dependants. These figures were the legacies of wars and military service since the Crimea, but already in 1912 there was fighting between Italy, Turkey and the Balkan States and in England the expression 'in the event of war' was becoming almost a commonplace. When, for example, the Secretary reported to the Executive Committee that 'he had been called on by the War Office, in the event of war, to act as an Assistant Cable Censor in London during hostilities', this was 'duly noted' without comment. There can be no question that by 1913 there must have been, in the minds of the distinguished members of the Executive Committee, great disquiet concerning probable future calls, surrounded as they were with widespread preparations for war and by the lining up of alliances of the Great Powers in warlike attitudes.

Footnotes

1. Just over 12s a week: or an increase of up to 20% in many instances.
2. A temporary restriction because of the number of calls on the Fund.

12 A World War and a Nation's Debt

Bearing in mind the devastation in the lives of scores of millions of people brought about by the events in 1914 and the immediately following years it would seem superfluous to describe the time as a unique period in the Corporation's history, but the consequences wrought on the organization were not all obvious, and were appropriately weighty. The traditional long-term policies and machinery to operate them were supplanted by the force of immediate and overriding need, involving a drastic change of pace and policies. At the same time these events brought into being such a close relationship with the Government that the Corporation could almost be said to have become the first Quango[1], though it would be another fifty years before the expression was coined.

If the Crimean War had been an 'unnecessary' war, and the Boer War a 'provoked' war, the 'European' war of 1914 which developed into the first 'World' war was an almost 'inevitable' war. Europe had reached the situation of being a number of armed camps in which the main protagonists had their war plans prepared and refined. The inevitability of war was so widely recognized that by 4 August 1914, when German troops invaded Belgium, and Britain, in consequence, declared war on Germany, this potentially significant event appears to have received little notice in the annals of the Corporation since its significance and probable effects on the Corporation's work had clearly already received considerable thought. The Vice-President and Chairman of both the Executive and the General Purposes Committees, the Right Honourable W. Hayes Fisher MP, was able to address the House of Commons on 6 August on the place of the Corporation in the immediate task of helping widows, orphans and other dependants of soldiers and sailors who at that time had not yet embarked for France as the British Expeditionary Force.

Immediately on the outbreak of war the Duke of Connaught had been asked, by cable to Ottawa, whether his name could be used in any fund-raising for the Corporation for the 'European' War. To this he had gladly assented, but the Prince of Wales on 6 August launched a 'National Relief Fund' appeal, following the pattern of the Corporation in 1899 for the Transvaal War in working through the Lord Mayor of London, and clearly a competing appeal was out of the question. The question thus became how the Corporation and its machinery was to operate in relation to this new fund.

With the opposing forces already heavily engaged in Belgium and France, it was clearly essential that some interim arrangements for immediate relief should be established. The public was responding generously to the Prince of Wales' appeal (£2 million had been raised by early September) so that it was primarily a question of how best to transmit financial help to those in need. The two organizations best able to do this were the Royal Patriotic Fund Corporation and the Soldiers' and Sailors' Families Association. Both had a network of volunteers throughout the country and a central organization of trustees qualified to supervise the management and disbursement of large sums. The Corporation had Mr Hayes Fisher as one of the trustees of the Prince of Wales' Fund, and its customary committee membership of some twenty distinguished trustees. Its Honorary Local Agents, first appointed in place of the local committees used in the Boer War and as a result of an Executive Committee decision on 5 December 1906, numbered over eighty and provided fairly good cover over most of the United Kingdom. This was made more comprehensive, with the help of the Soldiers' and Sailors' Families Association, the Distress and Relief Committees and the National (and Local) Relief Funds and other charitable organizations.

The considerable additional work needed to be performed by the office staff was carried out by voluntary helpers (there were nine of these by the end of 1914) and by the permanent staff working much overtime. The work itself was a matter of quantity rather than difficulty. The help provided from the National Relief Fund was in the form of standardized grants of £5 for widows, £1 for each child and £3 for other dependants, to be paid in one payment or sometimes in weekly instalments. Work was also simplified in the early weeks of the war by the decision that no new cases would be accepted on any of the Corporation's existing funds (though all commitments of existing allowances would be met). This decision was modified later in the year to the extent that new cases were accepted on the new funds established from surpluses, namely the 'Special Army and Navy' and 'Special Navy' Funds and the Transvaal War Fund 'Extension'.

In November 1914, the Secretary, Major Stanton, was ordered by the War Office to report immediately to Devonport in connection with the formation of a new battalion of the Somerset Light Infantry. With the support of the Trustees this move was postponed and subsequently cancelled since the Duke of Connaught, Governor-General and Commander-in-Chief in Canada had asked for Major Stanton to become his Military Secretary. Mr Hayes Fisher, as Chairman of the Executive Committee, had already been given authority to make any temporary secretarial arrangements that he saw fit.

He appointed as 'Acting Secretary' Lieutenant Colonel A. C. E. Welby who, Mr Hayes Fisher told the Council: ' ... learnt his soldier's duties and his knowledge of the Service when he commanded the Scots Greys, and who learnt administrative qualities and capacities both as a Member of Parliament and as a Member of the London County Council'.

As Colonel Welby's 'Honorary Assistant Secretary' the Chairman appointed a Mr F. N. Ashcroft to deal with Naval cases.

Although the Corporation had, as promised to the Government, made no separate appeal for funds, donations flowed in from all parts of the world so that before the end of 1914 over £3,000 had been credited to the Corporation's 'European War (Private Donations) Fund'. This Fund had reached almost £8,000 by the following June and the intention was to use it to help 'those deserving cases which inevitably arise out of the death of soldiers and sailors on service in war, but which for some reason are not eligible for relief by the Government Departments administering State Funds or out of any Public Fund'. Meanwhile about £3,000 of the 'Private Donation' funds had been loaned to some of the older funds which were showing debit balances; the Transvaal War Fund in particular being over £1,000 on the debit side. The fact that the Stock Exchange was closed at the end of 1914 made it difficult to realize investments, and in any event such action was unwise at the time because of the considerable fall in value of these.

At the end of 1914 £30,000 had been received by the Corporation from the National Relief Fund and 3,134 widows, 5,425 children and 1,436 other dependants had been helped. Perhaps, though, another figure that needs to be remembered is that by this time the total of British dead from the battles in Belgium and France (Mons, the Marne and Ypres) was over 40,000.

The number of wounded was much greater, and many of these would not recover. One of the wartime military hospitals concerned with caring for the wounded was London General Hospital No.3 at Wandsworth, in the premises of the Royal Victoria Patriotic School. The school, when it re-assembled after the August holiday (which had been extended because of the outbreak of war), was occupying several houses in Spencer Park only a short distance from the school building; eventually the Corporation managed to acquire seven of these.

The appalling casualty rate, particularly in contrast with previous experience of war, in addition to causing national distress, was giving rise to doubts in the National Relief Fund Committee as to whether the public response to its appeal, generous as it was, would be able to meet demands on such a scale. In consequence, in May 1915, with the fighting in Gallipoli and the second Battle of Ypres adding thousands to the total killed in action, the Committee asked the Corporation if it could estimate 'how many widows we think the National Relief Committee will have to provide for before the war is over'. This was what Mr Hayes Fisher told the Council at the Annual General Meeting on 10 June 1915, although other records show that the period referred to was

A World War and a Nation's Debt

'if the war continued twelve months more'. It is possible that the assumption was made that these times would be coincident.

The answer given by the Chairman of the Executive Committee was, not unexpectedly, that it was impossible to provide such an estimate. The detail of his reply in his address to the Council shows some of the reasons why:

> You can quite imagine that that is a question uncommonly difficult to answer. Now the number at present known to us of widows of soldiers and sailors that I have read out to you is 12,139 – and that, of course, is not including the widows of officers. You will have observed an answer given in the House of Commons yesterday by the Prime Minister on the subject of casualties; he gave the number in other ranks killed as 47,015[2] – call it 48,000. Say that we have relieved 12,000 widows, that means that 25 per cent of those men killed were married men, does it not? Yes, but then what is called 'Kitchener's Army'[3] have not yet really been tested in the firing line, to any large extent at all events, and we are told that 65 per cent of what is known as 'Kitchener's Army' are married men. So a very much larger proportion of the 'Kitchener's Army' are married than the proportion of the Expeditionary Force, or of what we used to know as our Regular Army plus the Territorials. Therefore, I do not think we can derive any data for making an estimate on those lines, and I will tell you what we have said to the Committee of the Prince of Wales' Fund:
>
>> 'Your Committee, you say, recognise the difficulty of forming anything more than an approximate estimate. Your Committee will no doubt equally recognise that the result of the past ten months of war can be no safe guide for the coming twelve months; that it is impossible to forecast what fleets and armies and what numbers in them will be engaged; what the nature of warfare will be; whether a supreme effort will be made to win victory at all cost in a given time, or, at far less sacrifice of life, to seek it by wearing out the enemy; that consequently any attempt to make even an approximate estimate of what the loss will be during the coming twelve months could only be to draw an inference from the figures furnished, which might be so affected by increased warfare and the composition of the Forces engaged as to become entirely falsified. Therefore my Committee do not venture to

make an estimate of expenditure, but feel that, having furnished the figures showing the expenditure of the last ten months, it is better to leave such estimate to your Committee, trusting that full provision will be made for continuing these grants to the widows, children and dependants of as many as are likely to die in this war.'

The overall financial position of the Corporation by the end of October in 1915 was that over-expenditure on all the pre 'European War' funds stood at £4,736 and that, although the 'European War (Private Donations) Fund' showed a credit balance of £9,674 it was anticipated that £2,000 of that would need to be borrowed to help the old funds before long.

Although the interim arrangements of the National Relief Fund dealing with the appeal and the income from it, then transmitting the latter to the Corporation, SSFA, and some other charities to disburse, had worked adequately for many months, once the more lasting nature and scale of the war became apparent the Government sought a more permanent system based upon statute. A Select Committee on Pensions was, therefore, established and recommended an Act of Parliament: 'to make better provision as to the pensions, grants and allowances made in respect of the present war to officers and men in the Naval and Military Service of His Majesty and their dependants, and the care of officers and men disabled in consequence of the present war, and for purposes connected therewith'.

The Act that emerged was the 'Naval and Military War Pensions, &C, Act, 1915 (Cap 83)' and was long and detailed but what it achieved in essence was a closer linking of the Government to the Corporation in relation to the payment of pensions, grants and allowances and the care of the disabled. It was a compromise between the ideas of many, including the Vice-President of the Corporation, that there should be one Pension Department with control over all matters of welfare of the Services, and the somewhat *ad hoc* arrangements of an Appeal Committee supplying funds as required to existing charities.

The Act established a 'Statutory Committee' of the Royal Patriotic Fund Corporation. This was to consist of the existing members of the Corporation as laid down by the Act of 1903 but strengthened to twenty-seven members and including, in addition to the previous representatives of the Treasury, the Admiralty and the War Office:

one appointed by the National Health Insurance Joint Committee,

one appointed by the Local Government Board of England and Wales,

one each appointed by the Local Government Boards of Scotland and Ireland,

two appointed by the Soldiers' and Sailors' Families Association.

Special provision was also made that of the twelve appointed by the Sovereign, 'some shall be women and not less than two shall be representatives of labour'.

In addition provision was made for the Chairman or the Vice-Chairman of the Statutory Committee to be paid 'out of money provided by Parliament, such salary as the Treasury may determine' and that 'All other expenses of the Committee (including such travelling expenses to members of the Committee as the Committee may determine) shall be paid out of the funds at the disposal of the Committee'.

The local representation of the Corporation, previously provided by Lord Lieutenants and Honorary Agents, was also to be strengthened by the formation of local committees established in every County and County Borough, and every Borough or Urban District having a population of not less than fifty thousand: these local committees to be appointed by the appropriate Councils and approved by the Statutory Committee; the latter being given the authority to appoint a local committee if the local Council fails to do so.

The other important change to the Corporation's responsibilities was the inclusion of care of disabled officers and men after they had left the service 'including provision for their health, training and employment'.

In the light of these very wide responsibilities and extensive organization it was not surprising that Mr Hayes Fisher, in his address to the council in 1915, expressed some misgivings about the ability of the new organization to meet these commitments. He said:

I will only say that so far as I and my colleagues are concerned, we are all desirous of doing anything we can to meet the wishes of the Select Committee, and to place our own services so far as we can at the disposal of the country for the purpose of carrying out the needs of the country as regards pensioning the widows, the orphans, and the dependants occasioned by war; but, after all there is a limit to human capacity and to human endurance, and I do want to say that although we may find many gentlemen ready to give up one day a week for this work, the Government must be careful in selecting the new men for the new duties, and the new women – because I hope there will be many women on this Body – so that they are men and women who really have leisure to give to the very difficult and arduous duties which will have to be performed. I am quite certain that this new Body will have to sit much more often than one day a week, and I am equally certain that while you might get men unpaid to do the old work, limited as it is to one day a week, you will not get men to sit for four or five or possibly six days a week and to do the work regularly in office hours unless at all events one, if not two or three, are paid administrators of the millions of money which, I understand, must be placed at their disposal if this work is to be done rightly.

In relation to the Vice-President's concern about future frequency of meetings, the year's total of Committee meetings in the period July 1914 to June 1915 had been:

Executive Committee	6
General Purposes Committee	21
(which dealt with applications for help)	
Finance Committee	9
School Management Committee	12

In spite of real concern as to the problems ahead, the Corporation lost no time in fulfilling its part in setting up the Statutory Committee once the Act of Parliament had been promulgated on 10 November 1915. At a special meeting of the Council on 1 December the Corporation's quota of six members were nominated to be:

Right Hon W. Hayes Fisher MP

B.B. Cubitt, Esq. CB – Assistant Secretary at the War Office

Admiral Sir Wilmot Fawkes, GCB, KCVO – C-in-C, Plymouth 1908–1911

A World War and a Nation's Debt

J.E. Raynor Esq. – Lord Mayor of Liverpool 1914–1915

The Countess Roberts – daughter of the late Field Marshal Earl Roberts

(a leading member of the Officers' Families Fund)

Mrs McKenna – wife of the Chancellor of the Exchequer (member of the Finance Committee of the Prince of Wales' National Relief Fund).

The other members of the Statutory Committee nominated by the Crown, Government Departments and the Soldiers' and Sailors' Families Association are listed at Appendix N. His Royal Highness the Prince of Wales was the Chairman and Mr Cyril Jackson (a Crown appointment) Vice-Chairman.

A special meeting of the Council of the Corporation on 1 February 1916 was addressed by the Prince of Wales (who was 'on very short leave from the Front'), the Right Honourable A.J. Balfour, First Lord of the Admiralty, and Field Marshal the Right Honourable Earl Kitchener of Khartoum, Secretary of State for War.

The Prince of Wales provided a general outline of the help to be given, comprising a flat rate of Government pension (this started at 10 shillings a week for a Private soldier's widow, rising to 12 shillings and six pence when she reached 35 years of age and 15 shillings at 45) together with supplementary grants or allowances to meet individual circumstances (since the services engaged in the war were 'drawn from all classes of the community' in widely differing financial situations). The flat rate of Government pensions would be paid by the appropriate State Departments financed by the Government: the supplementary grants and allowances by the Statutory Committee, through its local Committees, and voluntary associations; paid for by a combination of voluntary contributions and State grants. The Prince of Wales was able to announce that the Chancellor of the Exchequer had promised to ask Parliament for a million pounds 'to start us on our way'.

That every penny of this scale of financial support was likely to be needed was illustrated by Prince Edward by comparing the casualty figures of the previous, South African, war with the 'European War' up to the beginning of 1916. These were the total of all ranks killed in the South

African War 21,942 and in the 'European War' to date 128,138. In total casualties the figures were 44,876 and 549,467 respectively.

Somewhat later in the meeting the Vice-Chairman, Mr Jackson, dealt with a question with which many would sympathize (as much now as clearly did at the time) namely when large amounts of money are collected locally was it expected that all of this would be handed over to the central organization? Mr Jackson's answer showed a sense of realism – 'No, we do not' [expect that] 'First of all, we know you would not do it if we did. Secondly, it is not the scheme of the Act. The scheme of the Act is co-operation – co-operation between the central fund and the local funds.' He went on to say that where one area was richly endowed the Statutory Committee might ask for a proportion of their funds to help a poorer area, because the aim must be to have a fixed standard of supplementary allowances and grants – not one which varied from district to district. (Later in the operations of the Statutory Committee local 'War Pensions Committees' were authorized to make emergency grants not exceeding £3 to individuals.)

The Statutory Committee assumed responsibility for all 'European War' grants and allowances from 1 July 1916, so it was decided that purely 'Royal Patriotic Fund' grants for 'European War' cases should cease for any casualties notified after 30 June 1916 and any casualties notified as 'missing' before 1 October 1916.

The problem of officers and men reported as 'missing' (of which there were large numbers in the war of 1914–1918) had been carefully considered by the Corporation in the Spring of 1915 and it had been decided that where no notification of death had been received, either from evidence or decision of Court of Enquiry, a grant should be paid to the 'widow' after thirty weeks.

Prior to the Statutory Committee taking over the responsibility for the European War grants, the Corporation had distributed these to almost 40,000 widows, almost 85,000 children and almost 25,000 dependants, involving the expenditure of about £357,000; and this was before the Battle of Jutland and the Somme offensive with 2,750 widows and dependants added from the first and some 30,000 deaths

A World War and a Nation's Debt

resulting from the second.

Contributions from all over the world continued to arrive for the 'European War (Private Donations) Fund' and by mid January 1916 almost £11,500 had been received. These donations had all been unsolicited, nevertheless the Corporation arranged with the Statutory Committee that any future contributions which were not 'clearly intended for the Royal Patriotic Fund' would be handed over to the Statutory Committee.

The year 1917, which saw the return of the Duke of Connaught to England and to the Chair of the Council meeting in December of that year, also saw a further development in the handling of War Pensions.

Just before Christmas 1916, by the 'Ministry of Pensions Act, 1916 (Cap 65)' a Ministry of Pensions was established for the first time and this Ministry assumed the powers and duties of the two Service Ministries as regards pensions and grants, and it took control of the Statutory Committee. As a result, there followed in August 1917 the 'Naval and Military War Pensions & c. (Transfer of Powers) Act 1917 (Cap 37)' dissolving the Statutory Committee and transferring its functions to the new Ministry. This same Act transferred to the Royal Patriotic Fund Corporation 'All other property belonging to the Statutory Committee' to be 'held and supplied by them upon the trusts and for the purposes upon and for which it was held and applicable by the Statutory Committee' – which, in effect, meant £10,632 17 shillings and 10 pence being the balance of voluntary funds held by the Committee. This amount was brought to account by the Corporation in a new 'War (Transferred 1917) Fund' which embraced the same causes as when a part of the Statutory Committee 'Special Funds', namely:

'Sailors of the Royal Navy and their dependants'
'Jutland Battle'
'Minesweepers'
'Widows and orphans of Sailors and Soldiers'

Thus, three years after the outbreak of War the Royal Patriotic Fund Corporation was back to its separate role, though with the stronger Government links retained and with the addition of two new funds – the 'European War (Private Donations) Fund' and the 'War (Transferred 1917)

Fund': additions which still left the total market value of the investments of all its Funds standing only at £695,000 compared with a nominal value of £968,000.

The Corporation found itself so short of income that for the first time in its history, or that of its predecessor the Royal Commission, it had to refrain from accepting any new cases. 195 applications were received in 1917 and those which qualified for help were put on a 'waiting list'. There were also anomalies which the Corporation would have wanted to have corrected if the funds had been available. As the Duke of Connaught told the Council in December 1917, 'You will constantly see now in this country living in the same street the widow of a man who gave his life for the country in the Transvaal War, who, because her husband was killed by a Boer, only gets 7 shillings a week, while in the same street are the widows of men who have fallen in this War, who, because their husbands were killed by the Huns, get 13 shillings and 9 pence a week.'

1917 was the year of the battles of Arras, Messines, Passchendaele and Cambrai with British dead totalling over 200,000. It was also the year when the description 'European War' became inappropriate with the United States of America entering the war on the side of the 'Triple Entente', although it was to be many months before its major impact could be seen.

In contrast to all the bad news in 1917, 1918 saw a general brightening. The anomaly of widows of earlier wars being less well treated than those of 1914 to 1918, which was taken up by the Corporation with the Minister of Pensions, was corrected and all widows under 45 received 13s 9d a week while those over 45 received 15s, so that many whom the Corporation would have helped if funds had been available received State help instead.

In France, the German offensive on the Marne had failed and was followed by what the German General Ludendorff was to later describe as 'the black day of the German Army in the history of the war', the successful offensive by the British Army East of Amiens, using over 400 tanks in a surprise attack. German morale finally gave after this and although other battles followed the German Supreme Command was thereafter concerned with emerging from the war with the

A World War and a Nation's Debt

least possible further damage.

There were rewards for the Corporation too, apart from the success in persuading the Government to help widows from earlier wars. The Corporation's Vice-President and Chairman of both the Executive Committee and General Purposes Committee since 1907 and the latter Committee since the Corporation's foundation, Mr Hayes Fisher, was elevated to the Peerage as Lord Downham of Fulham, and Colonel Welby, the Secretary since his predecessor, Stanton went to Canada with the Duke of Connaught in 1914, was made a Knight Commander of the British Empire.

There also came in 1918 a time which the School Management Committee had been looking forward to with considerable eagerness: the return of the School buildings at Wandsworth so that the school could operate again in suitable surroundings rather than eight houses with inadequate facilities and recreation opportunities.

There can be no more proper ending to a chapter dealing with help for widows and orphans in the period 1914 to 1918 than simply to record that during that time the British Empire mobilized almost nine million men, of whom over two million became casualties and almost one million were killed in action or died of wounds.

Footnotes

1. Quasi-Autonomous Non-Governmental Organization – 'a semi-public body with financial support from, and senior appointments made by, Government.'
2. Officers' deaths were 3,327 but many deaths were also included in the figure of those 'missing' which was 53,747 all ranks.
3. The volunteers from civil life called for by Lord Kitchener in 1914.

13   Coming to Terms

The 'Great War' of 1914–18 had brought a considerable increase in mutual awareness between the British public and Service Charities as well as reinforcing the links between the latter and Government Ministries. The necessity for the Royal Patriotic Fund Corporation and the Soldiers' and Sailors' Families Association to act as agents for the distribution of grants from the National Relief Fund during the major part of the war had also strengthened the local representation of both organizations. This, together with the increasing interdependence between the Ministry of Pensions and the Corporation (there were now two representatives of the Ministry of Pensions appointed to the Corporation under the provisions of the War Pensions Act, 1918), made the Corporation a particularly suitable body to put forward proposals for improvements in the situation of Service widows.

The Pensions Acts of 1916 and 1917 had ensured that war widows of the Great War were receiving help appropriate to the current cost of living, but the rates of state pensions for those who had lost their husbands and fathers in the Boer War, and the level of allowances which the Corporation could afford to pay widows of earlier campaigns were very low in comparison.

Representations in 1918 and 1919 by the Corporation about the former were eventually successful in having their pensions raised to the same scale as that applicable to Great War widows; but there remained the problem of widows whose husbands had served in earlier campaigns and who were not eligible for statutory pensions. They had not gained from these pension increases, so the Corporation sought the Government's agreement that the latter would supplement

Coming to Terms

their allowances from the Corporation as necessary.

To ensure that their case had firm foundations, the Corporation had first to review its allowances and its own capacity to increase them. Once again the Institute of Actuaries showed itself to be generous in its help, by offering to value all the Corporation's individual funds free of charge. This valuation was very necessary because the war had severely depreciated the Corporation's investments and this had resulted in the decision not to accept new applications in several funds. Consequently, there were waiting lists of widows needing help; even at the previous low levels of allowances.

The result of the actuary's valuation enabled the Corporation to negotiate with the Ministry of Pensions the necessary supplementary grant from the Government to make it possible for the allowance paid by the Corporation to the widows of 'former wars' to be raised to rates compatible with the then current cost of living. On 17 February 1919, Mr Stanley Baldwin, then Minister of Pensions, was able to offer the Corporation a capital 'grant in aid' of £156,403 to permit these increased allowances to be paid. The Government had also already provided £25,000 towards the support of orphan girls at the Royal Victoria Patriotic School; now back in its old premises at Wandsworth. This was followed by a further grant of £10,000 in 1920.

The Institute of Actuaries carried out a further comprehensive valuation of all the Corporation's Funds to confirm that these new commitments, together with certain other proposals of the General Purposes Committee (increasing the age limit to 16 for the support of boy orphans, for example), could be afforded. This concluded that, while the value of investments continued to depreciate (by nearly £52,000 in just over a year) and while seven of the nineteen funds had a deficit, the overall position would allow the necessary additional £165,476 to be provided.

The existence of so many different funds, some of which had very small balances or were in deficit, had for some time appeared illogical to the Finance Committee. At various times it had been necessary to transfer sums from the more solvent funds to others in order to meet commitments.

Consequently it seemed only sensible to combine some of these funds as a permanent measure. Responsible legal opinion had been sought in 1906 and, based upon this, the nineteen funds were reduced to nine in 1920 by combining the Patriotic (Russian War), the 'Captain', the 'Eurydice', the 'Atalanta', the Zulu War, the Ashantee War, Patriotic (Army), County of Forfar, Indian Mutiny Relief, and Rodriguez Funds with the Patriotic General Fund. The 'Victoria' and Special Navy Funds were also combined and absorbed into the Royal Naval Relief Fund. The 'Zervudachi' Fund had already been absorbed by the Special Army and Navy Fund. As a result of these measures of rationalization the Funds administered by the Corporation (excluding those connected with schools) were:

Patriotic General
Soldiers' Effects
Transvaal War
Royal Naval Relief
Special Army and Navy
European War
State Supplements Account
Light Brigade (Balaclava)
Indian Army (Europeans') Effects

The last two funds, having very restricted application and Trust complications, had to remain separate.

The founding of the Royal Air Force as a separate service in 1918 also created new potential beneficiaries of Service Charities. As Queen Alexandra, Patron of the Soldiers' and Sailors' Families Association, wrote in a letter to the SSFA Chairman (Colonel Gildea) in July 1919 'our airmen having helped England so splendidly to win the great war – and the new Air Force, too, being now established as a distinct Service – we might, and perhaps ought, to add "airmen" to the name of the Association': so SSFA became SSAFA. The Royal Air Force had its own 'Royal Air Force Memorial Fund' but, in addition, the Soldiers' Effects Fund, which was not to be re-opened by the Corporation for new applicants until January 1925, in 1927 became the 'Soldiers' and Airmen's Effects Fund', after the necessary arrangements had been made with the Air Ministry; although from the time of the creation of the Air Force, it had always been possible for the Corporation to help the widows and orphans of men of the RAF by means of the 'European War Fund' (the 'Private Donations' Fund mentioned in the last chapter).

The increasingly close liaison with the Treasury which the Corporation had enjoyed since the days of the Statutory Committee continued to be to their mutual advantage. Since the end of the Great War the Corporation had been paying small allowances, as supplements to the old age pension, to those service widows whose husbands' deaths were not attributable to wars. In many cases the duplication of work by the Ministry of Pensions and the Corporation involved in obtaining the necessary information and 'Life Certificates', and in making payments, was out of all proportion to the amounts paid by the Corporation. In 1921 agreement was reached with Treasury that the Corporation's 'supplements' to the Old Age Pensions would be added to pensions by the Ministry itself, and the necessary adjustments made in bulk through the Corporation's 'State Supplements Account', which had come into being to handle the Government grants mentioned earlier.

In 1920 the field of Service Charities had lost two of its most prominent figures. On 2 July Lord Downham, who as Mr Hayes Fisher, had been untiring in his efforts as a Member of the Corporation since its foundation, and the Vice-President and Chairman of its Executive Committee since 1907, died and on 6 November the death occurred of Colonel Sir James Gildea, the founder and Chairman of SSAFA, and a member of the Corporation's Executive Committee.

In 1921 the Corporation received another legacy of the type that is particularly unexpected and pleasing because it came from a foreign country. The earlier contributions had been from Don Francisco Rodriguez in 1857 and Sir Constantine Zervudachi in 1883. The latter had been a Greek merchant in Alexandria and it was from Greece that perhaps one of the most unlikely donations came. The 'Greek White Cross' Fund was founded at the end of the wars between the Balkan States which preceded the war of 1914–1918. Its purpose had been to provide a 'marriage gift' for the daughters and sisters of Greek soldiers who died for their country in those wars. Mr Spiros Matsoukai, the founder and president of the Fund, presented 'fifty leaves of laurel and fifty thousand drachma' (equivalent in 1921 to just over £1,600) with the request that the recipients should be fifty daughters of British soldiers who lost their lives in the Great War.

The Corporation was asked by the Foreign Office to administer this gift and reacted to this unusual plea with considerable aplomb. The Finance Committee set up a temporary fund account, and the General Purposes Committee chose fifty daughters who had married after the death of their fathers who had lost their lives on the Macedonian front: to each was sent £32[1] and one laurel leaf and an additional grant of £28 was made to one other daughter to absorb the small balance remaining.

The wartime fall in the value of the Corporation's investments was beginning to show some signs of recovering by 1921 but the total market value was still some £300,000 less than the cost. The further appreciation of gilt-edged securities in 1922 made it possible for the Corporation to realize sufficient numbers to accept new applicants from the waiting list in the Royal Naval Relief Fund but most of the other older Funds were being quite rapidly diminished. The Patriotic General Fund was showing an income of just over £5,000 against an expenditure of £19,500; the Transvaal War Fund payments of about £30,000 against receipts of not quite £18,000, and the Soldiers' Effects Fund with an income of £3,500 had outgoings of £9,700. The Corporation decided that new applicants could not yet be accepted for allowances from the latter but there were 'indications that this Fund may receive important additions in the near future'.

The expected reinforcement to the Soldiers' Effects Fund came in 1923 from the War Office and totalled nearly £19,000. However, the future of the Fund was not an encouraging one. As the Corporation reported in July 1924, 'We have reason to believe that in a few years' time, after the transfer to the Corporation of the unclaimed balances standing to the credit of soldiers who died during the Great War, the annual amounts to be received will be comparatively small.' In consequence, the decision was made that 'in future the capital of the Fund should be kept intact, to ensure that a permanent fund may exist'. The expectation was that new cases could soon again be accepted in the Fund. Bearing in mind that there was a waiting list of applicants as far back as 1914, however, the decision was made in 1924 that, until the Fund could be reopened to new applicants, these should be helped by allowances from the European War Fund.

There were other important developments in the mid 1920s. In April 1925 the Army Council decided that the Corporation would be the best organization to receive and administer the balance of the 'South African War Fund'. This Fund had been established by Field Marshal Lord Roberts from church collections taken on 'Peace Sunday' when thanksgiving services were held at the conclusion of the South African War in 1902. The Council welcomed this, and formed the 'Transvaal War (Emergency) Fund' which, with the Army Council's approval, was to be used 'to give temporary help, when in ill-health, to widows, children, and dependents of deceased officers and men of the Royal Navy and Army who served in the Transvaal War (1899–1902), the marriage of the officer or man to have taken place before that campaign'.

With the arrival of this new Fund came the departure of an old one. 'The Light Brigade (Balaclava) Fund' which had been taken over by the Royal Patriotic Fund Commissioners in 1892 was exhausted in 1925 with one beneficiary still receiving an allowance of 25s a week. The 13th Hussars' Society, Lloyds' Patriotic Fund and the Incorporated Soldiers' and Sailors' Help Society, together with a fund administered by the Army Council, kindly assumed the responsibility for paying this old soldier's allowance for the remaining years of his life. He died in 1927 aged 95.

The other event in 1925 was the expiry of the lease at Seymour House (17, Waterloo Place) where the Corporation's offices had been since 1904. The Corporation would like to have stayed in this central position on the corner of Pall Mall and Lower Regent Street and opposite the Cox's and King's Branch of Lloyds Bank, but the cost of renewing the lease was too high,[2] so the Corporation continued to go West.[3] Suitable premises were found at 28 Sackville Street, W1 where a lease of nearly twenty years was acquired at the same rent as at Seymour House. At the same time the Treasury guaranteed to continue its help with the rent as far ahead as 1932.

In 1928 the Corporation was entrusted with the administration of another small Fund – the 'Royal Army Medical Corps War Memorial Fund' – a 1914–18 War Fund which had been raised as a memorial to those of the RAMC 'who gave their lives in the Great War'. The balance handed over was £4,612 and its use was 'primarily for the benefit of necessitous widows, orphans and dependants of deceased officers and other ranks of the Royal Army Medical Corps who served in the Great War, and who married before the 21 August, 1921, and for such other purposes connected with the war as have been specially designated by the donor'. A representative of the Fund was co-opted as a member of the Executive Committee.

Another cash injection to the Corporation's resources at this time was a bequest under the terms of the will of Miss Elizabeth Carew. There were no special conditions attached to this legacy so it was credited to the 'Special Army and Navy Fund'[4] which, because it was able to help those who, for one reason or another, were excluded from other Funds, had more demands upon it than funds to meet them.

Towards the end of the 1920s there were two more deaths of important members of the organization. Just before Christmas in 1928 the 'Lady Superintendent' of the Royal Victoria Patriotic School died suddenly at the school. She had held the appointment for eighteen years and had seen the School through all the difficulties of the wartime move and subsequent improvization. Then in the spring of 1929 the school also lost the Chairman of its Management Committee. Lieutenant-General the Honourable Sir Frederick Stopford, KCB, KCMG, KCVO had been a distinguished soldier, serving in the Boer War as well as the Great War, and he had also been a devoted member of the Corporation from 1909, and since the death of Lord Downham in 1920 he had been Vice-President and Chairman of all the Corporation's Committees.

Although there could never be a 'good' time for the Corporation to experience two such losses, these were particularly difficult times. As the decade came to its close the economic depression began to have its effect. The capital value of investments, which had begun to recover from the wartime recession, once again began to diminish. At the same time, the increase in the number of unemployed meant that the families of widows, who had in the past been able to help their mothers, were themselves struggling to meet their own expenses. If there had been no counterbalancing factor the Corporation might well have been unable to meet all the resulting demands. Fortunately, the 'Widows, Orphans and Old Age Contributory Pensions Act, 1929', which came into operation in July 1930, relieved the Corporation of the need to provide full allowances to large numbers of widows of 55 and upwards, who would not previously have received State pensions until they were 70.

The Corporation at this time continued to uphold the principle that some Funds should be 'permanent', from which only the income could be spent, while others could be diminished by spending capital. The Soldiers' and Airmen's Effects Fund was one of the former and in recent years the Patriotic General Fund had been in the latter category. As a result of the continuing depreciation in the total capital under its control, the Executive Committee decided that some kind of safety margin should be maintained and that the Patriotic General Fund should not be run down below £50,000. There was good reason for concern. With the market value of the Corporation's securities well over 20% below their cost, and with few signs of the state of the economy recovering in the near future, the sale of securities to raise capital was clearly to be avoided if possible.

The need to keep a careful watch on expenditure was particularly applicable to managing the Patriotic School, and to the cost of helping to support children at other schools. During the latter part of the Great War and for some years afterwards State help in the shape of War Pensions was helping to meet the costs of orphans' education but as these children grew up and new generations needed to be educated this was no longer the position. In addition the school, having been used as a hospital during the 1914–18 war, much needed modernizing in its school role: modern bathrooms and additional playrooms being particularly necessary. One solution proposed to reduce the scale of the problem was to reduce the number of pupils at the school from 300 to 250. The Executive Committee instead adopted the more gradual approach that the new entry should be regulated to fit the modernization process. This latter continued into 1934, with the School divided into 'Houses', each with a 'House Mistress', redecoration carried out in brighter colours, and the school laundry re-equipped and reopened.

Although these were years between wars and of no great prosperity, the Services did not forget the help their families had received and on which they could continue to depend. General Sir Walter Braithwaite, who had been elected Chairman of the School Management Committee, had written to the Colonels of Regiments, reminding them of the work of the school and telling them of the difficulties encountered in maintaining and improving the conditions for orphans during the straitened circumstances of the 1930s. This resulted in a generous and sustained response from Regiments. It was, however, still necessary to support the School Fund to some extent from the Transvaal War Fund, the Soldiers' Effects Fund and the European War Fund and annual donations for the school were received from the proceeds of the Royal Tournament.

A more personal appreciation of the value of the help provided was a donation of £400 (equivalent to over £6,000 in 1990) from Lieutenant-General Sir Fenton Aylmer, VC. His father had served in the Crimea, and the Royal Patriotic Fund had helped his mother when she was left a widow with himself, still a child, to clothe and educate. This allowance to his mother and help with his education, and his uniform when he joined the Army, had really already been repaid by his own service to the country, but his additional generous recognition made sure that some successors to the general would also have the opportunity to benefit.

By this time, eighty years after the founding of the Royal Patriotic Fund, the total amount disbursed by the Fund had reached £5 million[5] (not including the £410,000 spent from the National Relief Fund in the Great War), and the Trustees saw it as an appropriate time to carry out a thorough review of the separate Funds. The Patriotic General Fund which was the 'pivotal' Fund of the

HRH Prince Albert chairing an early meeting of the Royal Patriotic Fund in the Guard Chamber at the Palace of Westminster

Ewer sold in aid of the Patriotic Fund in 1855 portraying a grief-stricken family being watched over by a Victorian angel

Queen Victoria laying the foundation stone of the Commission's Girls' School on Wandsworth Common, 11 July 1857

The completed Girls' School on Wandsworth Common. The buildings remain in the 1990s

The Royal Victoria Patriotic School, Essendon

Coming to Terms

Corporation and which, at that time, met all the costs of administration, was in a much better situation than ten years before when expenditure from the Fund had been almost twice its income. It was considered, however, that the number of widows and orphans who would qualify to receive help from the Fund would grow in the future and that the Fund should become a 'permanent' one, no longer spending any of its capital. The conduct of Adolf Hitler, the new German dictator, may have had some influence on this reasoning. The other Fund which the Trustees felt must continue to be 'permanent' was the Soldiers' Effects Fund and there were several small Funds[6] where the special conditions governing the Funds entailed keeping the capital intact. It was considered to be right that Funds which were intended to relate to specific wars or campaigns should be diminished by spending capital as well as income on those who qualified. This applied to the Transvaal War Fund, the European War Fund and the RAMC War Memorial Fund.

The Royal Victoria Patriotic School Fund and the Roman Catholic Orphans Fund because they involved permanent commitments, not only needed their capital maintaining, but, because of the increase in the cost of maintaining educational establishments, their financial backing needed constantly to be reinforced. Failing the ability to sustain this level of support, the alternative was to limit commitments and during the first half of the 1930s the maximum number of girls at the School was gradually decreased from 300 to 240 and in 1937 reduced to 200; but these 200 were educated in much improved conditions, and still a total of 4,000 girls had been maintained, educated and trained at the School since its foundation.

On 31 May 1935 a disastrous earthquake occurred in Quetta, a large town in Baluchistan. There was an RAF station in the area and among the many thousand casualties were over fifty all ranks. In co-operation with the RAF Benevolent Fund the Corporation helped these widows and families in financial straits in consequence of these tragic losses. This co-operation with other service charities was a feature of the Corporation's operations. Another example was the help given to the families of Servicemen who died abroad. On these occasions it was arranged that SSAFA representatives should meet the returning families at the British port and pass information about their special financial needs to the Corporation. This enabled the families to avoid any hardship that might arise between their arrival in the United Kingdom and the receipt of Government pensions. Another form of collaboration occurred with some Naval cases. In order to meet the needs of sailors' widows and orphans from the Royal Naval Relief Fund, the Trustees had been forced to erode the Fund's capital. In consequence some potentially long-term commitments on naval cases arose which the Corporation felt unable to meet. Instead of these having to be rejected, however, they were almost invariably accepted by another Naval charity, usually through the liaison afforded by the presence, as a member of the Corporation, of the Director of Greenwich Hospital, one of the Admiralty representatives. In addition, 'King George's Fund for Sailors' made regular grants to the Corporation to help with naval applicants – thus collaboration operated in both directions.

In 1931 the Corporation had accepted into the Royal Naval Relief Fund the remaining widows of some of the forty-eight sailors who were lost in a pinnace from HMS *Edgar* which had capsized in the China Sea many years earlier. Until then they had received allowances from the '*Edgar* Boat Fund' which had been administered by SSAFA, but that Fund had become exhausted.

The title page of the Corporations' Annual Report for 1935, published in July 1936, bore a black border, and surrounded by the same black border was another page recording the sorrow that the Corporation, in common with the rest of the British Empire, felt at the death of King George V in 1936 (the exchange of messages is reprinted at Appendix O).

Once Government pensions and supplementary grants started to be a factor in assistance provided to widows and others reaching certain ages, the problem had been created of ensuring that these State benefits and those from Charities were not duplicated. This was not to say that these two elements could not supplement each other; they often did, but it was important to both State and Charity that each knew the position. In 1936, therefore, the Ministry of

Pensions made a proposal that it should establish, and staff, a central registry to record all assistance given to applicants with a view to avoiding any overlapping. There was a meeting between representatives of the Service charities and the Ministry of Pensions, but it soon became clear that the majority of the Charities saw this as a time-consuming exercise which they were not staffed to carry out, and which would detract from their main purpose. There was some feeling that the Government funds which would need to be used to set up such machinery could be better employed to increase the pensions.

As the end of the 1930s approached the Corporation received a very generous legacy from Miss Julia Lindley. This amounted to £8,800 which included £2,500 for a swimming pool for the School, £500 towards the upkeep of the School and £5,000 for the Royal Patriotic Fund. The sadness was, however, that within months of this being recorded in the Annual Report, the School Management Committee was deciding that 'in the event of war the School should be closed; each child returning to her respective home, and provision being made for those children who have no homes to receive them'.

In September 1938 when, as a result of the German invasion of Austria and threats to occupy the Sudetenland by force, it appeared that the outbreak of war with Germany was imminent, the School was evacuated; some children to their homes and others to a home in Wales which the Corporation had rented. When the immediate threat had passed with the signing of the agreement in Munich by Hitler, Mussolini, Daladier and Neville Chamberlain, the School resumed its Autumn Term at Wandsworth.

Before entering the year in which war was once again to disrupt the life of the School, there was a pleasant small happening to record which had echoes more than forty years later. One of the girls at the school, Muriel Ferguson, who had not yet reached her sixteenth birthday, had nevertheless reached a sufficiently high standard of training to be employed by Princess Beatrice at Kensington Palace; to be the home of the President of the Corporation in 1980.

Footnotes

1. Equivalent in 1990 to almost £300.
2. Seymour House had belonged to Sir Seymour King and had been sold by him in 1924 to Williams Deacons' Bank.
3. The Corporation's westward moves were from Charing Cross to Waterloo Place to Sackville Street.
4. Funded in 1911 from surpluses from the Patriotic (Russian War) Fund, the 'Captain' Fund, the 'Eurydice' Fund, the 'Zulu War' Fund and the 'Atalanta' Fund.
5. The 1990 equivalent is of the order of £50 million.
6. Indian Army (European Effects) Fund, Special Army & Navy Fund, Roman Catholic Orphans' Fund.

14 Fresh Fields in War and Peace

There really cannot have been many people with eyes to see and ears to hear who did not regard the 'Munich Agreement' as simply providing a welcome deferment to the outbreak of war by which German tyranny had to be stopped; and in which Britain and the Commonwealth were bound to be heavily committed. The Territorial Army was being rapidly expanded, civil defence and evacuation plans and material preparations went ahead, and generally throughout 1939 Britain was moving on to something approaching a war footing.

Preparations as far as the Corporation was concerned included a search for a school premises in a relatively safe area; removed from the air raid threat which would exist in the London area. A suitable house was found near Tenby in Pembrokeshire, but it would provide accommodation for only about ninety, including a proportion of the staff. At that time there were 196 children at the School so, when the time came to move to the West Country, the plan was to take in the first instance only those children who had no homes and those whose homes were in dangerous areas – others would initially be returned to their homes.

The declaration of war with Germany was not the first to have been experienced by the Corporation's President, the Duke of Connaught, or some of the more senior members in their roles as trustees, and, as in 1914, the President wished that his name should be used 'in any appeal for funds for widows and orphans of this war'. In October 1939, however, a new situation had been created which had not existed at the start of previous wars. A Hospital Flag Day had been planned to take place on 10 October, but the Committee of the British Red Cross Society and St. John Ambulance proposed that this should be cancelled and replaced by a National Flag Day and Appeal for the British Red Cross and Order of St. John; the appeal to be run by the Lord Mayor of London. The difference between this and the Mansion House appeals in 1854 and 1914 was that while the Crimean appeal was for helping widows and orphans, and the Great War 'Relief Fund' was broad in its scope, including any case of hardship or distress arising from the war (whether among widows, orphans, dependants or the servicemen themselves) the British Red Cross appeal was, in contrast, to be administered by the Red Cross, and solely 'for the sick and wounded in the War'.

The restricted nature of the proposed use of the money raised was apparent from the Lord Mayor's own description that the scope of the Fund 'primarily referred to preparation for air attack', that, whereas 80% of funds provided for the Red Cross from the National Relief Fund 'during the last war was required for overseas work (prisoners of war, the wounded, etc.) but the county [Red Cross] branches in this country had had considerable expenses of late, and he personally had suggested that a certain proportion of the proceeds should be returned to the counties which collected on Flag Day'.

A letter to the Lord Mayor asking that a proportion of the money raised should, as in previous wars, be granted to widows and orphans through the Corporation proved fruitless; as did a personal interview with the Lord Mayor to the same end. The Lord Mayor was sympathetic to the idea 'but stated that on this occasion the matter rested with the Red Cross authorities *on whose sole behalf the appeal had been issued*'[1].

An exchange of letters with the Red Cross along similar lines to that to the Lord Mayor produced the response that the Red Cross Emergency Help Committee only dealt with cases of widows 'not primarily within the scope of some other voluntary fund or public authority'. After further attempts to explain the relevance of a national appeal in war to the statutory task of the Corporation of providing for the care of widows, orphans and dependants of Servicemen, the Executive Committee decided to give a direct reminder to the public.

Fresh Fields in War and Peace

Sir Ian Fraser, well-known for his work for men and women blinded on war service, wrote to *The Times* on 3 November 1939 on the subject of the control of War Charities, urging that there should be a new 'War Charities Act' to replace that of 1916 because 'we may expect new charities to arise from this War, and there should be some machinery for limiting them if they are redundant, or securing that they are properly founded and conducted if they are required'.

Since this letter appeared apposite to the difficulties being faced by the Corporation, the Executive Committee agreed to follow up with a letter signed by Lord Fitzalan of Derwent[2], a member of the Committee, drawing the public's attention to the fact of the existence of the Corporation 'created by Act of Parliament, which for eighty-five years has administered funds raised for the relief of widows and orphans'. This was followed up by a short article in *The Times* on 15 November[3], four days later, appealing for funds for the Corporation – the appeal being necessitated because 'it is understood that the Lord Mayor's Fund is to be devoted entirely to the Order of St. John and the Red Cross and cannot be shared by any other organization'.

Bearing in mind that the public had already responded generously to the Lord Mayor's Red Cross appeal which had reached over £900,000 by the end of the year, it was not surprising that the outcome of this unobtrusive article in *The Times* was minimal. The trustees were concerned that at the beginning of such a major conflict, the scope of which could not be forecast, their funds were particularly limited. This was due in part to the fall in the market value of investments as a result of the war, which made it both unwise and unprofitable to realize any to provide more cash, and in part to the continuing annual excess of payments over receipts in the older Funds, in total amounting to a net £18,000 in 1939. In order, therefore, to ensure that calls on the Corporation's funds arising from the current War could be met, the trustees felt bound once more to refuse for a time any new applications for help from the Patriotic General Fund, The Royal Naval Relief Fund, the Special Army and Navy Fund and the Transvaal War Fund Extension. New grants and allowances continued to be given from the Soldiers' Effects

Fund and the European War Fund, but other applications had to be placed on waiting lists. At a time when the Corporation was providing long-term help for 1,545 widows, 772 children and 28 other dependants and short-term grants for 650 other beneficiaries it is understandable that the Corporation's Executive Committee 'took grave exception' to being denied any help from a National Appeal attributed to the 1939 War.

Other economies practised by the Corporation in early 1940 were savings in printing of the Annual Report, and the reduction of Council meetings from three to one each year.

It was inevitable that the outbreak of war would interrupt the Corporation's routine in other ways. Lieutenant Colonel Manly, who had been appointed Secretary in 1938 on the death of Lieutenant Colonel Maughan, had been recalled to his Regiment and Colonel Stanton, the Secretary at the outbreak of the 1914 War, stepped into the breach. Various Committee members were called to fulfil wartime tasks including Alderman Sanger who had represented the Ministry of Pensions, and Mr Widdows, Assistant Under Secretary of State at the War Office. In addition, some of the older members had been given appointments in the 'Local Defence Volunteers' (later to become the 'Home Guard'); Major-General Sir Cecil Pereira, as organizer for London, and Admiral Sir Studholme Brownrigg as organizer for Chatham.

During 1940 the financial situation of the Corporation showed some improvement. The Public Trustee, Sir Ernest Fass, who was also the Treasury representative on the Council, provided £2,450 for the Corporation and £1,000 for the Royal Victoria Patriotic School under the terms of the will of a Mr James Stewart Henderson. The latter amount was credited to the School Endowment Fund, but it was decided that the £2,450 and any subsequent donations received in connection with the current war should be put into a new Fund with the title 'War 1939–' – the closing date to be added when it was known. This would not include any donations for specific purposes. For example, at this time King George's Fund for Sailors provided a grant of £1,000 for the benefit of dependants of officers and men of the Royal Navy who lost their lives in the war, and this was credited to a separate 'KGFS (War) Fund'.

Fresh Fields in War and Peace

The other factor in 1940 which eased the financial strain on the Corporation was the extra help being provided by the Government to the elderly. The Old Age and Widows' Pensions Act of 1940 reduced the age of entitlement for women from sixty-five to sixty years, and the Government also instituted supplementary pensions for those in need of them. This meant that instead of the Corporation providing up to 12s a week to supplement the 10s of pensions, applications could be made to the State by pensioners for supplements of up to 12s 6d; indeed the Corporation insisted that qualifying widows being helped by the Fund should do this. These statutory developments relieved the Transvaal War Fund and the Patriotic General Fund of commitments to the total value of nearly £4,000.

The School was evacuated to Saundersfoot, near Tenby between 26 and 28 August; three months after the British Army's evacuation from Dunkirk. The largest number of girls were accommodated in Hean Castle, kindly lent by Lady Merthyr, which housed forty-six girls and twelve of the staff, and the remainder in two rented houses nearby; twenty, with five staff, in 'Elm Grove', and twenty, with three staff, in 'Cwm Wennol'. For the girls, their comfort and their health, this move to Wales was clearly beneficial. The Honourable Mrs Adeane, a member of the School Management Committee, visited the school twice during 1940 and reported that 'the girls were living in a state of comfort and amusement not less than that enjoyed even by Princess Elizabeth herself'.

In addition to the benefits to the girls of this country life, the reduction in numbers to be maintained at the school and other economies resulting from the evacuation added to the improvement in the Corporation's finances. The Trustees, therefore, anxious to pass on these gains, were able during the year to:

provide small maintenance grants to the mothers of girls from the school who had now to be kept at home:

notify Regimental Funds, which were still contributing regularly to the School expenses, that 'in view of economies in the School expenses through the evacuation to Wales of reduced numbers, the Committee of Management would refrain from asking for further

assistance for the period of the war, as Regimental Funds must be having unusually heavy calls made on them':
re-open the four Funds, closed to new cases in 1939, and to grant allowances to the ninety-five widows whose names had been put on the waiting list.

The School buildings and grounds at Wandsworth were taken over by the Government in March 1940. Previous to this, while the girls were still at Wandsworth, the School sanatorium had already been requisitioned as accommodation for the RAF No. 2 Balloon Centre. The main new occupants, however, were members of the War Department, and the initial role of the building was to provide a 'clearing station for aliens'. The military Commandant expressed 'his appreciation of the School's comforts' and promised that every care would be taken of the premises and its contents.

The Germans, however, had made no such promises, and several bombs had been dropped in the grounds in 1940, demolishing the engineer's cottage, greenhouse and potting shed but only causing superficial damage to the school building.

The frequency of air raids in 1940, which initially had resulted in the decision to have less meetings, and then to give the Vice-President and Chairman of the Executive Committee, Sir Bertram Cubitt, plenary powers to carry out the work of the Corporation, had, by November that year led to the Executive Committee being circularized as follows:

TO THE MEMBERS OF THE EXECUTIVE COMMITTEE

In view of the persistent raid warnings the Chairman of the Executive Committee had decided that both the Executive Committee [meeting], fixed for 12 noon on Wednesday November 6th, and the General Purposes Committee [meeting], transferred to the same date, should not be held.

The usual reports of the General Purposes and Finance Committees are, however, sent herewith; the report of the R.V.P. School Committee will follow. A slip asking for approval of these by post, in lieu of in person, is attached.

Fresh Fields in War and Peace

It is with regret that the death of Brigadier-General W. H. Usher-Smith, Secretary of Lloyd's Patriotic Fund and a member of the Executive Committee, is announced as a result of enemy action.[4]

Also that Engineer Rear-Admiral Whayman, member of the School Committee, has had his house bombed, and both he and Mrs Whayman are in hospital with injuries, but both are reported as progressing favourably.

By arrangement with the Office of Works, and in view of the intensified bombardment of London, it has been decided to evacuate the office in part to the Chairman's address, Hillstead, Weston, Bath for the duration of the war.'

Accordingly, the bulk of the Corporation's office moved to Bath early in November where it was housed in Sir Bertram Cubitt's house at Weston free of charge. The Accountant's element remained in Sackville Street because the frequency of dealings with the Paymaster and the Postmaster-Generals[5] would have been too difficult from the Bath area.

In January 1942, His Royal Highness the Duke of Connaught, the President of the Corporation since its inception in 1903 died, aged 92, and because he had taken such a personal interest, often taking the Chair at Executive Committee meetings, there was no doubt that the letter of condolence sent to his daughter, Lady Patricia Ramsay, was truly sincere in concluding 'His loss to us is irreparable and we can only thank Almighty God for sparing His Royal Highness for so long and so valuable a period to this Corporation.' In his place the King appointed the Princess Royal's husband, the Earl of Harewood.

The move to the West Country had proved a peaceful solution as long as London and the industrial centres had remained the main targets for German bombers, but in April and May 1942 the Germans began a series of air raids on British cities which had been specially indicated in German 'Baedeker' Guide Books as being of particular interest and beauty (the 'Baedeker Raids'), and Bath was one of these.

At the General Purposes Committee meeting on 14 May 1942, which Sir Bertram Cubitt chaired, it was reported that 'as a result of air raids on Bath on the nights of Saturday and

Sunday, 25 and 26 April, the Corporation's offices at the residence of Sir Bertram Cubitt were seriously damaged, windows being blown in, ceilings brought down, and the roof partly blown away by blast from a 500 lb bomb which fell only 30 feet from the front of the house.

'The books and papers were salvaged from the debris by the staff and work continued until temporary accommodation was found in a private garage in the vicinity.'

The Committee congratulated the staff on the way in which work had continued in spite of damage both at 'Hillstead', Sir Bertram Cubitt's home, and at No. 2 Royal Crescent, Bath, the home of Colonel Stanton, the Secretary.

Later that year, in October, Sir Bertram Cubitt died suddenly and it was decided that, although through the kindness of Lady Abbot-Anderson, an office in Madeira House, Park Gardens, Bath had been made available at very little cost, it would be best for the Corporation's office to return to London. The Admiralty carried out the move without charge.

The following spring the Treasury approved a further three year lease of 28, Sackville Street from the date of its expiry in June 1943.

The close working relationship between the Corporation and Government Departments was further demonstrated at this time; firstly by the Ministry of Pensions undertaking to transmit the Corporation's allowances to Canadian beneficiaries through the Ministry's representative in Ottawa, and, secondly, by the Corporation helping the Ministry to deal with the problem of helping certain widows and orphans of the 1939 war whose circumstances excluded them from normal assistance from either the Ministry of Pensions or the Ministry of Health under the Contributory Pensions Scheme.

The Corporation agreed to start and operate a special Fund, with the title 'War 1939 – Non-pensioned Widows' Fund', and to contribute 5% of the sum of the total allowances issued and the administrative costs. The allowances would be paid monthly and in advance, and the Ministry of Pensions would provide the funds, less 5%, ahead of the time when payments were due. The payment of these Ministry allowances would not debar the beneficiaries

Fresh Fields in War and Peace 147

from additional help from the Corporation if the widows or orphans qualified for this from one of the Corporation's other Funds. It took some time for the Ministry of Pensions to approve this scheme, but the first payments from this new Fund were made by the Corporation in December 1943.

The fact of establishing new Funds (three since 1939), and the inevitable creation of widows and orphans by a major war, would lead to the expectation that there would have been a considerable increase in the numbers of beneficiaries of the Corporation. A comparison between the figures for 1933 and those of 1943 shows that this was not the case:

1933		1943
1,356	Widows being given continuing help	1,225
1,052	Orphans being given continuing help	492
54	Dependants being given continuing help	8
1,303	One-time grants given	426
£62,756	Total Expenditure	£39,498

The reasons for this situation were the combination of the death of so many widows of wars before 1914, together with a number of those of the 1914/18 war; the maturing of the orphans; and the large numbers of beneficiaries taken off the books of the Corporation by the establishment of statutory help in the form of pensions and supplementary grants. The Corporation did its best to ensure that the gains from this reduction in the numbers of those dependent on it were passed on to those who remained. This was achieved in the form of increased benefits. In 1943, for example, maximum allowances from the Patriotic General Fund were raised from 10s a week to 15s, or £1 in exceptional circumstances.[6] The grant towards funeral expenses had already been increased from £5 to £7 10s[7] to bring it into line with statutory grants when these were given.

As the Allied fortunes prospered with victory in the Middle East, the successful invasion of Sicily, and the strong foothold in Italy, the School was also making its mark in its war effort. The Chairman of the School Management Committee was able to report that 'besides the ordinary routine of work the School has gained a pre-eminent place on account of its magnificent contributions to the National

Spitfire Fund, for salvage work, and for knitted comforts sent to all branches of the Forces. It was singled out for special mention on the BBC, and has received many tributes from Commanding Officers, from the British Red Cross and from the Women's Voluntary Services'.

The performance of the pupils and staff at the School, the benefit they were sharing from their rural situation, in spite of not being in purpose-built accommodation, and the fact that twice in twenty-five years the premises in London had had to be evacuated, must have all played their part in prompting the trustees of the Corporation to consider the whole question of where to site the School when the war was over. It was clear, too, that much would need to be spent on the Wandsworth buildings to make them suitable for a twentieth-century school.

Towards the end of 1943 the School Committee's ideas on this subject were:

to return to Wandsworth with the present numbers of eighty to eighty-five girls as soon as possible after the end of hostilities:

in the meantime to try to procure a suitable mansion and sufficient acreage to provide playing fields and room for three additional houses; the whole to take 120 girls and staff and to have reasonable access to good educational facilities and social amenities:

if a suitable existing mansion with the requisite facilities could not be found, then the alternative would be to buy land and build a complete new school.

The search for a suitable property began in earnest in 1944, with the additional prerequisite that it should be within thirty miles of London. Meanwhile the existing school at Saundersfoot was benefiting from the very co-operative attitude of both the Pembrokeshire and London educational authorities, and from the decision of the Ministry of Labour and National Service that employment on the school staff was considered to be 'work of National importance' – the latter helping greatly to maintain an efficient team.

As 1944 passed it became clear that any plan for an interim move back to the Wandsworth building was probably unsound. Apart from it having received more damage from bombs, its use by 'the War Office' – for MI5, or by 'the Home Office' – for aliens, was likely to preclude it becoming available to the Corporation again until well after the end of the war.

The School Committee thought that they had found a suitable house for the School at Maiden Erlegh, near Reading for £35,000 with possession by 1 January 1945, but it turned out that the sale had already taken place through another agent. In the event this was all for the best because the school Estate Agents, Messrs Drivers Jones & Co., found Bedwell Park, near Hatfield in Hertfordshire which apart from meeting the initial specifications, already mentioned, would cost only £17,250.

The plea by Sir Ian Fraser at the end of 1939 for a new War Charities Act to replace that of 1916 had been answered to some extent by the passing of the War Charities Bill, 1940 calling for the registration of all charities concerned in raising money for purposes related to the war, and prohibiting such activities without registration.

This Act contained an interesting acknowledgement of the Corporation's status in making it an exempted charity on a par with government-administered organizations. In Section II of the Act, defining war charities, paragraph (3) appears the following:

> The provisions of this Act, except in so far as they provide for the extension of the objects of certain war charities and make it an offence for any person ... (here there are listed offences involved in irregular appeals for funds and false representation) ... *shall not apply to the Royal Patriotic Fund Corporation or to any war charity administered by a government department* [author's italics].

The 1940 Act also contained provisions designed to facilitate proper control of such charities, and some safeguards against proliferation. However adequate the Act may have appeared in theory, there were clearly those who detected shortcomings in practice. The Soldiers', Sailors' and Airmen's Families Association felt that the Act needed provision for 'more rigid control over the formation of new and unnecessary wartime Funds' and sought the support of the Corporation in making representations to this effect. While sympathizing, the Corporation's Executive Committee felt that such representations would be more effective if initiated by the 'Central Council of Service Organisations' under the Chairmanship of Lord Rushcliffe.

There was no noticeable outcome to this proposal and very shortly afterwards, in October 1944, the Army Benevolent Fund was created under the authority of the Act. The other Services had possessed benevolent funds for some time but the Army had hitherto depended on individual regimental Funds. The stated object of the Army Benevolent Fund was: 'To assist to the full extent of its resources in the provision of financial support for Service and ex-Service men and women of the British Army who may be in need of it.'

It was not intended that the Fund should deal with individual cases but that it should make donations to Regimental and other approved voluntary organizations which dealt with individuals.

The Corporation approached the Army Benevolent Fund in the summer of 1945 with a request for a donation towards the Corporation's 'War 1939 Fund (Officers)' which helped the widows, children and dependants of Army officers whose deaths were attributable to that war. However, the Army Benevolent Fund regretted that it did not feel justified in making a donation to the Fund because the A.B.F. was substantially assisting the Officers' Families Fund for a similar purpose.[8] Subsequently, however, in 1948 the Army Benevolent Fund provided £1,000 which was put in a special 'War 1939–1945 Fund' by the Corporation, for widows and orphans of the war.

As 1945 advanced and the war in Europe ended with the German surrender, the Corporation made firm post-war plans for the Royal Victoria Patriotic School. The contract between the Corporation and the London County Council whereby the Council paid a rent for some of the classrooms at Wandsworth was terminated, and the Corporation's agents were instructed to negotiate a seven-year lease of the whole property with the Ministry of Works in view of the continued occupation by Government Departments. Although occupation of the new premises at Bedwell Park could have taken place during the Christmas holidays, it was thought best to wait until March 1946 while the necessary improvements and alterations were carried out, and to give more time for the necessary arrangements to be made with the local education authorities and schools. Fortunately, the owners of the castle and homes in Pembrokeshire had proved most co-operative and the Pembrokeshire education authorities had agreed to continue to provide the girls' education.

In the event the School started at Bedwell Park in June 1946 with some of the improvements still incomplete and with the maximum accommodation for only seventy girls, pending further construction. For their education the senior girls attended Queen Elizabeth's Grammar School, Barnet, and the Secondary Modern School, Hatfield, and the juniors were taught at Bedwell Park by teachers supplied by Hertfordshire County Council.

The old school premises at Wandsworth had eventually been leased to the Ministry of Education as a Teacher Training College and at a rent of £4,750 a year.

At this time of steady progress in establishing the School in good premises and arranging suitable State education in Hertfordshire the Governors of the Royal Soldiers' Daughters' School at Hampstead put forward a proposal that it and the Royal Victoria Patriotic School should join together, since both had similar aims, and the Soldiers' Daughters' School was unable to meet the heavy financial burden of maintaining a boarding school for small numbers at Hampstead. Pending the development of more accommodation at Bedwell Park, the initial plan would be to have the juniors of both schools there, keeping the Hampstead premises for the seniors – financial responsibility to be assumed by the Corporation. The proposal was acceptable to the Corporation but the Royal Soldiers' Daughters' School Governors were not able to accept that tuition should take place at outside State schools, and the Ministry of Education was not prepared to provide teaching staff at both schools, bearing in mind the small numbers involved. The proposal was, therefore, dropped and instead the Corporation agreed to make grants at the rate of £50 a year 'for each fatherless girl at the Royal Soldiers' Daughters' School who is eligible under the conditions of the various Funds of the Corporation'. The situation would be reviewed in 1955.

On 27 May 1947 the comparatively short period of the Earl of Harewood's Presidency of the Corporation ended with his death. In his place King George appointed his brother, His Royal Highness The Duke of Gloucester.

Footnotes

1. Author's italics.
2. Lord Fitzalan's letter is reproduced at Appendix P.
3. The short article in *The Times* is reproduced at Appendix Q.
4. The Brigadier-General's wife was killed at the same time.
5. In relation to payments to beneficiaries.
6. The 1990 equivalents would be £5 to £7.50 or £10.
7. The 1990 equivalents would be £50 to £75.
8. Generous assistance was, however, provided later. See Chapter 15.

15 Dependants and Interdependence

Nothing could be quite the same after a worldwide upheaval on the scale of the war that had ended in 1945. Many long established arrangements and practices were bound to be reviewed in the light of the many modern developments which had been accelerated by war. The remarkable improvement in communications of all types had its effects in almost every field. It was natural that those arrangements that stemmed from the earliest days of social development in Britain and which affected the majority of its citizens would be among the first to be overhauled.

Prior to 1940 the machinery by which British society maintained those who could not support themselves had its origins in the Poor Law, which was Elizabethan in character, dating from 1601. The care of the very poor was in the hands of Boards of Guardians composed of local worthies; and their instruments for providing the necessities for living were the Workhouse and Parish Relief, both of which were accompanied by a degree of humiliation: for the dead there were 'paupers' graves'.

The first advance for nearly 300 years came with the Workmen's Compensation Act of 1897 which was modernized to some extent in 1906. Thereafter further stages had been:

Non-contributory Pensions (at 70) – 1908
Compulsory Health Insurance – 1912
Unemployment Insurance – 1912 (amended in 1920)
Contributory Pensions (for widows and orphans) – 1925
Unemployment Assistance – 1934
Old Age and Widows' Pensions (at 60) – 1940

These various Acts had certainly improved the lot of very large numbers of citizens. Individual benefits increased considerably and the total outlay illustrates the widening scope of the State assistance; expenditure on the various forms of assistance reached only £4 million in 1900/1, but £25 million in 1914/15, £111 million in 1921/2 and £280 million in 1938/9. There were, however, many anomalies and considerable danger of overlapping and duplication of overheads: two different Ministries were involved, the Ministry of Pensions and the Ministry of Social Security, and they were both frequently involved in helping the same beneficiaries.

The wartime National Government decided in 1941 that, despite all the preoccupations of war, it was essential to review the whole question of State assistance and to rationalize its administration. The task was given to William Beveridge, a liberal economist, who headed a team which produced in 1942 the 'Report on Social Insurance and Allied Services'. This 'Beveridge' Report became the basis for the National Insurance Act of 1946. The scope of this Act was to provide the organization and administrative regulations covering benefits to meet the needs of unemployment, sickness, maternity, retirement, widowhood and death. All these became the responsibility of a Ministry of National Insurance.

There remained those aspects of welfare which had in the past, under the Poor Law, been a responsibility shared between local authorities, Boards of Guardians and local private charities; namely, accommodation, both individual and community, welfare and facilities for the disabled, marital financial problems (affiliation and maintenance orders) and burials. The National Assistance Bill, 1947 replaced the Poor Law and established a National Assistance Board to direct and administer the provision of these services. The Board, however, was responsible to the Minister of National Insurance so that the aim of having one Ministry to control all these functions and, it was hoped, reduce overlapping and duplication, had been achieved.

The effect of this rationalization and modernization of the many aspects of help for those in need was that social welfare became much more of a State responsibility, with Charities assuming a reinforcing role. A reversal of the situation which had prevailed in the days of the Royal

Dependants and Interdependence 155

Patriotic Fund Commission, when the Fund was the main instrument of welfare and received encouragement, but little financial help from the Government, until 1901 when the first State pensions were paid to Service widows.

This much greater part taken by the State after the Beveridge Report created such a significantly new environment that in 1950 the Corporation felt that there was a need for 'a comprehensive review of the conditions regulating all the Funds'.

As a result of the earlier combining of Funds (recorded at Appendix R) the remaining separate Funds at that time were:

The Soldiers' Effects Fund
The Patriotic General Fund
The Royal Naval Relief Fund
The Indian Army (Europeans') Effects Fund
The Special Army and Navy Fund
The European War Fund
The Roman Catholic Orphans' Fund
The Transvaal War Fund

Although it had been possible for the Corporation to provide help for the widows, orphans or other dependants of airmen from either the Patriotic General Fund or the European War Fund since the formation of the Air Force, it was only since 1926 that the 'Soldiers' Effects Fund' had received funds from the Air Ministry in the shape of the unclaimed effects of airmen. Up to 1925 expenditure from the Soldiers' Effects Fund had exceeded income and it had been necessary to limit new cases, subsequently, however, there had been a substantial injection of unclaimed estates from the War Office, so that by January 1925 the Fund had been able to accept new cases without abnormal restrictions. With the receipt of unclaimed estates from the Air Ministry, help from this Fund for airmen's widows and orphans was practicable. As a result, the title of the Fund had been misleading for some time. In addition, the increasing help provided by the State which led to the 1950 review had resulted in under-expenditure for the Fund so that the original qualification for help (that the soldier had to have died on service or within six months of his discharge) could be lifted. This broadening of the Soldiers' Effects Fund was all regularized by means of the Royal Patriotic Fund Corporation Act, 1950 of 12th July, and by Royal Warrant on 26 July 1950 when the Fund became 'The Soldiers' and Airmen's Effects Fund'. The new conditions applying to this Fund enabled it to cover the same field as the 'Indian Army (Europeans') Effects Fund' so that this, too, was absorbed, with the agreement of the Secretary of State for Commonwealth Relations.

The Patriotic General Fund had already absorbed the surplus balances of many of the small, specialized, Funds which no longer had the commitments for which they had been intended. To these, as a result of the 1950 review, were added 'The Special Army and Navy Fund' and 'The Roman Catholic Orphans' Fund'. Thus the Patriotic General Fund became even more of a 'catch-all' Fund, both as regards sources and beneficiaries: the latter including all those qualifying under the conditions of the special Funds as well as the more general cases, described as:

(a) Widows who, except in especially deserving cases, were married before the expiration of the husband's colour or regular service;
(b) orphans, and (c) other dependants, of deceased officers and other ranks of the Naval, Military and Air Forces of the Crown.

The Royal Naval Relief Fund had been derived from surplus balances of older, specialized Naval Funds and its more general application had been more restricted than the scope of the Patriotic General Fund quoted above. As a result of the 1950 review the qualifications for general Naval cases were slightly broadened to have similar eligibility to those of the Patriotic General Fund.

The 'European War Fund' had originated from the unsolicited donations which had been sent to the Corporation during the 1914–18 War outside the National Relief appeal. It had never exceeded £45,000 and consequently had never been able to meet all the applications for help stemming from the war, even though it had been limited to providing grants. Although the Corporation could have prolonged its life further by

Dependants and Interdependence 157

continuing these restrictions, it was thought that there was no merit in this since all allowances, and eventually all grants too, would have to come from other Funds. It was decided, therefore, to bring the qualifications in line with those of the Patriotic General Fund with only the added condition that the serviceman had served in the 1914–18 War.

As a result of these changes the Corporation had far more flexibility in dealing with applications on their merits and according to needs and, with the much greater State participation in welfare assistance, it could afford to be more generous and to help those who, through misfortune, were excluded from State assistance. The latter were by no means isolated cases, because it is not really practicable to frame State schemes to meet all contingencies.

The Sub-Committee which conducted the 1950 review of Funds and whose recommendations resulted in the reconstitution of Funds already described, also looked at the general policy and principles of administration of these Funds. The Committee's recommendations on these were adopted and as they remain the basis of the Corporation's activities, with only minor modifications, they are recorded at Appendix S.

Two other events in 1950 were to have significant financial implications for the Corporation. The London County Council, which was due to start paying an increased rent of £5,500 a year for the school premises at Wandsworth, made an offer of £55,000 to buy the property. On the advice of the Corporation's estate agents, this offer was rejected, but in August 1952 the LCC paid a total of £70,000 for the School.

The second occurrence was the Corporation's decision to apply to the High Court for authority to broaden the range of its investments. This stemmed from the considerable reduction in the number of undertakings in which the Corporation could invest under the terms of the 1925 Trustee Investment Act; a reduction caused by the Government's nationalization of the four railway companies and the electricity undertakings in 1948, leaving only low-yielding Government stocks as authorized subjects for investment.

The Corporation's application was heard by Mr Justice Romer in Chambers on 30 October and was successful. The

Court gave the necessary authority for the Corporation to invest in stocks, shares and bonds listed in a schedule which included 'bonds, debentures, debenture stock, mortgages, obligations or securities, or guaranteed or preference or ordinary stock or shares or ordinary preferred or deferred or other stock or shares of any company incorporated under any general Act of the United Kingdom Parliament or the legislative of any such dominion, commonwealth, union, dependency, colony, province or state aforesaid ... '. An authority of which the Finance Committee took some advantage in 1951, but much more in 1952, when the proceeds of the Wandsworth School sale became available.

There was a big increase at this time in the number of applications for grants. Those paid out in 1951 totalled 1,413 against 857 in 1950. This was a natural consequence of the 1939–45 war casualties, the increasing activity of the War Pensioners' Welfare Service (of the Ministry of Pensions and National Insurance) – a new source, the broadening of the Corporation's rules of eligibility, and a marked increase in the cost of living.

The need to minimize restrictions on the eligibility of Service widows, orphans and other dependants for help from the Corporation had been the reason for the Corporation's Bill of 1950, but it had also been the cause of some doubts being raised during the Parliamentary debate of 28 April of that year, and some trenchant criticism. There were sharp, if brief, echoes of the hostile attitude of the MP for Devonport (Mr Kearley) and others from sea ports during the late nineteenth century.

Commander Galbraith (Conservative MP for Glasgow, Pollok) found it difficult to believe that the income of the Corporation could not, by 1950, be fully spent on those widows and families already eligible, without the need to extend the eligibility of the Soldiers' Effects Fund. In place of this, he thought that any excess of income should 'go to supplement the income of those suffering from some particular hardship, though they happen to be in receipt of a war pension'; also 'to enable dependants to add a little jam to the bread and margarine which the State pension provides'. He considered that 'To throw the door wide open, as the Bill proposes, would almost certainly produce so

Dependants and Interdependence 159

many claims of equal and comparable hardship as to reduce any grants that can be made to such minute proportions as to be almost useless, and, indeed farcical'.

Commander Galbraith was content, however, to support the Bill and to leave further study to the Committee stage, on reassurance from the Secretary of State for War, Mr Strachey, that the removal of the qualification that the serviceman had to have died on Service, or within six months of discharge, did not, of itself, compel the Corporation to meet all applications made by those who met this criterion, nor did it prevent the Corporation increasing help to other beneficiaries and form other Funds. Commander Pursey, Labour MP for Hull, East, remained an unsatisfied and swingeing critic to the end.

Commander Pursey's charges against the Corporation, as recorded in *The Times* on 29 April were:

> that money was frittered away in the organization. About £40,000 was distributed in 1948 and the expenses were about £4,000 or nearly 2s. for every pound disposed of.

> The Corporation's school should be closed down. The cost a head through an expenditure of £16,000 for 60 girls was over £250 a year, and with Government grants that would pay for the education of the girls in some of the best boarding schools in the country. They should not be segregated as orphans.

> There was a far bigger story to be told about the whole racket of the Fund than he had told the House. The House had control over the organization and also over other organizations which controlled large sums of money, some of which was frittered away in such things as offices in Pall Mall. He was prepared to make his statement about a 'racket' from any platform in the Country without any question of Parliamentary privilege arising. The organization in question was second only to the British Legion as being one of the biggest charitable scandals in the country.

Other, less eye-catching, criticisms in a very long speech (frequently interrupted by remarks such as 'To sum up' from restless MPs) were that:

> only one copy of the annual report to the Sovereign was sent

to the House of Commons. It was promptly filed away in the archives and nobody saw it. It should be presented as a proper Parliamentary Paper for the use of Honourable Members and for purchase by the public. The Royal Patriotic Fund Corporation was an analogous organization to Greenwich Hospital, administering charitable funds for ex-Service men and also a school in almost precisely the same way, and copies of the Greenwich Hospital accounts were available to members and had been the subject of debate:

One has to go to other official publications to find that there is a Secretary, who is a major-general, presumably only part-time employed, and who is paid £900 per annum to dole out half guineas to widows and orphans:

The organization of the Corporation was drawn up on a vast nationwide basis. It included Lord, Lieutenants, Mayors, Provosts and a host of other people.

Some of these people apparently came from distant places, such as Devonport and Portsmouth presumably with first-class expenses to attend meetings and possibly for a night in London. Consequently, every time the council or a committee meets money is frittered away which would otherwise provide more pensions, grants and allowances for the widows and other relatives who are in distress:

These charities can now pay only 10s 6d a week as the sum to be disregarded where State aid is received, and that is one of the reasons why they cannot get rid of their money. There are 800 ex-Service organizations with funds totalling £20 million and, provided the individual or his dependants know where to go, there should be no question of any ex-Service man or his relations being in distress at all.

There was no reason for 'cadging from the public for the ex-Servicemen by rattling tin boxes on street corners on Poppy Day and similar days. In the Navy we decided a quarter of a century ago to abolish this national and Service disgrace of cadging from the public'.
　　The funds under the Royal Patriotic Fund Corporation should be transferred to the Service funds or other funds. Alternatively, the funds should be transferred to the Minister of Pensions for him to administer as he administers the

Dependants and Interdependence 161

King's Fund.[1] In either case, great economies would be made and more money would be available for a greater number of widows and orphans. I intend to campaign in this House, as far as I am able, by Question and Motion, and outside wherever possible, to have the Royal Patriotic Fund Corporation closed down lock, stock and barrel ...

Sir Ian Fraser, the Chairman of St. Dunstans, who spoke generally in support of the Bill, nevertheless raised again the vexed subject as to the rights and wrongs of having, on the one hand permanent Funds from which the income only is spent and which contains money subscribed over many generations, and on the other hand, exhausting Funds which have been raised for specific occasions or periods.

In spite of all the rhetoric, the Bill received an unopposed second reading and went through its Committee stage unchanged. The Secretary of State for War, Mr John Strachey, did, however, indicate that the setting up of the 'Nathan' Committee[2] would probably cover some of the points made in criticism. The nature of the attacks on the Corporation (for all that they mostly came from a notorious source) had however caused some concern within the Corporation. To give the latter credit, the setting up of a sub-committee to review the conditions regulating all its Funds, had occurred in March 1950 before even the first reading of the 1950 Act. It could not, therefore, be said to have been done to satisfy the hostile comments at the end of April. The Executive Committee, meeting on 25 May, considered whether the charges made against the Corporation during the second reading of the Bill should be refuted by a letter to the Press, but decided that it would be more satisfactory to deal with the matter by arranging for some appropriate questions to be tabled in the House of Commons in order to set the record straight.

In the light of some of the criticism of the Corporation made during this debate, the following extract from the Nathan Committee's Report of December 1952, in dealing with the question of possible overlapping and duplication of effort in general, provides something of a rebuttal:

We do not suggest that in the meantime nothing is being done. The Royal Patriotic Fund, for instance, has recently (in 1950) gone some, if not all, the way towards reducing the number of separate funds administered by it and takes special care to ensure that full advantage is taken of services provided by the State. But we would like to see this reforming zeal operating among charities for Service and ex-Service men on a wider scale.

One of the examples of the difficulties involved in dealing with Funds raised for specific purposes had been quoted by Sir Ian Fraser during the House of Commons debate. In discussing the relaxing of the restrictions in the Soldiers' Effects Fund, he said that 'while there are any South African War Veterans – and there are many still alive and many still in need, as I know from letters I receive – and while there is any widow of a South African War Veteran still in need – and I hear that there are many – while this is so, it cannot be right to allow sums of money which should be used for his or her benefit to be distributed in driblets in millions of cases'.

It so happened that the need for helping widows and families of those killed in South Africa had been fairly continuously on the Corporation's agenda since the end of the 1939–45 War when a review was undertaken of the Transvaal War Fund and allowances from that Fund were increased by over 20%. Concurrently the Charity Commission was asked to approve a relaxation of restriction on the Fund to enable its scope to be extended among South African War widows. The Charity Commission's own commitments were not going to permit an answer until 1951 but, whether or not related to this activity in the Transvaal War Fund field, it was at this time that 'The South African War Veterans', through the House of Commons branch of the British Legion, approached the Corporation suggesting that help might be given to South African War Veterans from the Fund.

The Corporation's reply had to be that the veterans were outside the scope of the Fund as it was constituted (having been raised for widows and orphans) but that if the current review of the Fund and revision of scales of assistance disclosed an 'actuarial surplus, it may well be that such surplus might be applied, under the necessary authority, for the relief of the Veterans on whose behalf you plead'. After much further correspondence and discussion, Brigadier-General Spring, a nominee from the South African War Veterans was co-opted to the Executive Committee; though, as an individual, and not as official representative. In spite of this appointment, the South African War Veterans' Association wrote to the Corporation in 1950 accusing it of maladministration of the Transvaal War Fund and demanding explanations about the system of accounting and administration of the Fund. The sharp retort from the Corporation demanded the withdrawal of these accusations, reminded the Association that the Corporation was in no sense answerable to it, but, if the charges were withdrawn, offered a meeting with Association representatives.

By 1951 the Charity Commissioners had approved the proposed relaxation in some of the Transvaal War Fund restrictions so that the requirements that marriage should have been before 1 June 1902, and a Serviceman's death should have occurred during his Service or because of it, were both removed. Brigadier-General Spring resigned from the Executive Committee in 1951 and a further actuarial valuation of the Transvaal War Fund at the end of that year showed that there was now no surplus. In consequence any extension of the Fund to include the 'Veterans' was clearly out of the question. It was decided, however, that, bearing in mind that any widows or dependants arising from the South African War would qualify for help from some of the Corporation's other Funds, new cases would continue to be accepted in the Fund until it was exhausted when any remaining beneficiaries could be transferred to another Corporation Fund.

One of the special characteristics of Service charities, particularly those concerned with widows and children, is the deferred nature of the impact of wars upon them. As an illustration of this, while much relevant discussion was going on about the Transvaal War Fund a war was starting in Korea; a war which was to result in over twelve hundred Commonwealth Servicemen were killed but which would not seriously impinge on the Corporation's activities for some time to come.

Another subject which had been raised during the debate on the 1950 Bill was the cost of the School at Bedwell Park. Although the figure of £250 annual cost for each girl, quoted by Commander Pursey in 1950 had been wrong – the correct figure being just over £178 – the Executive Committee maintained a close watch on the School finances; increasing the numbers of pupils as the opportunity occurred. This was bound to raise capital costs in these early years in the new premises, because it entailed providing extensions to existing buildings and adding new facilities. However, the sale of the Wandsworth property in 1952 provided a strong reinforcement for the School Fund.

The Chairman of the Executive Committee in 1952 was General Sir John Brind and he took a special interest in the attempt to put the School on a more certain and permanently sound economic basis. A small Committee was set up under the Chairman of the Finance Committee to consider in detail various alternative courses, including even the closure and disposal of the School. The latter course was 'strongly deprecated', and not only because at that time there would have been a considerable loss in relation to the price paid for the property in 1946. The main conclusion was that the School numbers should be raised to 100 which would be feasible without excessive new capital expenditure. If a generous sum were to be received as 'compensation for the loss of development' at Wandsworth, however, the Committee thought that a maximum figure of 120 pupils should be considered.

The lease of the Corporation's offices at 28 Sackville Street ended in 1953 after twenty-eight years of occupation, and in September the move was made to 64 Victoria Street. The Corporation was happy to report to the new Sovereign, Queen Elizabeth, that these offices were 'provided rent free by Your Majesty's Government, as had been the previous practice, in return for the services which the Corporation renders to certain Government Departments'.

The year 1954 was an important one for the Corporation as it was the end of the Patriotic Fund's first century. It was also a prosperous year with the market value of the Corporation's investments greatly boosted by the holdings of equities which had been acquired as a result of the wider powers conferred by the Court in 1950, and which had appreciated from £60,000 to £90,000 since their purchase.

The accusations by Commander Pursey in the House of Commons in 1950 that 'every time the Council or a Committee meets, money is frittered away which would otherwise provide more pensions, grants and allowances for the widows and other relatives who are in distress' had little real relevance, since there was barely any substance in his assumption that large numbers of members from far afield would be claiming expenses for first-class fares and nights in London. In addition, attendance from great distances was never in large numbers. The Council did, however, come to the conclusion in 1955 that it was unnecessarily cumbersome to hold a special Council Meeting every three years of those appointed under Royal Warrant, simply in order to appoint and co-opt members. Apart from the extra meeting, the system had meant that large numbers of members ended their appointments simultaneously. The new procedure entailed about one third of the members being elected at the annual Council Meetings.

The number of Funds operated by the Corporation were reduced further in 1957 with the exhaustion of the RAMC War Memorial Fund, the small Army Officers (War 1939) Fund, and the European War Fund. This left the War 1939 (Non-pensioned Widows) Fund, with two widows on its books, and the Transvaal War Fund as the two non-permanent Funds still being maintained. The latter was valued by the Institute of Actuaries as at 31 December 1957 and this disclosed a deficiency against liabilities of about £15,000. It would have made sense at that time to meld the Transvaal War Fund into the Patriotic General Fund. The only way in which it could continue to meet its commitments until all the beneficiaries had died, would be by selling securities, and, at the market prices prevailing, this would have involved significant book losses. Application was made to the Charity Commissioners to merge the Transvaal Fund with the Patriotic Fund, but this was not sanctioned. To avoid unnecessary losses to the Funds the Finance Committee arranged transfers of stocks between Funds so that the Transvaal War Fund received short-dated gilts that would provide a proper return in cash realization in the near future. The necessity for this sort of manoeuvre seemed regrettable, and fortunately future developments were to make it unnecessary in the future.

The Transvaal War Fund was clearly approaching a time when beneficiaries and resources were dwindling and any remaining commitments would need to be assumed by one of the 'permanent' Funds.

At this time one such permanent Fund was added to the Corporation's resources. The Royal Military Benevolent Fund originally came into being in 1875 as a charitable private enterprise to help the dependants of Officers of the Army and Royal Marines who had died; also for maintaining a school for the education of their daughters. In 1901, after an investigation by a Royal Commission, the Charity ceased to be a private enterprise and the School was closed. The Fund was then taken over by a Committee, and since 1901 it was assisted by grants from the Army Council: a support which had been continued since 1945 by the Army Benevolent Fund. In 1960 the Chairman of the Royal Military Benevolent Fund Committee, who was also a member of the Corporation, asked whether the Corporation would be prepared to assume responsibility for this Officers' Dependants Fund. The reason for this request was that the cost of the Fund's administration had become out of proportion to the benefits provided. At this time the total number of annuitants was only thirty-eight, including two supported by a special trust known as the Robert and Ella Laver Gift, which had been assigned to the committee of the Fund by the Chaplain-General of the Army.

Once the Corporation was satisfied as to the financial soundness of the Fund and its ability to meet its existing liabilities, the commitment was accepted with the approval of the Charity Commission. The object of the Fund remained unchanged, namely 'to grant annuities to ladies in reduced circumstances, and being the widows or unmarried daughters of Officers of Her Majesty's Army, inclusive of the Royal Marines'. This Fund thus became the fifth of the Corporation's 'permanent' Funds, joining the Patriotic General Fund, the Royal Naval Relief Fund, the Soldiers' and Airmen's Effects Fund and the Royal Victoria Patriotic School Fund.

Dependants and Interdependence

The existence of the Robert and Ella Laver Gift in the Royal Military Benevolent Fund, because it was specifically for Protestant beneficiaries, prompted the Charity Commissioners to require it to be kept separate from the broader Fund. Fortunately the Commissioners were persuaded to accept the compromise that 'while they cannot legally agree to the two Funds being amalgamated, they would not object to one account being kept, provided there are appropriate footnotes'. This British solution, complete with footnotes, stood the test of time.

At this time, closely following the centenary of the Patriotic Fund and the Royal Victoria Patriotic School, there were developments which were to establish the general form of the Corporation's economic structure for more than a generation, and these warrant a separate chapter.

Footnotes

1. The King's Fund was transferred to the Royal Patriotic Fund Corporation and the Joint Committee of St John and the Red Cross in 1983 (See Chapter 17).
2. A Committee of Inquiry under Lord Nathan to consider the whole question of the operation of charities and role of trustees.

16 Money Matters

The beginning of the 1960s was a time of important development in the business of management of charity property. The Charities Act 1960 acknowledged the modern interdependence of charity trustees and government authorities, both national and local, and provided the foundation for this co-operation and partnership. It also provided for the modern need for more flexibility for charities to adapt themselves to new situations.

The need for corresponding flexibility for trustees in their management of charities' funds had also been recognized by the Nathan Committee Report in 1952. This had underlined the extent to which trustees were handicapped by being limited largely to fixed income stock which became much reduced in value in time of inflation. This restriction not only prevented charities from maintaining the capital value of permanent Funds, but it meant that Funds for specific situations were usually exhausted sooner than necessary. The Nathan Committee had recommended that:

> The range of investment should be extended to comprise, with certain safeguards, debentures and the stocks and shares, including equity (i.e. ordinary) stocks and shares of financial, industrial and commercial companies quoted on the Stock Exchange, London. Trustees should be permitted thus to invest, say, fifty per cent of their endowment, and also to invest in freeholds and long leaseholds subject to the consent of the central authority.

It took nearly ten years and a change of government before this relaxation in the rules for investment became a reality in the Trustee Investments Act 1961, although wider investment powers for individual charities could be granted in the meantime by Court Order, as had been provided for the Corporation in October 1950.

The Trustee Investment Act is not the easiest piece of legislation to interpret, so that any brief summary such as follows must carry with it a warning that it is in broad terms and that there are many qualifications in the detail. In general, the Act authorized two categories of investment; a 'Narrower Range' and a 'Wider Range'. The former including all the fixed interest stocks allowed under the previous 1925 Trustee Investment Act, but broadened to include debentures, preference, loan and other fixed interest stock of companies incorporated in the United Kingdom; always provided that their capital was over £1 million, and that they had paid dividends in each of five years. The 'Wider Range' included all ordinary shares of companies which had similar qualifications. An additional category, 'Special Range' stocks, were permitted to be held as special dispensations. These were 'non-trustee' stocks similar, and in addition to, 'Wider Range' holdings, 'inherited' from other Funds. When sold, however, the proceeds had to be divided equally between the 'Narrower' and 'Wider Ranges'; also any reductions in the 'Narrower Range' holdings had to be replaced by a compensating increase.

As in the Nathan Committee's suggestion, the basic initial proportions of 'Narrower' and 'Wider Ranges' needed to be equal. If, however, the investments had been separated from some other Fund, or Funds, the division might either be equal or in the same relative proportions as in the original Fund, as long as these were not greater than three to one in favour of the Wider Range.

The Corporation's Finance Committee saw no need initially to take advantage of the 1961 Act because the 1950 Court Order permitted an adequate degree of flexibility. As an illustration, as early as 1954 a deficit of £146,000 between market value and cost of investments at the end of 1952 had been cancelled out; helped by gains in 1954 of £40,000 in equities, contrasting with only £18,000 in gilt-edged stock. Also, at this time separate investment accounts were having to be maintained for each of the five remaining Funds, and division of each of these into 'Ranges' would have caused complications which would not have been warranted by benefits. At the time that the 1961 Act came into force, for example, to have disposed of fixed interest stocks in order to have the money to re-invest in an appropriate proportion of equities would have entailed considerable book losses. However, the fact that the Corporation did not immediately take advantage of the two Acts of 1960 and 1961, did not diminish the role that these eventually played in the form of its finances.

Early in 1961 the Corporation's Executive Committee concluded that the 1960 Charities Act provided an opportunity both to enable the Corporation to break free from the complications of being governed by some four different Acts of Parliament and to bring its operations more in line with modern practices and requirements. A draft of a new Bill, which, it was hoped, would achieve these objectives was referred to the Treasury Solicitor and the Charity Commissioners in the hope that it might be possible for the latter to approve the changes under the provisions of the increased scope in the 1960 Act. It was considered that the need for change was justified and, if it could not be achieved by this method, that it warranted an approach to the Secretary of State for War to ask him to pilot a separate Bill through Parliament. First reaction from the Charity Commissioners was not unfavourable to the idea that change through the 1960 Act might be possible, but disappointing as far as any early decision was concerned; their commitments at this time were far in excess of their resources to perform their tasks.

In the event, the answer, not received until 1968, was that the Commissioners did not feel able to proceed with the proposed scheme. Some consideration was then given by the Corporation to the possibility of operating under Royal Charter as a way of loosening some of the tight restrictions stemming from the various Patriotic Fund Acts. Eventually, after receiving discouraging views from the Clerk to the Privy Council, the Corporation in 1970 decided that further efforts to change the rules were not warranted.

The Finance Committee's ability to achieve results within the framework of the 1950 High Court authorization, and without needing to take advantage of the 1961 Trustee

Money Matters

Investment Act, had been well demonstrated in 1959. In November of that year there were thirteen equity holdings (purchased under the dispensations of the 1950 Act) which had cost about £70,000 and the market value of which was about £205,000. At the same time the yield from them was less than 3%; bringing in only about £6,000 a year in dividends. This was a time of quite substantial overspending, so that the need was for maximum income. Government gilt-edged securities were yielding up to 5%, and were standing at substantial discounts in many instances. The equities were sold, raising £208,518, and these proceeds invested in 4% Consolidated Loan at 78. This increased the annual income by over £4,000.

This sort of operation could as easily have been carried out in the opposite sense, to achieve capital growth at the expense of income, and still using only the scope provided by the 1950 Court Order. The Corporation could afford, therefore, to delay making use of the 1961 Trustee Investment Act until there was some compelling reason to do so.

In 1963 the balance of the Transvaal War Fund was exhausted. There remained on the books of the Fund 178 widows being provided with allowances. Their liability, of the order of £20,000, was taken over by the Patriotic General Fund. The Transvaal Fund had served South Africa War widows well. There had been 5,282 beneficiaries, and in the sixty-three years of the Fund's existence £1,125,000 had been disbursed although the public's contribution to the Fund had been less than half this amount.

There were other sources of income for the various Funds administered by the Corporation. Apart from the initial public contributions, specific legacies, government grants and donations for specific purposes, gradually there became established regular contributions from the three Services.

Initially it was the Royal Victoria Patriotic School that benefited from regular donations. Many Regimental Funds had become long-standing contributors and the three Service Ministries each provided a proportion of their profits from the annual Royal Tournament performances. The United Services Fund and the British Legion also made generous annual donations to the School.

An application for a donation for the School made to King George's Fund for Sailors in 1931 had not been successful, but in 1932 this Fund had begun a series of annual donations to the Royal Naval Relief Fund which is still maintained, together with similar annual contributions from the First of June Appeal for Naval Officers' Charities which started to provide help for the Corporation in 1940. Apart from the Naval contribution from the Royal Tournament proceeds, both Greenwich Hospital and the Royal Naval Benevolent Trust provided financial help for the School in proportion to the number of girls of Naval families attending.

The Royal Hospital, Chelsea provided some help for the School on a proportionate basis according to the number of girls from Army families it nominated, but until 1954 other Army donations remained on a Regimental basis and were for the School Fund only. From 1954 onwards the Army Benevolent Fund added substantial donations for the School to those of individual Regiments, and after the Corporation's assumption of responsibility for the Royal Military Benevolent Fund the Army Benevolent Fund provided an annual contribution for this in addition.

Both King George's Fund for Sailors and the Army Benevolent Fund are Funds which have public appeals and make block grants to those Charities which help individuals. To this extent, therefore, the Corporation acted in the role of distributing agent for beneficiaries of these grants. The Royal Air Force Benevolent Fund, however, has, from its inception, helped individual beneficiaries. Nevertheless, the RAF Benevolent Fund began an annual contribution to the School in 1933.

Once the Corporation no longer had a School, King George's Fund for Sailors and the Army Benevolent Fund continued to make donations based upon the number of their respective service widows and orphans being helped by the Corporation. The RAF Benevolent Fund, which was still helping its own individuals, returned to making an annual donation to the Corporation once the latter assumed responsibility for specialist help in the 1980s.[1]

The disposal of the School in 1972, which is described in Chapter 17, removed a major and increasing liability and freed a very substantial sum for investment. With the number of Funds within the Corporation reduced to four[2] and some £245,000 available for investment it was decided that it was an appropriate time to obtain the better spread of investments which the Trustee Investments Act 1961 authorized. This entailed considerable book losses in disposing of a number of undated gilt-edged securities and small holdings of public board stocks, but resulted in a portfolio with the holdings of ordinary shares and convertible stocks in British companies being some 50% of the total compared with just over 3% prior to the new structure. The division of the investments into the 'Ranges' required by the 1961 Act was carried out in March 1973 after a valuation of the investments. The 'Special Range' investments, all in the Patriotic General Fund and 'inherited' from the Royal Victoria Patriotic School Funds, amounted to £231,924 in book value and to 20% of the book value of the total portfolio. The remaining investments were divided equally, by market value, between the 'Narrower' and 'Wider' Ranges; the market value of each being £245,923.50. The respective book values of the 'Narrower Range' (Gilts, Loans and Convertibles) were £497,765 and of the 'Wider Range' (all types) £463,211.

Although this considerable change in the pattern of the Corporation's investments gave much greater flexibility, and, because of the much larger sum available for investment a significant increase in the importance of investment income, there remained scope for one further advance in the Corporation's financial structure; the attainment of simplicity. Until 1975 the resources,[3] including investments, in each of the four Funds administered by the Corporation had to be dealt with separately which involved considerable extra work in the accounting procedures and administration generally. In 1974 the Corporation took advantage of the Charity Commissioners' 'scheme making' procedure and applied for a scheme to allow the consolidation of the resources of the four Funds into a combined pool.

This was accomplished by a Charity Commission Scheme 'sealed' on 9 January 1975, which created the 'Royal Patriotic Fund Corporation Common Investment Fund' which constituted one trust fund for the purposes of the

Trustee Investments Act 1961. The proportion in which each Fund was 'interested in' the Common Investment Fund, and thus the benefits in the way of dividends and interest obtained from it, was set out in general terms in the Scheme to be 'an appropriate undivided aliquot portion of the fund'. In practical terms this was determined by a valuation in June 1974 of market values as follows:

	Market Value	Percentage Proportion
Patriotic General Fund	£442,270	80.49
Royal Naval Relief Fund	£6,310	1.15
Soldiers' and Airmen's Effects Fund	£83,305	15.16
Royal Military Benevolent Fund	£17,609	3.20
Total Assets – Royal Patriotic Fund Corporation Common Investment Fund	£549,494	100.00

The Scheme made provision, however, for these proportions to be 'from time to time revised as circumstances may require by the said body corporate' by means of fresh 'valuations and calculations'. This action was first taken in 1976.

Thus, by the mid 1970s the Corporation had a modern financial structure which provided its trustees with the necessary scope and flexibility to vary its financial resources according to the needs of its beneficiaries: consequently less, if any, need in the future to limit eligibility because individual Funds could not meet commitments.

Footnotes

1. Described in Chapter 17.
2. Royal Patriotic Fund; Royal Naval Relief Fund; Soldiers' and Airmen's Effects Fund; Royal Military Benevolent Fund.
3. In legal terms 'property'.

17 New Looks but Old Values

During the next thirty years the Corporation's offices moved four times. This was not a price exacted by creditors, but a minor inconvenience brought about by its continuing willing dependence upon the provision of accommodation by the Ministry of Defence. In 1960 the move took place from 64 Victoria Street to Wellington House, Buckingham Gate.

The developments recorded in the last chapter, stemming from the Nathan Committee Report and the subsequent legislation, meant that the 1960s constituted a period of review and adjustment of the Corporation's field of assistance; both as regards those to be helped and scales of support. In addition to the larger part being played by the State in providing assistance, the number of widows resulting from the Boer and 1914–18 Wars was dwindling, and the number of children orphaned by the war of 1939–45 and still needing help, was very small. At the same time the cost of living had increased by some 50% during the previous ten years. For all these reasons it was considered that the Corporation could afford to, and should, be more liberal in its one-time grants and could also relax its eligibility rules to some extent. It was felt, however, that an increase in the value of maximum regular allowances to widows up to the full amount 'disregarded' by the State, of £1 a week, could cause Funds to be closed to new cases by 1983. In consequence, the maximum figure was maintained at 15s (or £0.75) for the time being.

As regards eligibility, the Corporation had often been compelled to make use of restrictions on this when funds had been short, but it had always relaxed these limitations as soon as possible. It was therefore decided that the qualifying period of service of the serviceman which would enable his widow to receive an allowance should now be reduced from fourteen years to ten years. Other rules as to eligibility for help had been modified over the years and, in brief, were to remain as follows:

1   Widows and Children

Marriage should have taken place before final expiry of service with the colours – though exceptions would be made where marriage had occurred shortly after discharge from the Service, provided that there had been long or distinguished service or the serviceman was disabled.

2   Dependants

In those days before ambiguity and euphemism became commonplace, there had been no problem in definition. Orphans were children who had lost one or both parents, and there was no age limit for them. Other members of the family might be dependent relatives. Once the 'dependent' adjective was dropped in favour of the 'dependant' noun it had become necessary for the Corporation to spell out the rules for these, which were:
- a) Dependants should be limited to near relatives (mothers, sisters, father, brothers) and it should be a condition that they had been, or would have been, bona fide dependants.
- b) Dependants of servicemen of the Dominions who could be defined as members of the 'Naval and Military Forces of the Crown' were clearly eligible, and applications from other dependants of Dominion Forces who were not so obviously identifiable would be considered on their merits.

3   Polish Forces Under British Command

Bearing in mind that the Soldiers' and Airmen's Effects Fund had benefited from a large contribution from unclaimed estates of members of the Polish Resettlement Corps, widows and orphans of servicemen of these forces who had been under British command would be eligible for help.

4 Overseas Beneficiaries
Applicants from Eire, Malta, India and Pakistan, who were otherwise eligible, would be accepted; as would dependants of other overseas members of the British Forces provided that they lived in a country where there existed an accredited organization that could administer the benefits.

The early 1960s were anxious years for the Royal Victoria Patriotic School. There had been a natural and welcome change from the Wandsworth days. In the first place the education of the girls was directed to realizing their potential as individuals for any variety of occupations, not just the domestic type. Then, the wartime evacuation had led to the use of some local education facilities and, on the move to Bedwell Park, this trend had developed into the exclusive use of local schools. As a result the girls were being educated at the following establishments:
Five at Queen Elizabeth's Grammar School
Six at East Barnet Grammar School
One at Hatfield Grammar School
Thirty-seven at Southern Secondary Modern School
Two at Pitman's College Finchley
Twenty-two at Ladbrooke Primary School

As far as educational achievement was concerned, the results were far beyond the modest ambitions at Wandsworth, but these welcome changes in the character of the Royal Victoria Patriotic School were obtained at a price which threatened its future existence. The maintenance of what amounted to 'hotel' accommodation in such large premises and grounds for about seventy girls was resulting in disproportionate overheads, so that the total annual cost for each girl was averaging over £350 in the mid sixties. Although there were many grants and donations made to the School, the only ways in which these per capita costs could be made more of an economical proposition were by increasing the amounts to be contributed by parents and building up the numbers of pupils at the school. Modern trends were not helpful in either of these directions. The improvements in State help for widows meant that it was easier for them to keep their children at home, and to use the free transport available from there to State schools; and for a very large majority this was their preference in any event. In addition, as the 1939–45 war orphans matured so the numbers of fatherless children decreased who were in need of help and eligible.

All these factors convinced the Corporation that it would be unlikely that all the vacancies at the school would ever again be filled by fatherless orphans. So, bearing in mind that many Servicemen were either separated from their families for long periods or that these children had to move schools frequently, members of the Corporation considered that it would accord with the spirit of the 1903 Act in regard to help for children if eligibility for the School could be extended to the children of living Servicemen.

The Treasury Solicitor, Mr Burke, gave it as his opinion that the word 'children' in Clause 2 of the Patriotic Fund Reorganisation Act 1903 need not be interpreted as 'orphan children' but might include children of officers and servicemen still alive. Having regard to this, and the fact that all Acts of Parliament relating to the Patriotic Fund prior to 1903 had been repealed, and furthermore that no scheme had actually been approved for the Royal Victoria Patriotic School, he considered that the Ministry of Eduction could be approached to request that the restriction that the girls should be 'orphan daughters of deceased servicemen' should be removed.

The Ministry of Education endorsed the Treasury solicitor's view that there would be no objection to the school accepting 'daughters of any serviceman of the Armed Forces, dead or alive, and whether he is discharged from the Forces or still serving'. The Corporation lost no time in letting this extension of eligibility be known and, as a result, by the Summer Term of 1960 there were fifteen daughters at the School whose fathers were still alive and sixty who were orphans: by the Summer Term of 1963 the numbers were thirty-three and forty respectively. Five years later there were only fifty-three girls at the school and only nineteen of these were orphans or were from broken homes.

By 1968 the issue as to whether maintaining the Royal Victoria Patriotic School was the best use of funds available for helping in the education of Service orphans was a matter

New Looks but Old Values

for serious discussion. At this time there were fifty-nine children at the School, of whom only sixteen were orphans, at a gross cost of £583 a year for each girl (reduced to a net cost of £349 by parents' contributions, service pensions, donations and grants). At the same time there were fifty-six children being provided with bursaries or other forms of assistance at other established boarding schools and colleges at a cost to the Corporation of less than £150 a year for each child.

As Air Vice-Marshal Sir Bernard Chacksfield, the Chairman of the School Committee, was to explain to the General Purposes Committee in 1971 when efforts were being made to find a new Principal for the School, it was very difficult to find staff of a high standard for a school where no teaching was undertaken and which also had the disadvantage of being isolated. By that time there were only ten orphans at the school and it was felt that supposing the school were to be closed and sold there would then be ample funds available to help the children to attend other schools in a more economically sound manner.

After further study, and legal clearance for the expenditure of the proceeds from the sale, and other funds released, to be devoted to the 'general purposes of the Corporation' (which naturally included educational help which would continue on 'an increased scale') the decision was made to close the school at the end of the 1972 school year. There were five orphans left at the school then, and these were accepted by the Royal Alexandra and Albert School, Reigate: the Corporation paying the fees. These five were the last of some 4,500 girls who had attended the school in the hundred and fifteen years of its existence.

The school was sold by tender in 1973 for £251,125, less £5,528 for agent's and solicitor's fees and, as already recorded in Chapter 16, this large injection of cash provided the appropriate occasion for the Corporation to take advantage of the 1961 Trustee Investments Act. The Ministry of Defence marked the school's closure with an appreciative letter from the Defence Council:

> The Council has heard with some sadness of the recent closure of the Royal Victoria Patriotic School, Bedwell Park, Hertfordshire.

The Council feels that it would be wrong to let this occasion pass without conveying to the Corporation its appreciation of all the help which the School has given to the daughters of Servicemen of all three Services since its foundation at Wandsworth in 1857. On behalf of all Servicemen past and present, especially those whose children have passed through the School, I would be obliged if you would convey the thanks of the Council to members of your Corporation and the staff of the School.

It is pleasant to record that nearly twenty years after the School's closure there remains a flourishing Old Girls' Association.

It was also in 1973 that the Queen appointed HRH Princess Alexandra to succeed the Duke of Gloucester as the Corporation's President. The Duke had been President for an unprecedented twenty-six years and his health had been failing for some time. His death occurred in 1974.

The Executive Committee (which had reduced its meetings in 1964 from three to one a year) at its 1968 meeting touched on a subject which had surfaced on occasions in the past and, as personalities change, will no doubt continue to do so: the possible revision of the Corporation's Act of Parliament.

In 1961 various ideas had been put forward for replacing the original Patriotic Fund Re-organisation Act 1903, together with the Royal Patriotic Fund Corporation Act 1950, the appropriate clauses in the Naval and Military War Pensions Act 1915, and the War Pensions (Administrative Provisions) Act 1918, by a new Bill, on the basis that these four Acts introduced complications and had been 'found on several occasions to be out of line with modern practices and requirements'. The Charity Commissioners had produced one or two tentative drafts over the years but in 1968 'now informed the Corporation that they did not feel able to proceed with the proposed scheme for the Royal Patriotic Fund Corporation which had been initiated in 1961 with a view to bringing the legal authority for the Corporation more into line with current practice'.

The Executive Committee, which did not seem to have been unduly hampered by this seven-year delay, decided, nevertheless, to investigate the possibility of operations under a Royal Charter in place of an Act of Parliament, and to consult the Clerk to the Privy Council on this. The decision was also made to abandon an idea of reducing the membership of the Corporation.

This last notion had been an element in the package of criticisms which Commander Pursey had levelled at the Corporation during the debate on the Corporation's Bill of 1950. 'The organization of the Corporation was drawn up on a vast nation-wide basis' was his description, but while he deduced from this that large sums were wasted from the Corporation's funds in paying expenses for this 'nation-wide' membership to attend meetings (which was not true) others were to argue from time to time that this large membership

> caused unwarranted costs in printing and postage when sending out papers and the Annual Reports:
>
> meant that an 'unwieldly board'[1] was involved in decision making:
>
> might have been realistic and of value in the past but was an anachronism at the end of the twentieth century.

Fortunately, it did not take long to conclude that a simple and, it proved, entirely acceptable answer to the excessive printing costs was to provide the draft report and accounts only to those who planned to attend the Council meetings and to those who otherwise specifically requested them; subsequently to provide printed copies of the Annual Report and Statement of Accounts on a limited scale.

The 'unwieldly board' argument was more apparent than real since from the outset the Executive Committee of some twenty members had always dealt with the Corporation's business satisfactorily on the Council's behalf. This Committee included all the officially 'appointed' members so that the Government Departments' views were given due weight alongside these of co-opted and elected members.

As regards the idea that the nation-wide membership was out of harmony with modern practice, it was recalled at various times that:

> it was in answer to the years of criticism and enquiry that

this broadly based national organization had been established 'representing the chief local authorities in the Kingdom' as well as the 'persons appointed by the Crown':

at various times in its history the Corporation had needed its nation-wide representation to facilitate the raising of funds and, in the event that this might be regarded as unlikely to recur, the possibility of needing to make further appeals was considered by Committee members on three occasions after 1960:

the existence of the Council, and its annual meeting where it calls its Committee members to account for the year's operations, is the equivalent to an economical compression of both Branch and Annual General Meetings of other large organizations.

These counter arguments on matters of principle and theory were against a background of the practical difficulties of change. As General Sir Charles Keightley, Chairman of the Executive Committee, reported in 1969: 'A Charter could not constitutionally alter powers given by Parliament, and amending or revoking legislation would be needed before application could be made for the grant of a Charter.' After there had been further discussions with the Treasury Solicitor, it was reported in 1970 that: 'it had been agreed that the difficulties of changing were too great to be contemplated. The only practical way of altering the Constitution was by another Act of Parliament.'

Bearing in mind that the necessity for change was not established, the economy in printing and postage had been simply achieved, and that the practical difficulties of change were great and costly, it was not surprising that the organization, which had certainly stood the test of time, remained unaltered.

Attendance at the Annual Council meetings by Lord Lieutenants, Chairman of Councils, Lord Mayors and Mayors was fairly consistent in numbers and widely representative geographically over the years: falling away in times of war or in the face of a clash of other commitments and on occasions reaching high totals as a result of special promptings. The total audience for the Royal President and the Chairman of the Executive and Finance Committees at

New Looks but Old Values 183

Council meetings remained at about fifty. The place of the meeting varied over the years: the Middlesex Guildhall, the United Services Institutions (later the Royal United Services Institution), and finally the splendid State Apartments at the Royal Hospital, Chelsea, have all provided fitting venues for the Council.

In 1974 're-development' came to Wellington House so that after fourteen years in Buckingham Gate the Corporation's offices had to find another home. This time, with the help of the Property Services Agency of the Department of the Environment, suitable accommodation was found at No.1 Cambridge Gate which was Crown Estate property.

In the roughly thirty years since the 1950 Act of Parliament and rationalization of the Corporation's various Funds much had changed, but much had remained the same. The amount of help that could be given in regular allowances without causing the State to reduce its benefits had risen to £4 a week from 10s. 6d., which was about equivalent to the increase in cost of living. The Corporation's income and capital growth had not managed to keep pace with this rate of inflation but it continued to do its best to maintain its allowances and grants at realistic levels. The comparative figures were:

Numbers being Helped	Education		Continuing Allowances		One-time Grants		Total Expenditure	
	1950	1980	1950	1980	1950	1980	1950	1980
Widows	–	–	1,077	331	876	316		
Children	134	69	346	3	–	–	62,296	82,618
Dependants	–	–	9	7	–			

Two of the widows being helped at about this time warrant special mention. One was the last Transvaal War widow. She died in 1981 aged 96, her slightly senior colleague from that war had gone a year earlier after reaching her fortieth year of receiving a Corporation allowance and at 100 years of age. The Transvaal War Fund had been exhausted in 1963, after sixty-three years of helping widows, orphans and dependants of South African War. The public had subscribed £515,170 to the Fund and the Corporation had provided £1,125,000 for beneficiaries, excluding Government help. The remaining Transvaal War beneficiaries had been transferred to the Patriotic General Fund which had provided over £20,000 since 1963 for them.

The other widow who was no longer on the books of the Corporation was the 'Lady of the Lake'. As General Musson, then Vice-President, told the Council:

> For twenty-seven years we had helped to make life just a little better for her in the house-boat in Kashmir which was all that was left of the worldly goods her husband was able to leave her when he died in 1940. There will not be many occasions on which the Corporation's funds will have been spent – quite correctly – on a grant to keep a leaking houseboat afloat: something which, in two or three storms, all our efforts sadly failed to do. Fortunately, on these occasions our friend prudently abandoned ship well ahead of disaster.

At the end of her second three year term of office as President of the Corporation, HRH Princess Alexandra felt that other commitments were preventing her playing her full part in the Corporation's work, so that in 1979 HM The Queen appointed HRH Prince Michael of Kent to succeed her. This was a particularly happy choice because, as Prince Michael told members at his first Council meeting: 'I feel particularly at home here with the Corporation because your first President[2] was the first Colonel-in-Chief of my old Regiment, 11th Hussars. We appointed him in 1854, which was the year of the charge at Balaclava in which my old Commanding Officer, Lord Cardigan, was fairly heavily involved.'

In addition to taking the Chair and conducting all the subsequent Council meetings of the Corporation, Prince Michael took a close interest in all the schools at which the Corporation had nominations for places in return for financial help. Most of these were of very long standing such as Wellington College (since 1857), the Royal Naval School, Haslemere[3] (since 1857), the Royal Caledonian Schools, Watford (since 1857), the Royal Soldiers' Daughters'

School, Hampstead (now the Royal School, Hampstead) (since 1864), the Royal School, Bath (since 1902)[4], the Royal Alexandra & Albert School (since 1966). Another with whom the Corporation had established close links and arrangements for bursaries was the Royal Hospital School, Holbrook (since 1977 – previously at Greenwich).

During the first ten years as President of the Corporation Prince Michael visited all these schools with very beneficial results to the relationships between the Corporation and the schools. He also visited the newest additions to the schools linked to the Corporation by bursary arrangements, the Duke of Kent School (since 1980) and the Gordon School (since 1981 – when it was the Gordon Boys' School).

A considerable bonus in February of 1981, which provided extra latitude for the Corporation in extending its educational help, had come from an unusual source. Prince Michael had presented awards in one of the entertainment worlds' ceremonies, and the sponsoring Mecca Organization had asked if the Prince would nominate a charity for a donation. His response provided the Corporation with a most generous gift of £5,000.

The 1980s were times of rapid development; also, fortunately, of financial boom so that when opportunities arose to extend the Corporation's help to Service widows and orphans the financial resources were available to provide the scope necessary. As far back as 1966 the Corporation had recognized that 'a television and connected expenses should be considered an essential for elderly widows and this should be taken into account when authorizing assistance'. In addition, therefore, to a television set and licence being regarded by the Corporation's members as a legitimate essential expense for widows, grants were often made to provide these amenities. For many years the Corporation had enjoyed a close relationship with Queen Mary's (Roehampton) Trust, so when that Trust wished to hand over its scheme for providing television sets and licences for war widows it was natural that it should turn to the Corporation where the operation of the scheme would so neatly fit its normal dealings with individuals, as well as its philosophy.

The Trust had started the scheme in order to soften a

double blow that had previously faced widows whose war-disabled husbands had been provided with free television sets and licences by the 'Not Forgotten' Association. Because this Association's Charter did not extend to helping widows, the death of these disabled ex-servicemen would have brought also the loss of the television help. So the Trust had started its scheme originally to assume responsibility for continuing this form of assistance. This provision of television help for 'ex- "Not Forgotten" Association' widows had then been extended by Queen Mary's Trust to embrace all war-widows who were unable to afford to provide their own sets and licences.

The reason why the Trust had wanted to hand over the operation of the scheme was to rationalize all its charitable operations into a system of 'block' grants, thus economizing in administrative costs. In undertaking responsibility for the scheme in 1981 the Corporation absorbed it into its existing pattern of work without any increase in staff. No separate Fund was established, but separate records were maintained of income and expenditure for the scheme to ensure that it did not become a heavy charge on the Patriotic General Fund (or any other). Queen Mary's (Roehampton) Trust provided generous block grants and each of the main Service Grant-making Funds[5] contributed grants on the basis of the numbers of their Service widows being helped.

This provision of television help, by the 'Not Forgotten' Association for disabled ex-Service men and women and by the Royal Patriotic Fund Corporation (as for Queen Mary's [Roehampton] Trust), was made a simpler and more economic proposition by the wholehearted co-operation of the supplier, the Thorn EMI Group.

Thorn EMI had maintained close relations with the Armed Services for many years while co-operating in the research, production and trials of electronic defence and security equipment. It was a logical development that that part of the Group concerned with the provision of television sets should enter into contracts with Service Charities when supplies of these were needed.

Within Thorn EMI the business of renting television sets to individuals is handled by 'Radio Rentals', but the 'Business Communications' element deals with similar products and functions in the general business market. This is the element which the Group deploys to help charities because the cost savings resulting from the larger scale of operations can thus be passed on to the charities. In consequence, the Royal Patriotic Fund Corporation has been able to pay for the provision of some 600 excellent colour television sets for Service widows at an annual rental of about £30,000, which includes installation costs and replacement in the event of breakdown. This is about one third of the normal rate from a 'high street' business and enables the Fund to look after more than a thousand war-widows with television licences and sets at an affordable cost.

The next addition to the Patriotic General Fund was a transfer very much in the pattern of the 'War (Transferred 1917) Fund'[6] in that it was a wartime Fund which had been operated by the Government. 'The King's Fund (1940)' was an extension of a Fund founded in 1918 by King George V, with its scope enlarged by King George VI to cover the 1939–45 War, and, in its later stages, also extended to include those disabled or bereaved in other operations. The Fund's trustees were members of the Department of Health and Social Security and it had been operated by civil servants of that Department. It was something of an anachronism as a 'State Charity', its resources were being rapidly diminished and it was clear that if no Charity could be found to assume responsibility for the proper administration of the funds that remained, there was a danger that these would be dissipated more with the aim of early exhaustion than of the best use of the money.

The King's Fund covered assistance to disabled ex-Servicemen as well as to their widows and children, and this extended beyond the Corporation's scope. The solution to this difficulty reached in negotiations between the Department of Health and Social Security was for the balance of the Fund to be divided between the Corporation, for the widows and children, and the Joint Committee of St. John and the British Red Cross Society, for the men. The amount received by the Corporation was just over £22,000 and since its purposes were similar to those of the Patriotic General Fund it was credited to that Fund.

The transfer was made in 1983, and at that time the Corporation was spending some £200,000 a year on the provision of continuing allowances, one-time grants, and television help for a total of over 1,800 widows, and assistance with the education of almost 100 children.

There were about to be some major changes in environment affecting the Corporation, both geographical and philosophical. For the first, Ministry of Works needs had meant that the Corporation's offices had had to exchange one view of Regent's Park for another as it had to move in 1976 from 1 Cambridge Gate to 9 Gloucester Gate. Then in 1982, for similar reasons the Corporation's headquarters came to Golden Cross House; to within a few hundred yards of where it had been a hundred years earlier.

The other changes were of a totally different nature. On the purely financial side the need for the City of London to maintain a major and profitable role in European and World finances brought about the so-called 'Big Bang' in the London Stock Market in 1987. Its operations were extended in time to enable it to react to markets at such extremes as USA and Tokyo, and, in order to be able to compete on equal terms, many Finance Houses grouped together in large conglomerates. Operations were computerized and a large number of stockbrokers introduced fee-charging systems in place of the previous commission basis.

The nature of the Corporation's foundation and its strong links with Government institutions had meant that its financial operations had always involved the Bank of England, the Paymaster-General, the Auditor General, and, as stockbroker, the Government Broker, Mullens & Co. At 'Big Bang' Mullens & Co ceased to be the Government Broker, joined a conglomerate based upon the merchant bankers, Warburg, and introduced a fee system. After a trial period it became clear that the system of charges operated by this conglomerate would involve the Corporation in excessive costs, so it became necessary to change to a firm of appropriate standing which retained a commission system. The decision was made in 1988 to employ Cazenove & Co: a decision which owed nothing to the coincidental early connection with the trustee of the Indian Mutiny Relief Fund (taken over by the Royal Commission in 1902) the stockbroker, Philip Cazenove. A coincidence but, like the return to Charing Cross, a happy one.

The other environmental change, however, was of much greater magnitude: the transformation of Charities into big business.

Footnotes

1. From the Nathan Committee Report in 1952 'Unwieldly boards are not unknown already. We have in mind, for instance, the 350 odd members of the Council of the Royal Patriotic Fund Corporation – partly attributable to its early history'.
2. Prince Albert, the Prince Consort, who had been first President of the Royal Commission.
3. Originally at Richmond as the 'Royal Naval Female School'.
4. The bursaries at the Royal School, Bath, originated from '119 votes for nominations' inherited with the Indian Mutiny Fund.
5. The main Service grant-making funds are King George's Fund for sailors, the Army Benevolent Fund and the RAF Benevolent Fund.
6. See Chapter 14.

18 Constancy and Consistency

In July 1853, just before the Royal Commission of the Patriotic Fund was founded, the Charity Commission consisted of four Commissioners, one secretary and two inspectors. In 1986 it had increased to a staff of about three hundred and thirty, but this still did not enable the Commission to exercise the control and produce the prompt action which the times and modern practices demanded. By 1990 there were some 170,000 registered Charities and the rate of increase in registrations had risen to over 4,000 a year. This is a far cry from the earliest days of Church and Parish Charities, and educational endowments, and it is on a vastly different scale to the relatively gradual increase in the nineteenth century when the Charity Commission was formed to create a permanent body to control what was regarded then as 'a proliferation' of charitable bodies. Those were the days when, apart from any domestic regimental funds or naval base voluntary efforts, Service Charities consisted, in the main, of Greenwich Hospital, the Queen Adelaide Naval Fund, the Royal Naval Fund, Lloyd's Patriotic Fund and the Royal Patriotic Fund; a time when Colonel Gildea's Zulu and Afghan War appeals and his Ladies' Committees were sowing the seeds of the Soldiers' and Sailors' Families Association. The British Red Cross, the Army Benevolent Fund, King George's Fund for Sailors, the British Legion (now the Royal British Legion) and the Royal Air Force Benevolent Fund were still to appear later in the twentieth century.

The greater emphasis on welfare engendered in part by the Beveridge Report and partly by the rapid increase in the cost of living, together with the marked improvement in communications of all types, were main factors in the increase in the numbers of Charities from the Second World War onwards, but it was in the 1970s and 1980s that the whole field changed so markedly. There were two sides to this transformation, which was a change in character: what *The Financial Times* called 'The Charitable Face of Business' and its obverse, the business face of charity. Although both sides were manifest, it was the latter which was both dominant and, in the view of many, harmful.

Perhaps the most significant move in the direction of commercialization was the introduction and spread of the professional fund-raiser. This, although entirely helpful for raising money for specific purposes, and harmless in itself, led inevitably to the involvement of other business organizations through the public relations and publicity channels. Commercial involvement meant commercial practices; competition for funds, higher salaries (£30,000 a year or more)[1] for competitive performance, and, in the boom years of the 1980s, pursuing the business pattern of 'big is beautiful' and how to be first to 'conglomerate' status.

For those accustomed to the traditional voluntary and co-operative face of charity this struggle for 'business' seemed to be a somewhat twisted form of beneficence. As for the fashion for spontaneous appeals, and those partly sponsored for the benefit of the entertainment industry, these seemed to be positively against the interests of those in need who depended on long-term assistance from established Charities; both from the point of view of reducing the public's contribution to these, and from the aspect of equity. The difficulty can be imagined of explaining to the widow of a serviceman killed in Aden, Malaya or Borneo why she has only a war-widow's pension and some occasional help from the Royal Patriotic Fund Corporation, while a 'Falklands War' widow obtained, in addition, a massive lump sum from the 'South Atlantic Fund'.

The charitable face of business included the various forms of corporate giving, a degree of sponsorship; and future development seemed to be in the direction of 'contract' giving in which, in return for fixed contributions, Charities would be committed to the provision of specific help to public bodies. While corporate giving such as 'Gift Aid' and 'Payroll Giving' was certainly a welcome addition to Charity income, 'contract giving' seems likely to lead to virtual control of charitable work by professional, and possibly, commercial organizations. *The Financial Times* also saw the possibility of other questions arising, such as: 'Are big businesslike charities likely to be any more efficient and responsive to individual needs than the big public authorities they replace? Would voluntary workers continue to give their time, and donors their money, to businesslike charities that compete with each other and with commercial organizations for contracts?'

Where all this may lead one cannot tell, but any development which militates against the long tradition of voluntary effort meeting the real needs of unlucky individuals in a selfless way, and not for commercial reasons, must be a matter of regret.

As the Royal Patriotic Fund Corporation entered its 137th year its record of assistance rendered since its Crimean inception, in prosperity and hard times, read like this:

Public Subscriptions for Crimean War	£1,471,375
Other Funds created prior to 1900	£ 414,034
Part of public subscriptions for South African War	£ 515,170
Securities and cash from War Office, Air Ministry and Ministry of Defence for Soldiers' and Airmen's Effects	£ 349,166
State supplements paid by the Treasury prior to Ministry of Pensions taking over	£ 156,135
Voluntary subscriptions from the public for the First World War	£ 43,656
Funds handed over by other Charities for disbursement	£ 66,032
Miscellaneous donations, legacies, grants, etc.	£1,328,366
Total receipts:	£4,343,934*
Total disbursements:	£9,198,516*

on account of:	44,140 Allowances to widows*
	45,758 Grants to widows*
	24,234 Allowances for children*
	952 Allowances for other dependants*
Remaining Assets:	£1,856,517 (Market value £2,708,431)

* Not including £408,993 administered on behalf of the Government from the National Relief Fund to 44,869 widows, 96,413 children and 29,419 other dependants at an administration cost of 1.6%.

So, after helping almost 135,000 widows and about 150,000 orphans and other dependants with over nine million pounds since the war with Russia in 1853, this Victorian charity finds itself in an environment of Charities with commercial outlooks and modern business methods. Before bringing this history to a close it is perhaps right to see how the Corporation is coping with this situation as it approaches its 150th anniversary and looks towards helping a widow who will be the 150,000th widowed beneficiary.

First as to the nature of its assistance: this remains entirely true to its traditional beneficiaries, the widows, orphans and dependent relatives of officers and men of the Armed Services; providing them with both continuing and immediate help. The way in which it has been accommodated to the modern 'quality of life' is that the earlier necessities of clothing, food and fuel have largely been replaced by help to support housekeeping which includes central heating, dishwashers and washing machines, and, for war widows, television sets.

The management of the Corporation's finance has been a model of adaptation, but also without departing from the prudent direction which was the basis of the generations of husbanding which had gone before. Rather earlier than the majority of Charities, the Corporation realized that the need to maintain capital, yet still provide the requisite income, called for investment in appropriate equities. The knowledgeable management of large investments in equities, without the type of risk which would be unjustified for a Charity, calls for skills among Trustees not needed in the days before the Second World War, when investment was limited to Government Securities, fixed interest stocks in national undertakings and local authorities, debentures, loan and preference stocks – indeed what were known as 'Trustee Stocks'.

The Corporation had been in a favourable position to undertake this more advanced management since it began its close links with the Institute of Actuaries. This relationship, which had begun through the regular actuarial valuations of individual Funds, had developed into the ex-officio appointment of successive Presidents of the Institute to the Corporation's Finance Committee. The profession of actuary, besides providing the skills necessary for insurance operations, also ensures the expertise which is in demand for many other appointments in the field of other financial institutions, such as Banks, Trusts and Pension Funds. This means that there was, and is, a large reservoir of capable men of standing with a wide knowledge of investment in all types of stocks and shares. The Corporation has been very fortunate over the years in having a succession of such actuaries holding office for long periods as Chairmen and members of its Finance Committee.

The appointment by the Sovereign of representatives from the Treasury and senior civil servants from the Ministry of Defence has also meant that there has been a sound foundation of financial management ability available in the Finance Committee since the Corporation's earliest days. There has also been available to the Corporation since its inception the 'blue chip' advice, first of the Government Broker's firm of Messrs Mullens & Co, and latterly of Messrs Cazenove & Co. With all this talent available to supervise careful, but profitable, investments, it is not due to chance, or a particularly favourable market that the Corporation has not only been able to meet its commitments to the full, but has, in addition, an invested capital of some £1.5 million at cost with a current market value standing at over £1 million more than this.

Any look at the way in which an old institution fits into a modern setting must include its structure, particularly when this was Victorian in design and when, on several occasions and at various times it has had its fervent critics. The criticisms that the membership of the Corporation is too wide, leading either to impersonal and cumbersome administration and unnecessarily heavy overheads, or, alternatively to decisions being taken by a small coterie behind a large 'front' organization and without adequate trustee involvement have been answered in general in Chapter 17. More specifically, the Finance Committee and the General Purposes Committee, each of between ten and twelve members, take the day-to-day decisions corporately in their own spheres, and where interim decisions are needed within existing policies, and Committee meetings would be too slow and unwieldly methods, individual trustees are specifically authorized to make these decisions, which are always subject to subsequent enquiry and endorsement. These Committees are sub-committees of the Executive Committee of up to twenty-two members and which represents, and answers to, the General Council.

As regards overheads, the cost of administration during periods of quite high inflation between 1980 and 1989 averaged 15% of the amount disbursed in allowances and grants to beneficiaries: a figure which bears comparison with any charitable body.

The criticism that there are too many Service Charities (Commander Pursey in 1950 alleged that he had counted 800) has arisen at various times during this century. As early as 1900 the Joint Parliamentary Committee under Lord Justice Henn Collins was delving into the possibility of there being overlapping and duplication in the work of the Service Charities then existing. In examining the Chairman of the Soldiers' and Sailors' Help Society, Lord Justice Collins remarked that, 'Your organization appears to run on very much the same lines as Colonel Gildea's.'[2] He was told 'Last year we endeavoured to bring about an amalgamation of the two societies. We got as far as forming a sort of alliance to work together. What we look to in the future is that these two societies may become amalgamated ... '. General Geary's forecast was approaching realization by 1990.

In 1900 Colonel Gildea himself had submitted a scheme for 'rationalization' in which the Royal Patriotic Fund would provide 'Permanent Help' for 'Widows, Orphans and Dependent Relatives', SSFA would provide 'Temporary Help' for 'Wives, Families and Dependent Relatives', Lloyd's Patriotic Fund would provide 'Permanent and Temporary Help' for 'Disabled Soldiers and Sailors' and the Red Cross Society would provide 'Temporary Help only in War' for 'Sick and Wounded'. However, none of the Select Committees seems to have concluded that anything more was needed than co-operation and exchange of information to guard against help for beneficiaries being duplicated.

It was not, however, this aspect which had caused Commander Pursey's outburst in the House of Commons in 1950 recorded in Chapter 15, or the sporadic impulse of those who, from Olympian heights, have observed many service Charities and concluded – possibly without acquiring either information in great detail or the point of view of beneficiaries – that: 'There are too many Service Charities, competing with each other for funds, and, in the era of modern big business, help for the Services would more effectively be carried out, at less administrative cost, if most of them combined.'

Most of those, however, with what might best be described as wide 'field experience' such as welfare visitors, both professional and voluntary, and those who are in need of help, would argue that Service families are particularly fortunate in having a wide variety of Charities to call upon, each with its different scope and rules, rather than some large conglomerate with a monolithic set of rules, and inevitably cumbersome office organization and the bureaucracy that goes with it. As General Gow, the Vice-President of the Corporation put it at the Annual General Council Meeting in 1987:

> Rightly, I think, Service families are particularly fortunate in the support they receive from those with their interests at heart. In these days of the domination by the large, impersonal, conglomerates in the world of commerce and most of the professions, I believe that Service families benefit greatly from having several organizations to support them – each with particular strengths and – if you will – specializations. There are the very large charities with their own appeal organizations and regular contributors – and without their generous grants most of the smaller charities would be very limited in the help they could give. But it would be difficult for some of those very large bodies to discover the needs of individuals throughout the United Kingdom and abroad. Here, those organizations with large numbers of 'field workers' such as SSAFA, the Royal British Legion and its connected charities (and I can speak also for the Royal British Legion in Scotland of which I am President) and Regimental Associations have their strengths and can provide the personal contact which is so necessary.

Apart from some very old hands among Service Charity Visitors, it is probably amongst the more experienced professionals – particularly in the War Pensioners' Welfare Service of the DHSS – that the strength of this pattern of Service help is most widely appreciated. They know where it

Constancy and Consistency

is best to go for the particular help that is needed, and when unusual problems arise they know that combined support from some of the smaller Funds may well provide the right answer. So I would like then, once again this year, to emphasize that our long experience in helping Service families leads me to believe that this interdependence and mutual support amongst Service Charities is a very precious asset indeed.

So, 'enacted' by the Sovereign, 'by and with the advice and consent of the Lords Spiritual and Temporal, and Commons, in this present Parliament assembled' the Corporation continues to administer 'the property of the Corporation' for the benefit of the widows, children and dependants of officers and men of the naval, military and air forces of the Crown; still in association with most of the same sister Charities, including schools, as for many past generations. As each annual report to the Sovereign and Parliament shows, the help may have changed in its nature with changing circumstances, the individual amounts have arisen to match modern needs, but consistently the Corporation has maintained its principle of treating each application on its merits, and throughout the years the care taken has remained a very constant factor.

Footnotes

1. Even £30,000 a year is beginning to be regarded as '25% less than his or her counterpart in industry' according to *The Financial Times*.
2. i.e. 'Colonel Gildea's'; namely the Soldiers' and Sailors' Families Association.

Appendices

Appendix A

EXTRACTS FROM THE ROYAL WARRANT CONSTITUTING THE ROYAL COMMISSION OF THE PATRIOTIC FUND – 7TH OCTOBER 1854

1. The warrant opens with:

> Victoria, by the Grace of God, of the United Kingdom of Great Britain and Ireland, Queen, Defender of the Faith. To Our most dearly-beloved Consort, His Royal Highness Francis Albert Augustus Charles Emmanuel, Duke of Saxony, Prince of Saxe Cobourg and Gotha, Knight of our most noble order of the Garter and Field-Marshal of our Forces.

It then addresses the remaining thirty-seven members of the Commission, namely:

The Duke of Newcastle
Lord Seymour
The Earl of Aberdeen
Rear Admiral the Earl of Hardwick
Horatio, Earl Nelson
Viscount Palmerston
General Lord Hardinge
Rear Admiral Lord Colchester
General Lord Seaton
General Lord Raglan
Colonel the Honourable
   James Lindsay
Henry Lowry Corry
Robert Vernon Smith
Sir Robert Throckmorton, Bt
Lieutenant General
   Sir John Burgoyne
The Lord Mayor of London
John Gellibrand Hubbard
Edmund Burke Roche

The Duke of Wellington
The Earl of Derby
The Earl of Shaftesbury
The Earl of Chichester
The Earl Grey
General Lord Combermere
Major General Lord Rokeby
Lord Panmure
Lord St Leonards
Sidney Herbert, Secretary-at-War
Sir James Graham, Bt
Edward Ellice
Sir John Pakington, Bt
Admiral Sir William Parker, Bt
Lieutenant General
   Sir Hew Dalrymple Ross
Thomas Baring
John Wilson Patten
Samuel Martin Peto
John Ball

2. The Warrant, acknowledging the desire of 'Our loving subjects throughout Our Kingdom and Dominions' to provide 'a just and generous benevolence towards the widows and orphans of those of Our soldiers, sailors, and marines who have been so killed, or who may hereafter die amidst the ravages and casualties of war, and also by their gifts and subscriptions to contribute a portion of those means with which Our nation has been blessed towards the succouring, educating, and relieving those, who, by the loss of their husbands and parents in battle, or by death on active service in the present war, are unable to maintain or to support themselves', recognizes the need to take measure for the safe custody and application of the money raised and lays the responsibility for this upon the nominated Commission.

3. Specifically the Warrant provides for the Commission to:

> ... make full and diligent inquiry into the best mode of aiding the loyalty and benevolence of Our loving subjects, and of ascertaining the best means by which the gifts, subscriptions, and contributions of Our loving subjects can be best applied, according to the generous intentions of the donor thereof, and from time to time to apply the same as you, Our Commissioners, or any three or more of you, shall think fit, or direct either for this immediate relief of such special objects of destitution as may come within the meaning and purpose of such benevolence; ...

4. The Commission was granted 'to any three or more of you, full power and authority to call before you, or any three or more of you, all such persons in connection with Our civil, military, and naval service, as you shall judge necessary, by whom you may be better informed of all matters and think most desirable to be done and performed, and to inquire into the premises and every part thereof by all other lawful ways and means whatsoever'.

'For the purpose of aiding you in the execution of these premises' the Warrant appointed 'Edmund Gardiner Fishbourne, Esquire, Captain in Our Navy' and 'John Henry Lefroy, Esquire, Captain in Our Royal Regiment of Artillery' to be joint Honorary Secretaries to the Royal Commission.

5. To ensure that local committees to further the Commissions task 'may the more readily and speedily be formed throughout Our Kingdom and Dominions of all Our magistrates, justices of the peace, the clergy, and other of Our loving subjects within all cities, parishes, boroughs, and places in Our Kingdom and Dominions, and in Our Colonies, possessions, and territories abroad', Queen Victoria's Warrant appointed 'Commissioners in Aid' 'to encourage, aid, and assist the establishment of all such Local Committees as may be useful or necessary in every town, parish, or place within the jurisdictions aforesaid, for the several purposes of collecting from time to time all or

Appendices

any gifts, subscriptions, and voluntary contributions as aforesaid, and transmitting the same when so collected to our Paymaster-General'.

6. For the safe custody of 'all monies which may hereafter be received' and 'of all sums of money already subscribed' the Warrant appointed 'Edward John, Baron Stanley of Alderley, Our Paymaster-General, or Our Paymaster-General for the time being, to receive and safely keep all and every sum and sums of money' which may be received. To this end the Paymaster-General was 'to open and keep a separate account at the Bank of England, and to 'pay to the credit of such account, which shall be called and known by the name of the "PATRIOTIC FUND", all and every sum and sums of money which he may at any time hereafter receive ... ' He was also to 'cause payments to be made therefrom by virtue of such drafts or orders as may be addressed to him by or on behalf of you Our said Commissioners, and, subject, to your direction and authority, by your said Secretaries or either of them, or by the said Executive and Finance Committee, or by any two or more of such Committee for the time being'.

7. For the purposes of carrying out the purposes of the Commission the Commissioners were authorized 'to nominate and appoint any three or more persons whomsoever, as to you shall seem meet, to be an Executive Committee in the premises;' and that 'such Executive Committee shall also be a Finance Committee, with power to select their own Chairman, and having the direction and control, under such orders and regulations as may hereafter from time to time be made by you', over receipts and expenditure.

8. It was Queen Victoria's 'further will and pleasure, when and so often as need or occasion shall require, so long as this Our Commission shall continue in force' that the Commissioners 'do report to Us in writing, under your hands and seals respectively, all and every of the several proceedings of yourselves.'

Appendix B

ROYAL COMMISSION OF THE PATRIOTIC FUND

Notice

The Offices of the Royal Commissioners of the 'Patriotic Fund' are for the present, at No. 16A Great George Street, corner of Parliament Street, Westminster.

The hours of attendance will be from 11 a.m. till 4 p.m. daily. The 'Commissioners in Aid' of the 'Patriotic Fund' are earnestly requested, without further notice, to take immediate steps for giving publicity, within their several jurisdictions, to the Royal Commission, in order that Local Committees be formed, whenever practicable, with the least possible delay,

'Local Committees' will, according to their discretion, obtain Contributions to the Patriotic Fund, either by public Meetings, establishing Subscription Lists, or otherwise.

The acknowledgement of individual donations, where obtained through the 'Commissioners in Aid' or by 'Local Committees', must in all cases, to avoid error and expense, be left exclusively to the 'Local Committee'.

Local Committees are requested to make up their first Subscription Lists and Accounts in or before the first week in December next, and to remit the amounts in or before the following week, by drafts payable to the 'Patriotic Fund', crossed 'Bank of England', to the Secretaries of the Commission, or direct to the Bank of England.

Total amounts only, as transmitted by Local Committees will be acknowledged at fixed periods in two London daily newspapers.

Donations, Subscriptions, and Contributions, to the 'Patriotic Fund', other than those paid to Local Committees, will be received by the Secretaries at the Offices of the Royal Commission as above, at the Bank of England, and by all London Bankers. Acknowledgements of the receipt will appear, from time to time, in the London papers above mentioned; but it is hoped that no separate receipts or acknowledgements will be required from the Honorary Secretaries, whose duties will be otherwise sufficiently laborious.

Appendix C

PROPOSALS FOR GIRLS' SCHOOL SUBMITTED BY THE REVEREND F C COOK H M INSPECTOR OF SCHOOLS JULY 1856

Suggestions submitted to the consideration of the Executive & Finance Committee of the Royal Commission of the Patriotic Funds, with reference to an Institution for 300 girls between 5 and 15 years of age.

The object of the Institution is to afford such a practical education to the girls as may qualify them for domestic service, or other similar occupations.

The course of instruction should include the subjects taught in a good National School. It has been found by repeated experiments that the habits and attainments of girls so educated, do in point of fact make them valuable and trustworthy servants, when due attention has been paid to practical and economical matters.

In addition to that course, a complete system of industrial training is desirable, and should be made the characteristic feature of the Institution.

The two points of most importance in the organization of such an Institution are:

1. The character and functions of the Managers, Teachers and other Officers.
2. The classification of the pupils.

For reasons hereafter to be assigned I would recommend the appointment of the following Officers, with salaries and other advantages here specified.

With Board and Lodging

Superintendent & Housekeeper	£80 to increase to £120 or £100 to £130
Cooks	£14 to increase to £16
Laundry woman	£14 to increase to £16
3 Housemaids	£40
3 Governesses	£120
3 Assistant Teachers	£60

With Lodging and other prerequisites, Coal, Gas, etc.
Chaplain & Secretary   £150 to increase to £200*
Medical Attendant   £50
Porter   £30

*This salary may not be sufficient to secure the permanent services of an efficient Chaplain. It may be well to begin with £200 and increase to £250.

In the Field and Dairy, it will be necessary to employ a married couple – the man as gardener and labourer, the wife as dairymaid. I understand that their wages ought not to exceed £60.

Duties of these Officers

1. The Superintendent will be charged with the entire management of the household, and the domestic order and discipline. Her duties will, in all essentials, be those which I have described in my last report on normal Schools for Mistresses, p.20-21. The authority of this Officer must be clearly defined, and be felt throughout the Institution, as paramount in all matters not directly under the superintendence of the Chaplain.
2. The five servants will each be assisted by girls between 15 and 17 years of age, trained in the Institution. I am of opinion that 10 girls may be retained for that purpose if there is also a dairy.
3. Each Governess would have the chief charge of one division of 100 girls. They will be assisted by one younger Governess, and 4 Pupil Teachers between 14 and 19 years of age. These Pupil Teachers will be regularly examined by the Government Inspector, and apprenticed on the usual system, excepting that they will not be paid by the Committee of Council on Education.

    The Governesses will be under the authority of the Superintendent, excepting in the matters connected with the Instruction of their Pupils which will come under the cognizance of the Secretary and Chaplain.
4. The Secretary will prepare reports on all matters connected with the Institution for the consideration of the Committee of Management. He will have the sole charge of the religious Instruction and be responsible to the Committee for the observance of all the regulations which they may enact. He will visit all parts of the Institution regularly but not interfere with the Superintendent, nor on any account interpose his authority between her and any member of the establishment.

    It is not desirable that the Superintendent should be the wife of the Chaplain. But the orderly working of this Institution will, to a great extent, depend upon the adjustment of the claims of these two Officers to such authority as will enable them to do their work severally without let or hindrance; and I am of opinion that it may be secured, provided always that persons of high character and requisite ability be appointed, if the Chaplain be held responsible for the Instruction in

School, and the Superintendent for all other matters.

The Institution ought to be visited (1) once a month by a House Committee, who should see the Chaplain and Superintendent separately and examine their reports, etc., and (2) twice yearly by the Commissioners who would receive the report of the House Committee.

Classification of the Pupils

The Institution will be in three separate departments. Each department will contain 100 girls.

For these 100 girls there will be one dormitory with 4 wards, so arranged as to be under the immediate control of a Governess, Assistant, and 4 Pupil Teachers. The apartments of the Governess and Assistant in the centre, one Pupil Teacher in each ward.

One playground which, if necessary, may be subdivided.

One Schoolroom, with Class Room.

The girls in each department will not come into personal contact with those in other departments. They will only meet them in the dining room and at prayers.

The classification will be regulated by the following considerations.

Girls who enter between 5 and 8 years of age will proceed regularly through the classes of two schools, and as they advance be removed to corresponding wards in the dormitories. It may be expected that elder girls who enter the Institution will generally be more difficult to manage, and require a firmer and more vigorous system of discipline and instruction. They will thereupon be placed in the third division, under the charge of the most experienced Governess and under the more immediate superintendence of the principals. Some of the girls retained for domestic service may sleep in their wards, and every bed, as well as every small class should be arranged as to bring each of the girls into direct and constant contact with those who will exercise a strong moral influence upon their character. This can be done without difficulty on the plans here suggested.

General Remarks

Supposing the Institution to be full, and in a normal condition about 35 will arrive at the age of 15 each year. Ten of these will be retained as domestic servants and one or two as Pupil Teachers. The future prospects of the girls will be tolerably secure, the former will be thoroughly trained for any situation, and the latter will be admissible as Queen's Scholars to the Normal Schools for Mistresses. I do not suppose that the Committee will think fit to pay wages to these girls, but they should receive a small sum of money, and a complete set of clothes, etc. with a few well chosen books, as an outfit on leaving.

About twenty to twenty-five girls will moreover be prepared for other situations. Their qualifications on leaving will be as follows.

A good plain education.

Needlework of all kinds, including cutting out.

Practical knowledge of work done in the kitchen, scullery, laundry, dairy, etc.

It may be found desirable to have one department for girls not strong enough for domestic service. They may be instructed in ornamental straw platting, lace making, and other kinds of fine work. This department will not involve much expense, if one or more of the Assistant Governesses be specially trained to take charge of it.

There will be an infirmary. In this those girls who show peculiar aptitude may be trained as nurses.

Calculation of Expenses

Salaries	from £600 to £700
Board and Clothing	£3,000

Other expenses cannot be calculated without reference to site and buildings. 6 Acres may suffice for the buildings, playground, etc. For Dairy – 10 additional acres.

(Signed) F.C. Cook

H. M. Inspector of Schools

July 1856

Appendix D

RESPONSE TO CHARGES BY ARCHBISHOP CULLEN OF DISCRIMINATION AGAINST ROMAN CATHOLICS

ARCHBISHOP CULLEN'S PASTORAL

TO THE EDITOR OF *THE TIMES*

Sir, I have just read with much surprise and regret the contents of a letter in your journal of this morning written by Archbishop Cullen, dated from Rome, and addressed to one of his vicars-general, with the object, as it seems, of inducing Roman Catholics to withhold their aid from the Relief Fund for the Sufferers in India. If he really believes that there is danger that the fund may be applied 'by bigots in proselytizing purposes' his better course would be to raise by the subscriptions of Roman Catholics a separate fund for the relief of the sufferers of their own persuasion, in that respect following apparently the example of a higher authority in the Roman Catholic Church. But could anything be more unwise? Is this a moment to add a drop to the cup of bitterness between the two churches? The heart of every man beats warmly in favour of our suffering and brave soldiers and fellow-subjects in India without reference to creed. I cannot believe that any subscriber has considered whether his donation will relieve a Protestant or a Roman Catholic. The Sultan of Turkey has set us an example in his munificent subscription which may make us Christians ashamed of insisting upon differences between our churches as a ground for not subscribing to the general fund. Roman Catholic equally with Protestant blood has been freely shed with a noble daring in defence of our sovereignty in the East. Christians of all denominations have suffered torture and death in their most savage forms, and the object of the subscribers is to alleviate the sufferings of those who survive. It is treason to humanity to suppose that the fund will not be honestly dedicated to the sacred purposes for which it is designed.

Still, I should not have felt it my duty to make any remark on Dr. Cullen's letter had he abstained from attacking the management of the Patriotic Fund as regards the widows and orphans of Roman

Catholic soldiers during the period I had the honour of being chairman of the executive and finance committee. According to his statement applications were made by Catholic clergymen of Dublin to the managers of the fund in favour of the widows and orphans of soldiers killed in the Crimea, yet, as far as he could learn, not one shilling was then obtained by such applications. Now, I assert that no application for the relief of *any* widow or orphan of a soldier killed in the Crimea was ever rejected or neglected, although I think it probable that applications by Roman Catholic clergymen of Dublin for money to be remitted to them for distribution by them among claimants of their own creed were not complied with. But I say, without fear of contradiction, that in distributing relief no question ever arose as to the religious persuasion of the claimant, except so far as to make the mode of payment as agreeable as it might be to the recipient. Archbishop Cullen then states that when relief was granted in Dublin a parson was always employed to administer it, and he had heard that he generally selected a Protestant church or vestry as the place of doling it out. I never heard, during the many months of my attendance on the duties of my office as chairman of the committee, any complaint of the manner of the distribution, and the payments were made by the paymasters of pensions wherever their services could be obtained, and always so as to meet the convenience of the claimants as far as might be. Doctor Cullen then refers to the manner in which the funds were ultimately allotted, and he says that they seem to be all grants to Protestant institutions and for Protestant purposes. This only proves that Dr. Cullen is writing from Rome upon a subject dear to England and Ireland in regard to which he is ill-informed. At every step care has been taken to extend the same relief to the widows and children of Roman Catholics as to those of Protestants. But while religious belief forms no element in the claim to relief, due regard has been paid to the religious feelings and education of the Roman Catholics. Some attempt was made to obtain a separate allotment out of the fund, to be managed by a committee of Roman Catholic gentlemen, for the relief of Roman Catholic objects in Ireland, but this was resisted, and I certainly understood that the arrangements as they now stand satisfied all classes and every denomination of Christians. If the charge of unfair conduct in regard to relief from the Patriotic Fund should be persisted in, it may be found necessary to enter more particularly into facts in order to vindicate the conduct of the committee, which, up to this moment, has never been impeached.

I have the honour to be, Sir, your obedient servant,

Boyle Farm, Oct. 5. [1857]
ST. LEONARD'S.

Appendix E

NUMBER OF CHILDREN IN BOARDING INSTITUTIONS AT THE EXPENSE OF THE PATRIOTIC FUND, IN ADDITION TO THOSE IN THE ROYAL VICTORIA PATRIOTIC ASYLUM MARCH 1863

Barnet	353
Sailors' Orphan Girls' School, Hampstead	12
Royal Caledonian Asylum	27
London Orphan Asylum, Clapton	5
Infant Orphan Asylum, Wanstead	3
Convent of Our Lady of the Orphans, Norwood	39
St Mary's Orphanage, North Hyde	24
Bethesda Infant Orphan Asylum, Dublin	14
Kilmeague Orphan Asylum	6
Sisters of Mercy, Bagot Street, Dublin	6
St Clare's Orphanage, Harold's Cross	12
Mount Brown Orphanage, Dublin	16
St Patrick's Orphanage, Belfast	4
Royal British Female Orphan Asylum, Devonport	39
Devon and Cornwall Asylum, Plymouth	7
Birmingham Free Industrial School	88
Birmingham Blue-Coat School	1
Alresford Asylum, Hants	54
Portsmouth Seaman and Marines' Orphan House	28
Hants Orphan Asylum	5
Edinburgh Orphan Asylum	23
Perth School of Industry	2
Leicester Asylum	2
Tre-Wint, Hackney	4
Miscellaneous	9
Total	783

Appendix F

WILL OF DON FRANCISCO RODRIGUEZ

I, Francis Rodriguez, a Philippine Spaniard, widower by condition, and a Christian, being of sane and perfect judgement, but of broken health, and aware of the uncertainty of life, do resolve to make, and do make this my last and final Will and Testament, in the way and manner following, that is to say:

1st Item It is my will that my mortal remains be buried in the place called Loma, used for the burial-place of the English here, and that my funeral should be performed without luxury or pomp, or any unnecessary expense.

[Here the 2nd to 6th Items concern details of his assets]

7th Item It is my will that my houses be rented and occupied by English-men only; and if at any time my executors should decide on selling my houses, I desire that they be sold to English subjects; ...

8th Item It is my will that my moveable property and personal effects be sold after my decease in the way and to the persons that my executor may think proper, and they should apply the processed as I direct in the following clause, which is the ninth.

9th Item It is my will that, out of the proceeds of the revenues, rents or sales of my real and personal property, as also the sums existing in money, after paying the testimonial expenses incurred, the net balance should be applied to the succour of the families of English subjects wounded or dying in the wars; and if any individual who shall be considered entitled to this succour shall have no family, then it shall be paid to his nearest relation.

10th Item For the fulfilment of the aforesaid provision, my executors shall remit the said proceeds to some Society in England named by them; and my executors will take care that no one shall profit by this succour but such as are really indigent and necessitous.

[The 11th and 12th Items are concerned with his executors and in revoking any previous Will]

This Will was signed in the dwelling-house in the Collegion del Embariodero de San Gabriel, in Manila, 30th March 1857.

Appendix G

FIRST PAGE AND EXTRACTS FROM THE PATRIOTIC FUND ACT, 1867
ANNO TRICESIMO & TRICESIMO PRIMO

VICTORIAE REGINAE

C A P. XCVIII.
An Act to make better Provision for the Administration of the Patriotic Fund.

(12th *August* 1867.]

Whereas the Fund called the Patriotic Fund is administered under a Commission issued by Her Majesty the Queen under Her Royal Sign Manual, dated the Seventh Day of *October* One thousand eight hundred and fifty-four (in this Act referred to as the original Commission):

And whereas the Executive Committee of the Commissioners thereby appointed have appropriated Part of the Fund for the Erection and Endowment of a Girls School known as the Royal *Victoria* Patriotic Asylum, and have appropriated other Part of the Fund for the Endowment of a Boys School, and have appropriated other Parts of the Fund for the Purposes described in the Schedule to this Act, and the Appropriations aforesaid have been adopted by the Commissioners, and have been from Time to Time approved by Her Majesty, or been specified in the Reports of the Commissioners made to Her Majesty, and laid before the Houses of Parliament; and it is expedient that the Appropriations aforesaid be now confirmed by Parliament:

Some further specific provisions of the Act were as follows:
4. Such of the Acts of the Commissioners from time to time acting under the Original Commission as relate to the Application and Appropriation of the Patriotic Fund, and as have from time to time been approved by Her Majesty, or been specified in their Reports

made to Her Majesty and laid before the Houses of Parliament, shall be and be deemed to have been valid and binding and are hereby respectively confirmed.

5. It shall be lawful for Her Majesty, Her Heirs and Successors, from time to time, by Supplementary Commission under the Royal Sign Manual, directed to such Persons as to Her Majesty, Her Heirs or Successors, seem fit, to authorise and direct the Commissioners thereby constituted to apply the Patriotic Fund and the Income and Accumulations thereof, or any part or parts thereof, subject to the Appropriations aforesaid (in such Manner as any such Commission from time to time directs, or, in the absence of such Direction, or as far as such Direction, if any does not extend, as the Commissioners think fit), to the Purposes and in the Order following:

First, in Relief of Widows, and Maintenance, Education, Training, and Advancement of Children of Soldiers, Seamen, and Marines of Her Majesty's Army and Navy who lost their lives in Battle in the Late War with Russia, or in consequence of wounds received in or by or in consequence of other casualties sustained in or disease contracted in that war:

Secondly, in Maintenance, Education, Training, and Advancement of Children of Soldiers, Seamen, and Marines of Her Majesty's Army and Navy who have lost or hereafter lose their lives in Battle in any other War, or in consequence of Wounds received in or by or in consequence of other Casualties sustained in or Disease contracted in any other War:

Thirdly, in Maintenance, Education, Training, and Advancement of Children of other Soldiers, Seamen, and Marines of Her Majesty's Army and Navy who have lost or hereafter lose their lives in the Service of the Crown, or by or in consequence of Casualties sustained or Disease contracted in the Service of the Crown.

8. Any Supplementary Commission may direct that the First Lord of the Admiralty and the Secretary of State for War and the Paymaster-General shall be the Trustees of the Patriotic Fund, in trust to support the Appropriations in such Commission specified, and subject thereto in trust for any Purposes therein specified in conformity with the Provisions of this Act.

10. The Governor and Company of the Bank of England shall, when required by the Official Trustees of the Patriotic Fund, open and keep all Accounts of Annuities, Stocks, Funds, and Securities belonging to the Patriotic Fund, and standing in the Books of the said Governor and Company, as the Accounts of the First Lord of the Admiralty and the Secretary of State for War and the Paymaster-General for the time being (by their official Titles) ex parte the Patriotic Fund; and all Interest and Dividends accruing on such Annuities, Stocks, Funds and Securities shall, from time to time without any further Authority or

Appendices 215

Direction than this Act, be received by the said Governor and Company, and shall be carried by them to the Cash Account of the Paymaster-General in their Books.

There are four further paragraphs providing for the depositing of Securities and cash, and income and expenditure from the Patriotic Fund's funds, to be carried in the Paymaster-General's Account in the Bank of England's Books.

Further provisions of the Act are:
17. The Accounts of the Receipts and Expenditure of the Patriotic Fund shall be audited by such Persons and in such Manner as the Commissioners of Her Majesty's Treasury from time to time direct.
18. Any Supplementary Commission may authorise the Commissioners acting thereunder to employ a Secretary and Clerks at Salaries, the same, with other proper Expenses, to be paid out of the Patriotic Fund.
19. It shall be lawful for Her Majesty, Her Heirs, and Successors, from time to time, by Warrant under the Royal Sign Manual, on the submission of the Commissioners of the Patriotic Fund, to award to any Person who has been employed by the Commissioners of the Patriotic Fund, acting under the Original or any Supplementary Commission, such Pension or retiring Allowance as to Her Majesty, Her Heirs or Successors, seems fit, to be paid out of the Patriotic Fund.
20. All Rights of Nomination to Schools or Institutions possessed by the Commissioners acting under the Original Commission, or by the Executive Committee of those Commissioners and for the time being exercisable, and all Powers relative thereto, may be exercised by the Commissioners for the time being acting under any Supplementary Commission, or by the Executive Committee of these Commissions, as any Supplementary Commission directs: and in the event of the Original and any Supplementary Commission being superseded, or of the Discontinuance of the Commissioners under any Supplementary Commission, or of a Reduction of the Number of those Commissioners below Twelve, then the same may be exercised by such Person or Persons as Her Majesty, Her Heirs or Successors, from time to time, by Warrant under the Royal Sign Manual, is or are pleased to direct.
21. Any Supplementary Commission may direct that the Fund known as the Rodriguez Fund shall be applied for the same or the like purposes as the Patriotic Fund, and the same shall be applied accordingly.

Appendix H

SOME PROVISIONS OF THE SUPPLEMENTARY COMMISSION PATRIOTIC FUND 1868

As enacted generally in the Patriotic Fund Act, 1867 and more specifically in the Schedule to that Act, the Supplementary Commission included the following specific provisions:
- a. Confirmation of the actions of the Commissioners in founding the Royal Victoria Patriotic Asylum for Girls, and the endowment of a Boys' School:
- b. Retrospective approval of the Commissioners' investment:

  – £2,500 at 3% to provide, in perpetuity, for 13 boys at the Royal Naval and Military Free School at Devonport:

  – £2,500 at 3% to provide, in perpetuity, for 11 boys at the Royal Seamen and Marines' Orphan School, Portsea:

  – £25,000 to provide, in perpetuity, for 18 boys at Wellington College:

  – £1,000 towards building and £2,000 at 3% to provide, in perpetuity, for 5 widows of soldiers at the Cambridge Asylum, Kingston-on-Thames:

  – £5,000 to provide, in perpetuity, for 5 girls at the Royal Naval Female School, St Margaret's, Isleworth.

  – £8,000 to provide, in perpetuity, for 7 boys at the Royal Naval School, New Cross.

Otherwise the Supplementary Commission generally gave executive force to all the provisions of the Act of 1867.

Appendix J

APPEALS FOR TRANSVAAL WAR FUND BY THE DUKE OF CAMBRIDGE AND LORD MAYOR OF LONDON

ROYAL COMMISSION OF THE
PATRIOTIC FUND
53, CHARING CROSS,
October 21, 1899.

MY DEAR LORD MAYOR, – The engagement of our forces with the enemy in Natal yesterday resulted, so the telegrams state, in killed and wounded among our troops. This means soldiers' widows and orphans to be provided for. Parliament has placed upon the Patriotic Fund Commission the responsibility of appealing to the public for contributions for the benefit of widows, orphans, and other dependents of officers and men of her Majesty's Naval and Military Forces.

You my Lord Mayor, are yourself a Patriotic Fund Commissioner.

It is, therefore, my duty as President of the Patriotic Fund Commission to ask you to at once kindly open a Fund for the benefit of the widows, orphans, and other dependents of those who may lose their lives by wounds or disease in the war operations in South Africa.

Arrangements have already been made, as in the case of our recent war operations on the North-west frontier of India and similar operations in various parts of Africa, to afford immediate relief to the widows, and the War Office authorities will give us the earliest intimation of every casualty, so that the relief may be prompt.

I will only add that the object of the Fund will be to provide the widows with regular allowances during widowhood, according to their circumstances, and regular allowances to the children – boys under fourteen years of age and girls under sixteen years of age – as has been done by the Commission in the case of every widow and orphan of those who fell in the recent campaigns to which I have alluded. Such children as it may be desirable to place in orphanages will be placed in the Royal Victoria Patriotic Asylum for Girls or other available homes.

I have every confidence that the nation will respond liberally to this appeal if your Lordship will be so good as to open a Mansion House Fund, and thanking you in anticipation, allow me to remain, my dear Lord Mayor, yours very faithfully,

GEORGE
President.

The Right Hon. The Lord Mayor of the City of London.

THE MANSION HOUSE,
October 21, 1899.

TO THE EDITOR.

Sir, – In response to the accompanying appeal from H.R.H. the Duke of Cambridge, I have consented to open a Fund for the benefit of the widows, orphans, and other dependents of officers and men of her Majesty's Forces, who may unfortunately lose their lives in the war operations in South Africa.

At the same time I think it right to say that there are cognate objects for public philanthropy in connection with our gallant troops engaged in those operations. I allude to the soldiers themselves who may get disabled by wounds, and the wives and children separated at home here from their husbands and fathers by the exigencies of the war.

I therefore propose, in order to give the public the widest scope for their benevolence, that contributions for widows, orphans, and other dependents of those who may lose their lives shall be handed to the Patriotic Fund Commission for administration; those for sick and wounded while under treatment to the British Red Cross Society; those for soldiers disabled by wounds (for their benefit after they leave the service) to that excellent organization, Lloyd's Patriotic Fund, founded in the City in 1803; and those for wives and children separated, to the Soldiers' and Sailors' Families' Association. All contributions should, therefore, be clearly indicated by donors as follows: (1) Widows and Orphans; (2) Sick and Wounded; (3) Disabled Soldiers; (4) Wives and Children. Any not marked will be handed over for the benefit of widows and orphans, as it is upon the Duke of Cambridge's appeal that I ask the public to give liberally. As this is a national emergency, I would earnestly invite the cooperation and assistance of my brother Mayors, to whom I have already had occasion this year to apply for help in other matters.

Donations may be sent to the Secretary's Office, Mansion House, or to the Bank of England, to the credit of 'The Transvaal War Fund'. I would especially request donors to send their contributions in such a way that they may not be confused with the simultaneous appeal for the Transvaal Refugees' Fund, which, in spite of its great success, is still urgently in need of assistance.

I am, Sir, your obedient Servant,
JOHN VOCE MOORE, Lord Mayor.

Appendix K

DETAIL OF FINANCIAL HELP PROVIDED FOR AND BY THE ROYAL COMMISSION UP TO THE INCEPTION OF THE ROYAL PATRIOTIC FUND CORPORATION

Year of Origin	Name of Fund	Contributions to, or Amounts transferred to each Fund since its creation	Total Expenditure up to 31 Dec 1903	Balances in hand at 31 Dec 1903
		£ s. d.	£	£
1854	Patriotic Russian War / Royal Victoria Patriotic Asylum / Roman Catholic Orphans	1,471,375 10 8	2,688,978	298,507
1864	Rodriguez	6,212 15 10	5,839	15,225
1871	HMS 'Captain'	45,163 7 10	55,838	17,442
1878	HMS 'Eurydice'	19,000 0 0	18,441	9,424
1879	Royal Naval Relief	5,277 1 2	3,842	7,332
1879	Zulu War	27,360 17 2	25,560	18,790
1881	HMS 'Atalanta'	9,275 0 0	7,890	6,801
1883	Zervudachi	1,300 0 0	598	1,735
1884	Thurlow	506 8 5	131	757
1884	Soldiers' Effects	138,288 15 2	55,362	162,727
1886	County of Forfar	846 7 11	308	844
1888	Ashantee War	2,200 0 0	1,549	1,895
1890	Light Brigade	2,949 19 6	2,219	1,942
1893	HMS *Victoria*	73,265 12 11	35,762	54,669
1897	Patriotic General	190,085 19 11	51,266	171,572
1897	Indian Army Europeans' Effects	4,800 0 0	782	5,027
1899	Patriotic Army	2,390 0 7	277	2,354
1900	Transvaal War	492,820 3 3	123,326	408,800
1903	Indian Mutiny Relief	23,400 0 0	3,184	20,877
	TOTALS	2,516,518 0 4	3,081,152	1,206,720

Appendix L

LETTER FROM COLONEL YOUNG TO THE DUKE OF CONNAUGHT ASKING FOR A HIGHER SALARY

Sir, In the Report of the General Purposes Committee to be considered by the Executive Committee at Meeting on 1st May, over which Your Royal Highness will preside, there occurs the following passage relating to myself:

> '... Looking to the fact that all official salaries are drawn from philanthropic funds subscribed by the public, and that these funds are inadequate to meet the many deserving cases brought to our notice, we should not be justified in recommending any increase to Colonel Young's salary, although that salary may not be commensurate with his services and abilities.'

This decision was only communicated to me in the afternoon of the 24th instant, after the General Purposes Committee had closed their Meeting in the morning, and without my being given any opportunity of urging any grounds why such a decision should be adopted.

While I am greatly gratified by the high appreciation of my services which preceded this decision, I feel compelled to respectfully submit to Your Royal Highness and the Executive Committee that the decision, if carried into effect, will be *ultra vires* of paragraph 3 (b), Patriotic Fund Reorganisation Act, 1903, which ordered that the Royal Patriotic Fund Corporation should not, in its treatment of me in regard to salary, place me in a worse position than if the Act had not been passed.

That I have been, ever since the dissolution of the Patriotic Fund Commission on 31st December, 1903, in a worse position as regards salary than if the Patriotic Fund Reorganisation Act, 1903, had not been passed, I shall show cannot be gainsaid, for the Patriotic Fund Commissioners at a meeting held 9th December, 1903, to consider my position, if I agreed to accept transfer to the Royal Patriotic Fund Corporation, unanimously resolved, on the motion of Lord Davey, seconded by the Accountant-General of the Army:

> 'That Colonel Young's duties having been largely increased by the administration of the Transvaal War Fund, if this Commission had continued to be entrusted with its present duties the Commissioners

Appendices

would undoubtedly have recommended Colonel Young to His Majesty's consideration for a substantial increase to his salary.'

and the Commissioners awarded me, unasked £400 in respect of the years 1901, 1902, and 1903, as evidence of what they considered the increase to my salary should be.

I had been previously appealed to by a special Committee presided over by Lord Davey to accept transfer to the Royal Patriotic Fund Corporation as a matter of public duty, as the Commissioners felt that I was the only individual who had been connected with the Patriotic Funds who, under them, had mastered and successfully managed the Funds.

Lord Davey, in handing me the original draft in his own handwriting of the Resolution above quoted, told me any Judge would know what it meant, and would give a just interpretation to it.

I accordingly accepted, as a public duty, transfer to the Royal Patriotic Fund Corporation depending upon the provisions:

1. Of paragraph 3 (b) Patriotic Fund Reorganisation Act, 1903, that I should not be in a worse position in regard to salary, tenure of office, and superannuation allowance than if the Act had not been passed;
2. Of the Resolution of the Commissioners, 9th December, 1903, recording what my position in regard to salary, &c., would have been if the Act of 1903 had not been passed;
3. Of Royal Warrant for Office Establishment, 15th March, 1893, giving me the right to extra remuneration for extra work;

and upon the recognition recorded by the Patriotic Fund Commissioners of exceptional services rendered by me in many ways beyond the ordinary duties of a Secretary between 1887 and 1903.

Now the General Purposes Committee come along and by a stroke of the pen would place me in a far worse position than if the Act of 1903 had not been passed.

With all respect I cannot accept that their decision is other than *ultra vires*, and I could not accept in any case that the official salaries have any relation to any question of the inadequacy of the Funds 'to meet the many deserving cases brought to our notice'.

The funds would be inadequate in any case to meet such cases, for it would require a far larger amount than the public has shown any disposition to provide for such cases, which are cases, for the most part, of widows of men dying long after having left the Navy and Army, and who have no direct claims on any of the Funds administered by the Corporation.

The widows entitled to relief from the Patriotic Funds raised by Public subscription are all provided for adequately, and certainly none has had to be refused adequate provision since I have been Secretary because of the amount of the official salaries. On the contrary, all these have gained largely as the result of my personal initiative in management of their Funds.

What would be true to state, would be that all the official salaries have from the very year I became Secretary, 1887, been drawn from funds obtained as the result of financial and administrative reforms initiated solely by myself between the year and 1891.

The proof of this is ready to hand in a printed Statement which I was directed to make of the financial results of my reforms, in which the following paragraph occurs:

'Money gains, to say nothing of increased administrative and financial efficiency, resulted from the reforms introduced since 1887, as follows:

	£	s.	d.
for the year 1887 ...	119	19	10
1888 ...	741	13	8
1889 ...	1,033	9	4
1890 ...	1,443	16	2
1891 ...	1,705	6	8
	£5,044	5	8

or £233 more than the total cost, £4,808 5s. 6d., of the Office Establishment (including my own salary) for the same period.'

These gains were verified by the Executive and Finance Committee of the Patriotic Fund, and constituted the basis of the scheme for the Office Establishment for which I at the same time obtained approval under the Royal Sign Manual.

These gains have continued to be reaped annually, more or less in amount, ever since as a result of my reforms, and these facts show that I have literally poured thousands of pounds into the treasury for the relief of our widows and orphans, more than I have taken out or could possibly take out in future for my own salary.

These gains, moreover, could not be gained by my successor for he would have no opportunity of initiating such gains, inasmuch as he would find a house in order, up-to-date in financial, administrative, and executive management.

It remains for me, however, to show how unjust the decision of the General Purposes Committee would be in depriving me of all practical recognition for the immense increase in my duties and responsibilities which has taken place since my salary was fixed at £750 in 1898, for my then duties and responsibilities.

Since then there have been added:

The Transvaal War Fund, 1899;

The Indian Mutiny Fund, 1903;

and the number of cases accepted for relief from the

Patriotic General Fund;

Rodriguez Fund;

Royal Naval Relief Fund; and

Soldiers' Effect Fund;

have increased enormously in proportion to the number accepted prior to 1900.

This consequent increase of responsibility and work is easily proved by the increase in the number of letters received and respectively in 1898, the

Appendices

year before the Transvaal War – 3,810, and the number received in 1906 – 10,000; and by the number of 'cases' accepted for relief in the 45 years, 1854 to 1899 – 6,805, and the number accepted in the 4 years, 1900 to 1903 – 7,431.

The cost of management and distribution in relief

	per cent of expenditure.
in 1887, when I was appointed Secretary was ...	£6.34
in 1898 it had fallen to ...	£4.74
in 1906 it was only ...	£3.97

and it should be borne in mind that the allowances from the Transvaal War Fund and Soldiers' Effects Fund run, in hundreds of cases, from only such small allowances as 1s. to 2s. or 3s. a week in supplement of Army Pensions in the one case and in the other from 1s. 6d. to 4s. a week, whereas the allowances in 1898 ranged from 5s. to 12s. a week. Thus it follows that if the expenditure in 1906 had been for allowances at the rates in 1898, the cost of management in 1906 would have worked out at far less than £3.97.

In conclusion, I have to state that the Patriotic Fund Commissioners made it clear that they did not consider that my salary adequately recognised the special public services I gave in connection with the administration of funds for the benefit of Sailors' and Soldiers' Widows and orphans, for they placed on their Minutes that my services were deserving of recognition by an Honour, and His Royal Highness the President accordingly recommended me in 1896 to be so honoured, the recommendation being repeated twice afterwards, in 1902 and 1903.

Therefore if the Executive Committee feel any doubts about the just and fair interpretation of my rights as I have submitted them herein, I beg that the just and fair interpretation of my rights under the Act of 1903, the Minute of the Royal Commission, 9th December, 1903, and the Royal Warrant for the Office Establishment, 15th March, 1893, in regard to extra remuneration for extra work, may be referred to arbitration by a competent impartial authority, such as a Judge of the High Court of Justice, for although the action of the General Purposes Committee has forced me either to defend or abandon what I conceive to be my clear rights, I am quite as anxious as they are that what is right and can be justified only shall be done.

I have the honour to be,
Sir,
Your Royal Highness's
Most obedient humble Servant,
(Signed) J. S. YOUNG, Colonel.
Secretary
Royal Patriotic Fund Corporation.

Field Marshal His Royal Highness,
The DUKE OF CONNAUGHT, K.G.,
President
Royal Patriotic Fund Corporation.

Appendix M

Unto The King's Most Excellent Majesty

MAY IT PLEASE YOUR MAJESTY,

We, the Corporation of the Royal Patriotic Fund, desire to express our profound sorrow at the great loss we, in common with all Your Majesty's subjects throughout the Empire, have sustained by the death of our late beloved and revered Sovereign King Edward VII, and we humbly beg to tender to Your Majesty, to Her Majesty Queen Mary, to Her Majesty Queen Alexandra, and all the Royal Family, our deepest sympathy in your sad bereavement.

His late Majesty and Her Majesty Queen Alexandra always showed the kindliest interest and sympathy in the welfare of the widows and orphans of their sailors and soldiers, and this was recently evinced by their gracious attendance on July 24th, 1907, at the Royal Victoria Patriotic Asylum on the occasion of the commemoration of the Jubilee of that Institution, founded in 1857 by Her late Majesty Queen Victoria for the benefit of orphan daughters of sailors, soldiers, and marines.

In compliance with His late Majesty's command we have regularly submitted our Annual Report for His Majesty's perusal and information, and we know that he followed with sympathetic attention the work of the Corporation.

We beg further most respectfully to tender to Your Majesty our dutiful homage on your Accession to the Throne, with our earnest prayer that Your Majesty and Her Majesty Queen Mary may under God's Providence be spared for many years to enjoy a happy and prosperous Reign.

ARTHUR, *President.*
W. HAYES FISHER, *Vice-President and Chairman, Executive Committee.*
E. A. STANTON, *Major, Secretary.*

Appendix N

MEMBERS OF THE STATUTORY COMMITTEE OF THE ROYAL PATRIOTIC FUND CORPORATION – UNDER THE NAVAL AND MILITARY WAR PENSIONS ACT, 1915

Comprising 12 Crown Nominees, 6 Royal Patriotic Fund Nominees, 2 SSAFA Nominees, 7 Government Nominees.

HRH The Prince of Wales, KG Chairman
Cyril Jackson Esq. Vice-Chairman
The Rt Hon. A J Balfour, MP 1st Lord of the Admiralty
Field Marshal the Rt Hon
   Earl Kitchener of Khartoum. Secretary of State for War
The Rt Hon. Walter H Long, MP President of the Local Government Board
The Rt Hon. W Hayes Fisher, MP*
B B Cubitt, Esq, CB*
Admiral Sir Wilmot Fawkes, GCB, KCVO*
J E Rayner Esq*
The Countess Roberts*
Mrs McKenna*
Sir W Ryland Adkins, MP
A A Allen Esq, MP
The Rt Hon. G N Barnes, MP
C M Bruce Esq
Sir Henry Craik, KCB, MP
Miss Durham
H Gosling Esq, JP
The Marchioness of Lansdowne
Major-General Sir Ivor Herbert, Bt, CB, CMG, MP
Sir R MacLeod, KCB
The Countess of March
C J Mather Esq, KC
C H O'Conor Esq
Sir S B Provis, KCB
Lieutenant-Colonel Sir Donald Robertson, KCSI
Mrs Sidney Webb

* Representing the Royal Patriotic Fund Corporation.

Appendix O

Unto The King's Most Excellent Majesty

MAY IT PLEASE YOUR MAJESTY,

We, the Corporation of the Royal Patriotic Fund, desire to express our profound sorrow at the great loss that we, in common with all Your Majesty's subjects throughout the Empire, have sustained by the death of our late beloved and revered Sovereign King George V, and we humbly beg to tender to Your Majesty, to Her Majesty Queen Mary and to all the Royal Family, our deepest sympathy in this sad bereavement.

His late Majesty and Her Majesty Queen Mary always showed great interest and sympathy in the welfare of the widows and orphans of all ranks of the Royal Navy, Army and Royal Air Force, and in compliance with His late Majesty's command we have each year submitted our Annual Report to His Majesty knowing that the work of the Corporation was followed with sympathetic attention.

We beg further most respectfully to tender our dutiful homage on Your Majesty's accession to the Throne, with our earnest prayer that Your Majesty may under God's Providence be spared for many years to enjoy a happy and prosperous Reign.

ARTHUR, *President*,
BERTRAM B. CUBITT, *Vice-President
and Chairman, Executive Committee*,
F.G. MAUGHAN, *Lt.-Colonel, Secretary*.

BUCKINGHAM PALACE.
3rd February, 1936.

SIR,

The King will be glad if you will convey to His Royal Highness, the President, and the Members of the Corporation of the Royal Patriotic Fund His Majesty's sincere thanks for their kind expression of sympathy in his sorrow.

The King, who greatly appreciates their good wishes, will follow the progress of the Fund, as his beloved Father did, with unfailing interest and solicitude.

I am, Sir,
Your obedient Servant,
WIGRAM.

To SIR BERTRAM CUBITT, K.C.B.,
*Vice-President and Chairman, Executive Committee,
Royal Patriotic Fund Corporation.*

Appendix P

FROM *THE TIMES* 11th NOVEMBER 1939
WAR CHARITIES

THE ROYAL PATRIOTIC FUND

TO THE EDITOR OF THE TIMES

Sir,– The excellent letter from Sir Ian Fraser on the above subject in your issue of November 3 encourages me to draw attention to the fact that there is already in existence the Royal Patriotic Fund Corporation created by Act of Parliament, which for 85 years has administered funds raised for the relief of widows and orphans of sailors and soldiers dying in or by war, and was intended where possible to coordinate such funds. This corporation, which is under the presidency of H.R.H. the Duke of Connaught, having been made a statutory body in 1903 by Act of Parliament, is surely an organization which could be trusted to administer the necessary relief of widows, orphans, and other dependents by the present war. Their constitution, embodying every lord lieutenant, chairman of county council, lord mayor and mayor, lord provost and provost in the kingdom, apart from eight members appointed by the Government and numerous representatives of charitable bodies, should satisfy the most sceptical that the funds handed over to them will be properly used for the purpose for which they are given.

The defect of local appeals lies in the fact that donors somewhat naturally prefer to see their gifts spent on local cases, often in terms too generous. The inevitable result is that after a few years local funds become exhausted and the widows find the assistance given to them fails. As Patriotic funds are administered on actuarial bases it is possible for grants to be continued to widows and other dependents until they become eligible for old-age pension. If only the administrators of local funds could be got to realize that by entrusting a portion of their funds to the Royal Patriotic Fund Corporation they would ensure that, even if their own funds fail, their beneficiaries would be assisted until they become eligible for State pensions.

The corporation has the advantage of securing uniformity of treatment and saving in considerable overhead charges of numerous small funds.

I am your obedient servant,

FITZ ALAN of DERWENT
28, Sackville Street, W.1., Nov. 8.

Appendix Q

FROM *THE TIMES* 15TH NOVEMBER 1939

HELP FOR SOLDIERS' WIDOWS

FUND FOR RELIEF OF SPECIAL DISTRESS

An appeal for funds is made by the Royal Patriotic Fund Corporation which, as was pointed out by Lord FitzAlan in a letter published in *The Times* on Saturday, has for 85 years administered funds raised for the relief of war widows and orphans, and was intended where possible to coordinate such funds. The appeal is made because it is understood that the Lord Mayor's Fund is to be devoted entirely to the Order of St. John and the Red Cross, and cannot be shared by any other organization.

During the last war the corporation distributed £409,000 out of the National Relief Fund to 170,701 widows, children and other dependents to assist them while their Government pensions were being adjusted. Without any appeal voluntary contributions totalling £44,500 were received, which provided a fund for widows and dependents who failed to obtain pensions and for others in need who are still being assisted.

Money is now required to assist those who for some reason fail to qualify for pensions and whose need is as great as that of others. It is also required to provide grants for cases of sickness, rents in arrear through unemployment, clothing, coal, special surgical appliances &c., for education and apprenticeship fees of children of officers, non-commissioned officers and men – often £75 a year for three years – and for allowances in special cases over and above pensions.

The address of the Royal Patriotic Fund Corporation is 28, Sackville Street, London, W.1.

Appendix R

THE COMBINING OF FUNDS – MARCH 1920

1. As a result of the Actuarial Valuation of Funds carried out for the Finance Committee in February 1920, surplus funds remained available to meet foreseeable commitments in eleven Funds, namely:

    Patriotic (Russian War) Fund
    Zulu War Fund
    Rodriguez Fund
    Royal Naval Relief Fund
    Patriotic General Fund
    Indian Army (Europeans') Effects Fund
    Patriotic Army Fund
    Transvaal War Fund
    Special Army and Navy Fund
    Zervudachi Fund
    Special Navy Fund

   Funds with insufficient resources to meet planned commitments, however, were:

    'Captain' Fund
    'Eurydice' Fund
    'Atalanta' Fund
    Ashantee War Fund
    'Victoria' Fund
    Indian Mutiny Fund
    Soldiers' Effects Fund

2. It was considered logical and fair that the way to redress this imbalance of Funds would be to combine certain Funds, and that prime candidates for this would be those Funds which had previously shared resources. Transfers of surplus resources had taken place from time to time, as follows:

From	£	To
(1) Patriotic (Russian War) Fund	110,184 in 1897	Patriotic General Fund
Patriotic (Russian War) Fund	17,355 in 1911	Special Army & Navy Fund
(2) 'Captain' Fund	13,484 in 1900/1903	Patriotic General Fund
'Captain' Fund	2,500 in 1911	Special Army & Navy Fund
(3) 'Eurydice' Fund	4,800 in 1900/1903	Patriotic General Fund
'Eurydice' Fund	1,561 in 1911	Special Army & Navy Fund
(4) Zulu War Fund	7,945 in 1899/1903	Patriotic General Fund
Zulu War Fund	2,479 in 1911	Special Army & Navy Fund
(5) 'Atalanta' Fund	1,200 in 1903	Patriotic General Fund
'Atalanta' Fund	1,616 in 1911	Special Army & Navy Fund
(6) 'Victoria' Fund	19,130 in 1911	Special Navy Fund

3. It was concluded that:
   (a) Because of these earlier links the *Patriotic General Fund* should absorb:

   The Patriotic Russian War Fund
   The 'Captain' Fund
   The 'Eurydice' Fund
   The Zulu War Fund
   The 'Atalanta' Fund

   (b) Because the Ashantee War Fund, the Patriotic Army Fund and the Patriotic General Fund had kindred purposes and were not subject to special Trusts, they should be combined in the *Patriotic General Fund*.
   (c) When the Royal Commissioners accepted the administration of the Indian Mutiny Relief Fund they undertook to provide for the continued payment of existing allowances if necessary making up any deficiencies from other Funds, this Fund should also be combined with the *Patriotic General Fund*.
   (d) The Rodriguez Fund could also be combined with the *Patriotic General Fund* as legal opinion was that this would be in accordance with the Acts regulating the Royal Commissioners prior to the Corporation being constituted.
   (e) The 'Victoria' Fund should be combined with the *Special Navy Fund* as it had contributed towards it.
   (f) The Special Navy Fund should combine with the *Royal Naval Relief Fund* as they both had kindred purposes and were not subject to special Trusts.
3. The Zervudachi Fund had earlier been combined with the *Special Army and Navy Fund*.
4. Funds with special Trusts attached to them had, of necessity, to be kept apart. These were:

   The Indian Army (Europeans') Effects Fund
   The Transvaal War Fund
   The Light Brigade Fund (soon after exhausted)

5. The outcome of this combining of Funds in 1920 was that (omitting the School

Appendices

Funds) from 1920 the Corporation operated the following separate Funds:

The Patriotic General Fund
The Soldiers' Effects Fund
The Indian Army (Europeans') Effects Fund
The Royal Naval Relief Fund
The Special Army and Navy Fund
The Transvaal War Fund
The Roman Catholic Orphans' Fund
The European War Fund

Appendix S

GENERAL POLICY AND PRINCIPLES OF ADMINISTRATION AGREED UPON AS THE OUTCOME OF THE REVIEW OF POLICY ON THE ISSUE OF ALLOWANCES AND EXPENDITURE OF FUNDS APRIL 1949

1. The policy is to establish a standard of adequate relief according to the circumstances of the beneficiaries, based upon the encouragement in capable beneficiaries of a spirit of self-dependence instead of entire dependence upon a Fund, while increasing the provision in advancing age or in the event of premature infirmity or disability.
2. The funds of the Corporation, subject to any special Trust relating to any part thereof; are to be administered in accordance with the following guiding principles:
    - (a) *Widows and children (See Note A)*
      Marriage should have taken place before final expiration of service with the colours, though exceptions may be made in the following instances, where in each case marriage has taken place shortly after discharge (See Note D):
    - (i) Cases of long (See Note B) or distinguished (See Note C) service.
    - (ii) Cases where the officer or man concerned has been in receipt of a disability rate of retired pay or a disability pension.
    - (b) *Dependants*
      Should be limited to near relatives (mothers, sisters, fathers, brothers), and it should be conditional that they had, or would have, been bona-fide dependants.
    - (c) Assessment of awards should be primarily based on the need, and should take into account:
      (1) length of service, active service, distinctions, rank, etc., and also whether death was attributable to service, and
      (2) the circumstances of the applicant: ability to earn, health, special commitments, etc.
    - (d) Allowances should be restricted to those including children who by family ties, age, or infirmity, are not capable of earning a sufficient income in conjunction with the State pensions or allowances to which they are entitled.

Appendices

(e) Awards of grants and allowances should be made additional to, and not in substitution of, any State aid to which applicant may be entitled. The National Assistance Board scale, where applicable, should be used as a guide to the minimum income which the applicant should receive.

(f) The proportion of the total income of the Corporation's funds to be spent on officer cases should be determined from time to time in relation to circumstances.

Note A   Sons and daughters are technically children at any age.

Note B   Long Service is for this purpose held to constitute not less than 14 years service.

Note C   Distinguished service is held to constitute the award of a decoration, a mention in despatches, or any special commendation.

Note D   The term 'shortly after discharge' is intended normally to mean not more than two years after discharge.

Appendix T

Presidents	Chairmen of Executive Committee and Vice-Presidents
1854-1861 Field Marshal HRH The Prince Consort KG	1854-1856 The Rt Hon Lord St Leonards
1861-1864 His Grace The Duke of Newcastle*	1856-1863 Rear-Admiral Lord Colchester
1864-1865 His Grace The Duke of Somerset, KG*	1863-1867 The Rt Hon Henry Lowry Corry, MP
1865-1867 His Grace, The Duke of Wellington, KG*	1867-1874 General the Honourable James Lindsay
1868-1903 Field Marshal HRH The Duke of Cambridge, KG	1875-1878 The Rt Hon Lord Hampton, GCB
	1878-1880 Admiral W A Baillie Hamilton
	1881-1903 The Rt Hon The Earl Nelson
1904-1942 Field Marshal HRH The Duke of Connaught, KG, KT, KP	1904-1906 The Rt Hon The Earl of Dartmouth
	1906-1920 The Rt Hon W Hayes Fisher, MP (from 1917 became Lord Downham of Fulham)
	1921-1929 Lieutenant-General the Hon. Sir Frederick Stopford, KCB, KCMG, KCVO
	1930-1942 Sir Bertram Cubitt, KCB, DL, JP
1942-1947 The Rt Hon The Earl of Harewood KG, GCVO, TD	1943-1945 Colonel Sir Arthur Erskin, GCVO, DSO
1947-1973 Field Marshal HRH The Duke of Gloucester, KG.	1946-1948 General Sir Harry Knox, KCB, DSO
	1949-1953 General Sir John Brind, KCB, KBE, CMG, DSO
	1954-1962 General Sir John Crocker, GCB, KBE, DSO, MC
	1963-1973 General Sir Charles Keightley, GCB, CBE, DSO
1973-1979 HRH Princess Alexandra of Kent	1974-1983 General Sir Geoffrey Musson, GCB, CBE, DSO
1979 to Present HRH Prince Michael of Kent	1984-1988 General Sir Michael Gow, GCB
	1988-1989 General Sir Thomas Morony, KCB, OBE
	1989 to Present General Sir Martin Farndale, KCB
* Acting – Pending a Permanent Appointment by H M Queen	

Honorary Secretaries
and
Secretaries

1854-1866 Captain E Gardiner Fishbourne†
(Later Secretary)
Captain J H Lefroy, RA†
(Later Major, Colonel and Brigadier-General)
1867-1868 Brigadier-General J H Lefroy – Honorary Secretary
(Later member of Executive and General)
1868-1886 W H Mugford (Paymaster RN) – Secretary
1887-1909 Colonel J S Young – Secretary (Later Colonel Sir John Young)
1910-1914 Major E A Stanton, CMG (Later Colonel and Member of Executive Committee) Governor of Bermuda
1914-1921 Lieutenant-Colonel A C E Welby (Later Lt. Col Sir Alfred Welby)
1921-1938 Lieutenant-Colonel F G Maughan, DSO
1938-1946 Lieutenant-Colonel M U Manly
1946-1948 Major G E B Fawcett, MC
1948-1963 Major-General RRH Nalder CB OBE

1964-1979 Brigadier H E Boulter, CBE, DSO

1979-1990 Brigadier D C Blomfield-Smith, MBE

1990 to Present
  Brigadier T G Williams, CBE

† Joint Honorary Secretaries

Index

Abbot-Anderson, Lady, 146
Abel Smith, John, 39, 40, 42
Aberdeen, Lord, 11
Acts of Parliament
   1866 – Patriotic Fund, 44
   1867 – Patriotic Fund, 44–5, 49, 51, Appendix G
   1881 – Patriotic Fund, 57, 59
   1899 – Patriotic Fund, 86
   1903 – Patriotic Fund Reorganisation, 89, 178
   1915 – Naval and Military War Pensions etc, 118
   1916 – Ministry of Pensions, 123
   1917 – Nsaval and Military War Pensions etc (Transfer of Powers), 123
   1925 – Trustee Investment, 157
   1929 – Contributory Pensions, 153
   1940 – Old Age and Widows Pensions, 153
   1940 – War Charities, 149
   1950 – Royal Patriotic Fund Corporation, 156, 158
   1960 – Charities, 170
   1961 – Trustee Investment, 168, 173
Actuarial Calculations 1858/68, 45–7
Actuarial Calculations 1909, 106
Actuaries, Institute of, 86–7, 93, 99, 105, 127, 165, 194
Actuary of the National Debt, 45–7, 49, 55
Adeane, Hon. Mrs, 143
Aden, 191
Admiralty, 49, 51–2, 59–60, 90
Admiralty, First Lord of, 45, 59, 73, 77
Afghan Wars, 64
Air Ministry, 128
Albert, Prince, 11, 29, 39, 42, 43
Alcock, Samuel, 10, 13
Alexandra, Princess, 180
Alexandria, 64
Alma, River, 5, 9, 16
Annuities, 17, 47
Applications for Help, 62, 63
Archbishop of Dublin, 26, 32–4
Ardingly, St Saviour's Grammar School, 60
Army Benevolent Fund, 150, 166, 172, 190
'Army Compassionate Fund', 102–3
Ashantee (Ashanti), War, 53–4
Ashcroft, F.N., 115
Atalanta, HMS, 55, 100
Audit Office, 48, 188
Awdry, Sir Richard, 94
Aylmer, Lt. Gen. Sir Fenton, 134

Baedeker, 145
Balaclava (Balaklava), 5, 16
Balaclava (Light Brigade) Fund, 62, 128, 131
Baldwin, Stanley, 127
Balfour, A.J., 73, 76, 80–1, 121
Balfour, Lord (of Burleigh), 96
Balloon Centre, No. 2 RAF, 144
Baltic Sea, 7
Bank of England, 18, 45, 88, 90, 96, 97
Barnett, Charlotte, 35–9
Bath, 144–5
Bayley, T., 67, 69, 73, 75
Beatrice, Princess, 137
Bedwell Park, 149, 151, 179
Belgium, 113
Bengal, 49
Bermuda, 55
Beveridge Report, 154–5, 190
'Big Bang', 188
Black Sea, 6–7
Bloemfontein, 74
Boer War(s), 60, 80, 88, 94, 98, 102
Borneo, 191
Botha, General Louis, 67
Bowden-Smith, Admiral Sir Nathaniel, 99
Braithwaite, General Sir Walter, 134
Brind, General Sir John, 164
British Expeditionary Force (BEF) (1914), 114
British Legion (later Royal British Legion), 171, 190
British South Africa Company, 67
Brownrigg, Admiral Sir Studholme, 142
Buller, General Sir Redvers, 67, 74
Burgoyne, General, 11
Burnaby, Major-General, 83

Cambridge, Duke of, 40–2, 45, 80–1, 94
Cambridge Gate, 183
Captain, HMS, 51–3, 100
Cardigan, Lord, 184
Cardwell, Secretary of State (for War), 52
Carew, Miss Elizabeth, 132
Casualties, 5 and *passim*
Cazenove, Philip, 88
Cazenove & Co., 188, 194
'Central Council of Service Organisations', 150
Chacksfield, Air Vice-Marshal Sir Bernard, 179
Chairmen of County Councils, 101
Chancellor of the Exchequer, 79, 105, 121
Chancery, 25, 88

Index

Chamberlain, Joseph, 74
Chaplain, School, 28, 35–7, 39, 40
Charing Cross, 63, 100, 189
Charity Commission(ers), 111, 162, 165, 173, 180, 190
Charter, 170, 181
Chelmsford, Lord, 45, 60, 77
Chichester, Earl of, 45
Chief of the Imperial General Staff, 102
Childers, Secretary of State (for War), 59
China, 49
Clavell, Miss, 30
Colchester, Lord, 32, 37, 39
Colenso, 74
Commandos, 75
Commission, Royal, 5 and *passim*, Appendix K
Commissions, Supplementary, 1868, 45–6, 67, Appendix H
Commissions, Supplementary 1875, 52
Commissions, Supplementary 1897, 73
Commissioners, 12 and *passim*
Commissioners in Aid, 12, Appendix B
Connaught, Duke of, 95, 95, 103, 139, 145
Cook, Revd F.C., 27, Appendix C
Corry, H.C. Lowry, 37
Council of the Royal Patriotic Fund Corporation, 90, 99, 101, 104, 165, 181–2
Cox & Co, 54
Crimea, 8 and *passim*
Crimean War, 5 and *passim*
Cubitt, B.B. (later Sir Bernard), 120, 144–6
'Cwm Wennol', 143

Dalhous, Earl of, 45
Dardanelles, 6
Dartmouth, Earl of, 95
Daughters of Army Officers, School for, 44, 185
Davey, Lord, 78
Defence, Ministry of, 175, 194
De Grey, Earl, 45
De La Rey, General Koos, 67
Dependants, 153 and *passim*, 176
Derby, Earl of, 96, 104
Devonport, 71, 108
Devonshire, Duke of, 96, 104
De Wet, General Christiaan, 67
Disraeli, Benjamin, 45
Downham, Lord (of Fulham), 125, 129
Drivers, Jones & Co, 149
'Duke of Kent School', 185
Dunstans, St, 161
Durban, 74

East Barnet Grammar School, 177
'Edgar, HMS, 136
Education, Ministry of, 178
Edward, Prince of Saxe-Weimar, 82
Egyptian and Sudanese Campaign, 64
'Egyptian War Fund', 65
Eire, 177
Elizabeth, Princess, 143
'Elm Grove', 143
'European War', 113, 118, 122, 128, 156, 165
'European War (Private Donations) Fund', 115, 118, 123
Eurydice, HMS, 53, 100

Executive (and Finance) Committee, 16–19, 20 and *passim*
Expeditionary Force (1854), 7, 8, 9

Fass, Sir Ernest, 142
'Falklands War', 191
Fawkes, Admiral Sir Wilmot, 120
Fermoy, Lord, 45
Field, Captain, RN, 52
Field, Admiral, MP, 76
Finance Committee, 13 and *passim*
Finance for Girls' School, 23
Financial Times, The, 191, 192
Finlaison, Alexander Glen, 45–7, 61
Finlaison, Alexander John, 57, 87
Finnis, Alderman, 88
'First of June Appeal', 172
Fishbourne, Captain, RN, 13, 40, 61
Fitzalan of Derwent, Lord, 141, Appendix P. Appendix Q
Forfar, County of, Fund, 85
France, 6, 101, 114
Fraser, Sir Ian, 141, 149, 161–2

Galbraith, Commandzer, MP, 158–9
Geary, Colonel (Chairman, Soldiers' and Sailors' Help Society), 195
General Purposes Committee, 96, 99, 104, 127
Germany, 113, 144
Gibbs, Frederick W., 61
'Gift Aid', 191
Gildea, Colonel James (later Sir James), 54, 64, 70–1, 83, 99, 129, 195
Gilt-edged Securities, 18, 157–8, 169
Gladstone, William, 45
Gloucester, Duke of, 152, 180
Gloucester Gate, 188
Gold Coast Relief Fund, 54
Golden Cross House, 188
Gordon Boys' School (later Gordon School), 185
Governesses, 28
Government Broker (Mullens & Co), 188, 194
Gow, General Sir Michael, 196
'Great War' (1914–18), 126
'Greek White Cross Fund', 129
Greenwich Hospital, 136, 172, 190
Greenwich Schools, 24
Grey, Earl, 42, 45
Guardians, Boards of, 153–4

Haldane, Lord, 103
Hardwicke, Earl of, 45
Harewood, Earl of, 145, 152
Hartington, Marquis of, 42
Harvey (Clerk), 47
Hatfield, 149
Hatfield Grammar School, 177
Hawkins, Rhode, 27
Hayes Fisher, W., 94, 96, 103, 105, 115–20
Hean Castle, 143
Henderson, James Stewart, 142
Henn Collins Committee, 76–9, 82, 195
Henn Collins, Lord Justice, 76, 77
Herbert, Sidney, 11
Hertfordshire County Council, 151
Hibbert, Sir J.T., 68
Higham, C.D. (President of the Institute of

Actuaries), 87–8
High Court, Application to, 157
Hodge, General Sir Edward, 61
Hussars, 13th, 131

'Imperial War Fund', 65
'Incorporated Soldiers' and Sailors' Help Society' (later 'Soldiers' and Sailors' Help Society'), 131, 195
India, 177
'Indian Army (European) Effects Fund', 85, 128
Indian Mutiny, 49
Indian Mutiny Relief Fund, 88, 188
Inspector of Schools, 27, Appendix C
Institute of Actuaries, 86–7, 93, 99, 105, 127, 165, 194
Investment Income, 168
Investment Policy, 169, 171, 173–4
Investment Ranges, 169, 173
'Isandlwana and Rorke's Drift Fund', 54
Italy, 112, 147
Iveagh, Lord, 96

Jackson, Cyril, 121–2
James, Lord of Hereford, 81
Jameson, Dr L.S., 67
'Jameson Raikd', 67, 68
'Jutland Battle', 123

Kearley, H.E., 67, 68, 73, 75, 82, 94, 98–99, 107, 108
Keightley, General Sir Charles, 182
Kelly-Kenny, Lieutenant-General Sir Thomas, 94, 107
Kensington Palace, 137
Kimberley, 74
King Edward VII, 94, 109, Appendix M
King George V, 136, 187, Appendix O
King George VI, 152, 187
'King George's Fund for Sailors', 136, 142, 172, 190
'King's Fund (1940)', 160, 187
Kirkby, Revd William, 30
Kitchener, General (later Field Marshal) Lord, 67, 121
'Kitchener's Army', 117
Kneller Hall, 28
Korean War, 163
Kruger, Paul, 60, 67, 74

Ladbrooke Primary School, 177
Ladysmith, 74
Ladies Committee, 36–7, 39
Lauderdale, Earl of, 45
Laver Gift, Robert and Ella, 166–7
Lefroy, Captain J.H. (later Lt. Col, Col, Brig.-Gen., Maj.-Gen., Lt.-Gen. and General Sir Henry, 61
'Life Certificates', 63–4, 129
Light Brigade, 5, 62
'Lime Grove', Putney, 29, 30
Lindley, Miss Julia, 137
Lloyds' Patriotic Fund, 11, 70, 131, 190
Local Government Boards, 119
London County Council, 111, 115, 150, 157
London General Hospital, No. 3, 116
Lord Mayor of Liverpool, 121
Lord Mayor of London, 9, 10, 55, 75, 88, 95–7, 114, 140–1

Lord Mayors, 89, 92, 99
Lord Lieutenants, 12, 89, 92–3, 95, 98–9
Lord Provosts, 89, 92, 99
Ludendorff, General, 124
Lyveden, Lord, 45

Mafeking, 74
Magersfontein, 74
Maiden Erlegh, 149
Majuba, Battle of, 60
Malaya, 191
Malta, 17, 177
Management Committee, Royal Victoria Patriotic Asylum (later School), 95, 109, 120, 125, 137, 143, 147
Manila, H.M. Consul at, 43
Manly, Lieutenant-Colonel, 142
Mansion House, 10, 54, 75, 87, 97
Marzials, Frank, 94
Mashonaland, 68
Matabeleland, 68
Matsonkai, Spiros, 130
Maughan, Lieutenant Colonel (Secretary), 142
Maurice, Major-General J.F., 83
McKenna, Mrs (wife of Chancellor of the Exchequer), 121
Mecca Organization, 185
Merthyr, Lady, 143
Michael of Kent, Prince, 184
Middlesex Guildhall, 182
Militia, 14
Millington, James, 83
Milner, Sir Alfred (later Viscount), 67, 74, 104
Minesweepers, 123
Moldavia, 67
Morocco, 101
Mortality Rate, 35
Mowatt, Sir Francis, 94
Mugford, William Henry, 61
Musson, General Sir Geoffrey, 184

Natal, 69, 74
'Nathan Committee', 161, 168, 175
'National Health Insurance Joint Committee', 119
'National Relief Fund', 114–16
Nelson, Lord, 41, 42, 45, 58
Newcastle, Duke of, 11, 39, 40, 41
New Zealand, 49
Nightingale, Florence, 9, 13
Norfolk, Duke of, 26, 32–4
Northbrook, Lord, 59
'Not Forgotten' Association, 186
'Officers' Families Fund', 150
Old Age Pensions, 105–6, 129, 143
Old Girls' Association, 180
Orange Free State, 69, 74
Orphan Asylum, Wanstead, 23
Orphans, 20 and *passim*
'Orphans of Other Wars', 50, 53, 55
Orphans (placing), 21, 24, Appendix E
Ottawa, 114

Pakington, Sir John, 42
Pakistan, 177
Palestine, 6
Palmerston, Lord, 11
Panmure, Lord, 11

Index

Parish Relief, 153, 190
Parliamentary Select Committee, 57–8, 69–72, 81
'Patriotic (Army) Fund', 85
'Patriotic (General) Fund', 100, 128, 133
'Patriotic (Russian War 1854-6) Fund', 100
Paymaster-General, 18, 45, 90, 145
'Payroll Giving', 191
Pennefather, Revd. W., 23
Pensions, Ministry of, 124, 126–7, 137, 146, 154
Pensions, State, 79, 80
Pensioners, Staff Officers of, 63
Pereira, Major-General Sir Cecil, 142
Petre, Lord, 45
Pitman's College, 177
Polish Forces, 176
Poor Law, 153–4
Portsmouth, 7, 55, 70
Postmaster General, 145
Post Office Orders, 63
Powis, Earl of, 95
Pretoria, 74
Prime Minister (1905), 107
Prisoners of War, 14
Privy Council, Clerk to the, 181
Probyn, Rt. Hon. Sir Dighton, 97
Pursey, Commander, MP, 159–61, 181
'Quango', 113
Quartermaster General's Fund, 85, 91
Queen Adelaide Naval Fund, 190
Queen Alexandra, 128
Queen Elizabeth II, 164
Queen Victoria, 11, 29, 82
'Queen Elizabeth's Grammar School', Bsarnet, 151, 177
'Queen Mary's (Roehampton) Trust', 185–6
Quetta, 135

Radio Rentals, 186
Raglan, Lord, 11
Raids, Air, 139, 144–5
Ramsay, Lady Patricia, 145
Rationalization of Funds, 128, 155–7, Appendix R
Red Cross and Order of St John, 139–41, 190
Red Cross and Order of St John Joint Committee, 187
Rhodes, Cecil, 67–8
Roberts, Field Marshal Lord, 67, 74, 102
Roberts, Countess, 121
Rodriguez, Don Francisco, 43, 45, 100, Appendix F
Rokeby, Lord, 45
Roman Catholic Education, 26, 32–4, 54, 58, 60, 110, 135, 156
Rothschild, Lord, 95–6
Royal Air Force, 128
Royal Air Force Benevolent Fund, 135, 172, 190
Royal Alexandra and Albert School, 179, 185
Royal Army Medical Corps War Memorial Fund, 132, 165
Royal British Female Orphan Asylum, 24
Royal Caledonian Asylum, 24, 184
Royal Hibernian School, Dublin, 24
Royal Hospital, Chelsea, 183
Royal Hospital School, Holbrook, 185
Royal Military Asylum, Chelsea, 24
Royal Military Benevolent Fund, 166

Royal Military Tournament, 102
Royal Naval And Military Free Schools, Devonport, 23
Royal Naval Benevolent Trust, 172
Royal Naval Female School, Richmond, 23, 31, 184
Royal Naval Fund, 99, 190
Royal Naval Relief Fund, 52–4, 104, 128, 136, 156
Royal Naval and Royal Marines Orphan School, Portsmouth, 23
Royal Naval School, New Cross, 22, 31
Royal Patriotic Fund Corporation', 89 and *passim*
'Royal Naval Sailors' Rests', 71
Royal Soldiers' Daughters' Schools, Hampstead, 151, 185
Royal Tournament, 134, 171
Royal Victoria Patriotic Asylum, 26, 29, 55 and *passim*
Royal Victoria Patriotic School, 109, 127, 135 and *passim*
Rushcliffe, Lord, 150
Russell, W.H., 8, 9
Russia, Czar Nicholas I of, 6, 7
Russian Fleet, 6
Ryder, Rear Admiral, 52

Sackville Street, 131, 145, 164
St Leonards, Lord, 45, Appendix D
Sanger, Alderman, 142
Saundersfoot, 143, 148
School Endowment Fund, 142
School for Boys, 23, 24, 40, 58, 60
School for Daughters of Army Officers, 44, 185
School Superintendent, 28, 35, 37, 39
Scutari, 9, 13, 16
Seamen and Marines Orphan School, Portsmouth, 23
Sebastopol, 7, 9, 22
Serpent, HMS, 70
Seymour House, 100, 131
Shackleton, D.J., 95
Shaftesbury, Earl of, 45
Shrewsbury, Earl of, 45
Sicily, 147
Smuts, Jan, 67
'Soldiers' and Airmen's Effects Fund', 128, 156
'Soldiers' Effects Fund', 65, 80, 88, 110, 128
Soldiers' Infants Home, Hampstead, 24
'Soldiers' and Sailors' Families Association' (SSFA), 65, 70–1, 99, 114, 119, 126, 190
'Soldiers', Sailors' and Airmen's Families Association' (SSAFA), 128, 135, 149
Somerset, Duke of, 40–2, 45
South Africa, 60, 67, 79, 121–2
'South African War Fund', 92, 131
South African Veterans, 142–3
'South African War Widows and Orphans Fund', 103
'South Atlantic Fund', 191
Southern Secondary Modern School, 177
'Special Army and Navy Fund', 111, 115, 128, 132, 156
'Special Army Cases', 50–1
'Special Navy Fund', 111, 115
Spencer, Earl, 28, 29, 96

Spion Kop, 74
Spring, Brigadier-General, 163
Stanley of Alderley, Lord, 18
Stansfield, C.H.R., 94
Stanton, Major (later Colonel) E.A., 109, 115, 142, 146
State Supplements Account, 128–9
'Statutory Committee' of the Royal Patriotic Fund Corporation, 118, Appendix N
Stopford, Lieutenant-General the Hon. Sir Frederick, 132
Strathcona, Lord, 96
Sunday Times, The, 30
Symons, Major-General Sir W. Penn, 74

Talbot, Lieutenant-Colonel Lord Edmund, 94
Tenby, 139
Thorn EMI, 186
Thunderer, HMS, 54
'Thurlow Fund', 85, 91
Times, The, 8–100, 34, 70, 141, Appendix Q
Transvaal, 68–9, 74, 92
'Transvaal War Fund', 60, 75, 79, 87, 89, 93, 96, 101–3, 128, 165, 171, 183, Appendix J
'Transvaal War Fund, Extension', 115–16
'Transvaal War (Emergency) Fund', 131
Treasury, 1st Lord, 73, 79
Treasury, HM, 45, 68, 90, 100, 105, 194
Tremenheere, General, 88
'Triple Entente', 124
Trustee Investment Act (1925), 157
Trustee Investment Act (1961), 168, 173
Trustee Stocks, 194
Tully, Lieutenant-Colonel Thomas, 83
Turkey, 6, 112
Turkey, War with Russia, 6

'Uitlanders', 69, 74
United Service Institution (later Royal United Service Institution), 183
Usher-Smith, Brigadier-General W.H., 145

Van Dieman's Land, 19

Varna, 16
Victoria, HMS, 84, 100
Victoria Street, No. 64, 164, 175
Wales, Prince of, 98, 114, 121
Wallachia, 6, 7
Wandsworth, Boys' School, 24, 38
Wandsworth, Common, 28, 111
Wandsworth, Girls' School, 24, 148, 158
'War Charities Act', 149
'War Charities 1939 – Fund', 150
'War Charities 1939 – Non-pensioned Widows' Fund', 146, 165
'War Charities 1939 – Fund (Officers)', 150
'War Charities Office, 49, 51, 59–60, 65, 112
'War Charities Pensioners' Welfare Service, 158
'War Charities Pensions, 133
'War Charities Pensions Committees', 122
War Relief Funds, Committee, 76–9
War, Secretary of State for, 49, 66, 73, 77, 88, 90, 103, 110, 161
'War Charities (Transferred 1917) Fund', 123
Warrant, Royal, 10, 54, 65, 156, Appendix A
Waterloo Place, 100
Welby, Lieutenant-Colonel, A.C.E., 115, 125
Wellington College, 22, 31, 184
Wellington, Duke of, 7, 45
Wellington House, Buckingham Gate, 175, 183
Weston, Miss Agnes, 71, 83
Weston, near Bath, 145
Whayman, Engineer Rear-Admiral, 145
White, Lieutenant-General Sir George, 74
Woolley, Joseph, 61
Wolseley, Field Marshal Lord, 67, 74
Workhouse, 153

Young, Colonel John Smith, 57, 69, 100, 107, 108, Appendix L

Zervudachi, Sir Constantine, 64, 100
Zulu War, 54, 102
'Zulu War Fund', 54, 70
'Zulu War General Fund', 54